Mac® mini Hacks & For Dummies®

M000313007

Common Tools for Modding a mini

If you don't already have these most often used tools for modding a mini, take a trip down to your hardware or hobby store.

- 1½" metal putty knife
- Plastic putty knife or other thin, flat, nonmetal tool
- Jewelers' #0 Phillips screwdriver
- Philips #1 screwdriver
- Covered glass jars for keeping screws
- Bent-nose forceps for handling the mini screws inside the Mac mini
- Needle-nose pliers
- A Dremel (rotary handheld cutting tool) if cutting materials
- Well-lit workspace

Things to Avoid When Modding

You can do a lot of damage when modding a mini, unless you avoid harmful activities, such as

- Discharging static electricity inside the Mac mini
- Losing screws
- Touching a metal tool to the internal electronics
- Running the Mac mini in a hot environment
- Running the Mac mini with the bottom and rear air vents blocked
- Bending connector pins
- Getting paint on the inside of the Mac mini
- Neglecting to back up before hacking software

Handy Hardware

Here are the most common things you'll need to plug into or insert inside a Mac mini to make these mods work:

- External FireWire hard drive for storage of video, audio, or for backup
- External drive enclosure in which to keep your old internal hard drive or DVD drive
- A big RAM module (512MB, or better yet, 1GB)
- FireWire cables
- USB cables
- DVI-to-video (TV) connector cable
- Bluetooth adapter (if not internal)
- Remote control

For Dummies: Bestselling Book Series for Beginners

Mac® mini Hacks & Mods For Dummies®

Cheat Sheet

Keyboard Shortcuts

When you're using the Mac mini for nonstandard uses, choosing commands from menus isn't always easy. Use these key commands to get the job done faster.

Keys	Function
⌘+Shift+A (in the Finder)	Open the Applications folder
⌘+Shift+H (in the Finder)	Open home folder
⌘+Shift+U (in the Finder)	Open the Utilities folder
⌘+I (in the Finder)	Open the Info dialog for files
⌘+Shift+N (in the Finder)	Create a new folder
⌘+H	Hide the current application
⌘+Option+H	Hide all other applications (except the top one)
⌘+Option+D	Show or hide the Dock
⌘+Tab	Switch between applications
Control+Click	Bring up contextual menu (same as right-click)
⌘+W	Close window (or close tab in a web browser)

Different Startup Modes

Hold these keys while powering up or restarting the Mac mini to change the way the mini boots.

Keys Held	Result
C	Startup from optical disc. Lets you boot from the system DVD.
T	Startup in target disk mode. When connected to another Mac via a FireWire cable, lets the other Mac see the Mac mini's hard drive. Good for moving files between Macs.
Option	Choose a startup disk. Lets you select from connected hard drives and optical discs that have Mac OS X installed.
⌘+S	Boot in single-user mode, a command-line text interface for troubleshooting

For Dummies: Bestselling Book Series for Beginners

Mac® mini Hacks & Mods FOR DUMMIES®

by John Rizzo

with Arnold Reinhold

WILEY

Wiley Publishing, Inc.

Mac® mini Hacks & Mods For Dummies®

Published by
Wiley Publishing, Inc.
111 River Street
Hoboken, NJ 07030-5774
www.wiley.com

About the Authors

John Rizzo bought his first Mac in 1984, which came with 128 k of RAM and no hard drive. He soon began modding the Macintosh with a soldering iron to add RAM. Later, he cut some holes in the case and hacked in a new motherboard and a hard drive.

Since then, John has been writing about Macs (and Windows, too). His books include *Mac Annoyances* (O'Reilly), *Mac Toys* (with Scott Knaster; Wiley), *Customizing Windows XP* (Peachpit Press), and the *How the Mac Works* series (Que).

John writes about computer technology for Ziff Davis Online, which includes eWEEK.com and Publish.com. His columns, features, reviews, news, and analysis stories have appeared in every major Mac magazine, including *Macworld*, *MacAddict*, *MacHome*, and the no-longer-published *MacWeek* and *MacUser*. From 1988 to 1995, he was a staff editor and columnist for MacUser magazine. His stories have also appeared in the San Francisco Chronicle, CNET, and PC Magazine.

John is a leading authority on Mac and Windows integration issues. Since 1997, he has published MacWindows.com, the Web's largest resource for helping people get their Macs and Windows PCs to play nice together.

Before Apple invented the Mac, John worked as an engineer at Boeing in Seattle building aircraft electronics.

Arnold Reinhold has been programming computers since they had filaments. His first introduction to the hype/so-what?/wow! cycle that governs computer industry evolution was the invention of the transistor. He has gotten to do cool stuff in spacecraft guidance, air traffic control, computer-aided design, robotics, and machine vision. Arnold has been on the Internet for over twenty-two years and has been a loyal Mac user for twenty. Recent writing includes "Commonsense and Cryptography" in *Internet Secrets*, *E-Mail For Dummies*, 2nd edition, and *Internet For Dummies Quick Reference*, 8th edition (all by Wiley).

Arnold studied mathematics at CCNY and MIT, and management at Harvard. You can check out his home page at http://www.hayom.com/reinhold.html.

Dedication

To creative modders everywhere, who refuse to settle for the commonplace, and who are not afraid to void warranties. They inspire the geek and the artist within us.

Author's Acknowledgments

Thanks to Bob Woerner at Wiley for his understanding and accommodation during a time of unexpected obstacles. And to Nicole Sholly for bearing the brunt of the consequences with grace and acumen. Her guidance through the process was invaluable.

Thanks to my colleagues in the non-publishing world, who put up with my absences as I wrote this book.

Thanks to John Edwards for his suggestions about X10 hardware, and thanks to Pier Philipsen for streamlining some code for the Mac OS X hacks.

Thanks to Arnold Reinhold for writing the chapters on minis in your car (Part V) and the mini-in-your-kitchen, and for coming up with ten more things you can do with the mini.

Special thanks to Chris for her support of my work and of my work habits.

And, finally, thanks to Archive.org for helping to keep me at my most productive during the late nights and into the wee hours of the Morning Dew.

Publisher's Acknowledgments

We're proud of this book; please send us your comments through our online registration form located at www.dummies.com/register/.

Some of the people who helped bring this book to market include the following:

Acquisitions, Editorial, and Media Development

Project Editor: Nicole Sholly

Senior Acquisitions Editor: Bob Woerner

Copy Editors: John Edwards, Jean Rogers

Technical Editor: Pier Philipsen

Editorial Manager: Kevin Kirschner

Media Development Manager: Laura VanWinkle

Editorial Assistant: Amanda Foxworth

Cartoons: Rich Tennant (www.the5thwave.com)

Composition Services

Project Coordinator: Maridee Ennis

Layout and Graphics: Carl Byers, Andrea Dahl, Lauren Goddard, Joyce Haughey, Barbara Moore, Heather Ryan

Proofreaders: Leeann Harney, Shannon Ramsey

Indexer: TECHBOOKS Production Services

Special Help: Rebecca Senninger

Publishing and Editorial for Technology Dummies

Richard Swadley, Vice President and Executive Group Publisher

Andy Cummings, Vice President and Publisher

Mary Bednarek, Executive Acquisitions Director

Mary C. Corder, Editorial Director

Publishing for Consumer Dummies

Diane Graves Steele, Vice President and Publisher

Joyce Pepple, Acquisitions Director

Composition Services

Gerry Fahey, Vice President of Production Services

Debbie Stailey, Director of Composition Services

Table of Contents

Introduction

· ·

*I*f you ever stumble into some of the geekier discussion forums around the
Internet, you may come across a community of people who enjoy modifying, or *modding,* their PCs. They're keen on showing off how they changed the
look or function of their PC using cutting, painting, and soldering techniques,
or by adding stuff — some of it pretty weird — that isn't normally there.

There is a software equivalent of modding: *hacking.* This is programming
changes in software to make it look different or to make it do something it
wasn't designed to.

There is also a third type of computer change: using your computer for a radically different purpose, hacking your perception of what a computer is, or
modding your noncomputer possessions to fit the computer.

The mini was tailor-made for all three of these types of changes. Oh sure,
Apple wants you to think that the mini is perfect and complete the way it is.
But then, this isn't the book that Apple wanted me to write.

About This Book

Mac mini Hacks & Mods For Dummies gives you several different approaches
to information about modding. Some chapters give you specific projects to
work on. For these, I provide step-by-step directions on how to achieve a particular objective, such as upgrading the internal hard drive or modifying the
mini's outer casing. I've peppered these sections with plenty of tips and
tricks and lists of tools that you'll need.

With some other mods, however, there are just too many options to give you
a step-by-step procedure. For these, I present descriptions of what's involved
with a type of mod and show you the modding techniques for doing it. You
also find lists of what you'll need to acquire and where to get it.

In some parts of this book, I try to provide you with ideas for further mods,
or to help you come up with your own ideas.

I can't take all the credit, though. Writing this book was such a big task that I
enlisted the help of Arnold Reinhold to write six of the chapters, including
everything on installing a Mac mini in your car. He also tackled the chapter
on kitchens and the chapter at the end of the book that lists ten more things
you can do with a mini.

Foolish Assumptions

Unlike some other computer books, you won't find much filler here — no lectures on what's in the print dialog and no dissertations on obscure features that have no bearing on the task at hand. That's because I assume that you are already a computer user.

Don't worry if you are new to the Mac. I explain any Apple-specific terms and techniques that you need to know. For instance, I describe how you can use your old Windows keyboard on the mini. Experienced Mac users can skip bits of Mac-specific material. But I don't give you a test on your Mac savvy at the end of the book. The aim here is not to turn you into an expert Mac user, but to show you how to turn the Mac mini into something different than what you bought from Apple.

I also assume that you've already bought or are intending to buy a Mac mini. I assume that you're running Mac OS X v. 4, Tiger or later on your mini. I don't make any assumptions about what hardware options you bought with your mini.

Oh, yes, I make one more important assumption: You must have extensive knowledge of how to handle a screwdriver. If not, check out *Screwdrivers For Dummies* . . .

What You Don't Have to Read

When it comes down to it, you really don't have to read any of this book. Look at the pictures, hide a copy of Harry Potter inside of it to read on the subway, or use it as a prop under a kitchen table leg. As long as you buy it, I'm okay with it. (It makes a great gift, too, by the way.)

If you *are* going to read this book, however, you don't need to read the whole thing, or read it in any particular order. The book is organized in a logical manner from beginning to end, but it's not a narrative. Rather, it's modular. You only need to read the portions that apply to a specific project or technique that you may be interested in.

There are two exceptions. First, I tell you how to open the Mac mini in Chapter 4. Rather than repeat the procedure for every project that requires you to get inside the mini, I simply refer you to Chapter 4. The second exception is Chapter 5, where I show you how to remove the internal assembly that houses the storage drives. Again, instead of repeating this over and over, I just refer you to Chapter 5.

Mac experts don't need to read much of Chapter 2, which is a chapter on plugging different kinds of things into a mini. However, you may not want to skip it completely, because it includes information on some nonstandard ways of plugging things into the Mac mini. You may be surprised what you find there.

If you want, you can skip the text that's next to the Technical Stuff icons. I won't be insulted (well, not much), although I think you may enjoy some of the technical details.

You don't have to read the appendix for any modding project. It's there just in case your Mac mini starts acting sick and needs some help.

How This Book Is Organized

Mac mini Hacks & Mods For Dummies is split into seven parts, with a troubleshooting appendix tacked on at the end. You don't have to read the book sequentially, and you don't even have to read all the sections in any particular chapter. You can use the table of contents and the index to find the information you need and quickly get your answer. If you're going to open the mini, however, be sure to read Part II first.

Part I: Owning a Mac mini

I start the book with an introduction to Mac mini modding, describing what your modding options are, what your expectations should be, and what benefits you might get from different approaches. I also offer some recommendations that might help you plan and choose a mod.

I then start you off with the simplest projects — modding by plugging things in. This includes what the ports do and how to convert between different types of connectors, as well as how to do some rather unusual things with the ports. I round off this trio of chapters with tips on how to take your mini on the road.

Part II: Cracking Open the mini

Turn the mini around in your hands, and the question comes to mind "Where are the screws?" Well, you won't find any. Opening the Mac mini isn't something you can figure out by looking at it. That's why I provide detailed instructions with photos, and I tell you exactly what tools work best.

Don't let the title of Chapter 5 fool you. "First Mods Inside the Mac mini" includes hands-on instructions to help you begin disassembling the guts of the mini.

Part III: Upgrading the mini Yourself

This is where I debunk the myth that the mini is not upgradeable. Add more RAM; replace the internal hard drive with a bigger, faster model; swap out the internal Combo Drive for a DVD burner; and add wireless networking and Bluetooth. If that's not upgrading, I don't know what is.

Part IV: Mods for the Home

Here is home improvement, mini style. Expect to read about some very cool things that your mini can do in your house or apartment: the mini as a multi-purpose home appliance in the living room and in the kitchen. If that's not enough, have the mini control all your other home appliances.

Part V: Modding Your Car for the Mac mini

This part is Arnold's baby. Here, he takes you through the joys of having a mini installed in your car. You find out where to put it, how to power it, and how to display it.

Part VI: Maxi mini Mods

Want to do some radical stuff to your mini? I'm talking about using rotary saws, soldering irons, and spray paint. Don't worry if you've never handled these tools; I provide detailed instructions on the tools and techniques that you need. You'll find some cool pictures, too. See the photos of how I destroy the top casing of the Mac mini. There's no going back with these mods. I also show you some software hacks that let you do similar things to Mac OS X.

Part VII: The Part of Tens

Arnold and I describe ten places to visit on the Web to get more help and information, and ten more things you might want to do with a Mac mini.

The appendix

I couldn't write this book without telling you how to get out of a jam. This appendix gives you the troubleshooting techniques you need to nurse a sick Mac mini back to health.

Conventions Used in This Book

Flip through this book, and you'll find different uses of typeface to point out different things. Here's what I do with the typefaces:

- I use a monospaced font to point out Web addresses, like this: `www.apple.com`.
- To show you when to hack software, I also use a monospaced font to indicate `code` that you need to type at a command line, as in `fsck -fy`.
- On a Mac keyboard, the Command key is the key that has an Apple icon (🍎) and the Clover icon (⌘). This book uses ⌘ to represent the Command key. If you're using a Windows keyboard with your Mac mini, the Ô key is the same as the Windows key.
- In the step-by-step directions, the actions you need to perform are in bold type, **like this**. The explanations of what you can expect to happen after the action are not bolded.
- A new term uses italics, *like this*, to show that this is the first time it's being used and defined.

Icons Used in This Book

In addition to the typeface tricks, this book also uses four different types of icons to the left of the text. These icons are here to help you flip through the pages to browse for information. Think of them as signposts, each pointing to a different way to think about what's being said.

Tips are the parts of the instructions or descriptions that are the best bits to remember to make the job easier or better. They aren't always the only way to get something done, but they do point out the best way to accomplish a task. Sometimes you can reuse a tip for other tasks.

When you see this icon, it means that I'm flagging something that you shouldn't forget to do — or you may mess up your mod. Or, it could mean that I've mentioned this item before, but I'm repeating it for emphasis.

The Warning icon highlights lurking danger. With this icon, I'm telling you to pay attention to what you're doing — or to what you shouldn't do.

This icon marks a general interesting fact that is a techie explanation of what's going on or why you need to do something. Because I don't want to turn this book into one of my old college engineering textbooks, I keep the tech stuff short. Don't worry; I don't use any differential equations.

Where to Go from Here

The section "How This Book Is Organized," earlier in this introduction, gives you a good idea of where to begin with this book. You might want to have a Mac mini with you as you go through the book so that you can see what I'm talking about. I couldn't supply a mini with the book, unfortunately, so you'll have to supply your own.

Part I
Owning a
Mac mini

The 5th Wave   By Rich Tennant

"The Mac mini's a basic computer to which you connect other devices that might be important to your lifestyle, like a monitor, a keyboard, a fog machine..."

In this part . . .

The Mac mini offers so many modifying possibilities, it's hard to know where to begin. Modding the mini can be a means to an end or a hobby in itself.

In this Part, you find out where to start and what to expect, and get a glimpse of the range of hacking possibilities. You will also discover the most basic mods for the mini: plugging hardware into it for fun and productivity and for standard functionality and expanded horizons. I also show you how you can take the mini on the road with you.

Chapter 1

Modding a Mac mini: An Overview

The multipurpose mini is the most modifiable Mac on the market. If you don't yet have a mini, you will realize this as soon as you pull it out of its Styrofoam cocoon. Sure, there's the big expensive Power Mac with its expansion slots and room for more hard drives than any sane person needs, but its sheer bulk makes it destined to be tied to a desk or working as a network server in a closet somewhere. The Mac mini, on the other hand, is the size of a few CD jewel cases, as big as one of the Power Mac's hard drives, fitting inside the pocket of your cargo pants. Not only can you install things inside the Mac mini, but you can also install the mini itself inside of other places.

This book shows you how to *modify* (alter the hardware) and *hack* (change the look or function of software) a Mac mini to be more productive, to have fun, or to go where no Mac has gone before, at least in your experience as a Mac user. Or maybe you're a veteran Windows user switching to your first Mac and want to know what you can do with it inside and out. Perhaps you don't have a mini yet, but you think the minis are cool and you're looking for a reason to justify augmenting the Mac you already have.

Don't worry if you aren't daring enough to do the most radical mods described in this book. There are plenty of down-to-earth mods that won't cost more than the mini did. But the maxed-out mods described in Part VI are interesting and entertaining, even if you just read about them.

In this chapter, I cover what you should know before you do anything rash with your Mac mini. This chapter is all about scope, and it shows you how to find out if your mini has what you need for your mod. It also lets you know what you're in for, what you might need to investigate, and why you'd want to modify and hack your beautiful Mac mini.

What's a Mod?

If you ever saw the movie *Quadrophenia* by The Who, you'd recognize the term *mod* as the name of the trendily dressed, Vespa-driving, occasionally rioting British youth faction of the early '60s. Hyper and with attitude, the mods were doing something different.

A *mod* is also doing something different with your stylish Mac mini. Not just changing the look or feel, but using it for something that you — or even Apple — might not have thought about. And because your Mac is a tiny mini, it can go in places that you wouldn't ordinarily take a Mac, such as in your TV's entertainment center, in a cupboard, or in your car. I don't recommend using a Mac mini on a Vespa, however.

A mod isn't limited to working with the hardware. Changing or adding software can open up the mini to new uses just as changes to hardware can. Then there are *hacks,* which usually describe unusual techniques for changing software for good or for ill. I only talk about the good here.

Like the authorities facing an armada of mod-carrying scooters, some of the designers at Apple may cringe at the kind of mods and hacks you can do with and to your Mac mini. There's your attitude for you.

Why Mod a Perfectly Good Mac?

Apple loaded up the Mac mini with plenty of goodies, both in hardware and software. It already lets you do cool things with music, photos, movies, video conferencing, e-mail — the list is long. And, as Figure 1-1 shows, it looks pretty cool. So why mess with it?

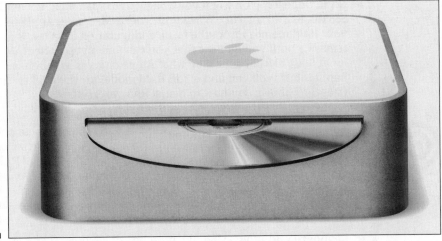

Figure 1-1:
Take your 2-inch high Mac mini to places where other Macs won't fit.

The answer is that there's no reason to let the marketing gurus and engineers at Apple decide what you should do with your mini. Their job is done, because you've already decided to buy a Mac mini. It's now time to Think Different, as Apple used to say.

This section looks at some of the big-picture reasons why you might want to mod your Mac mini:

✔ Save money

✔ Make it do something new

✔ Make it look different, on-screen and off

If you haven't yet bought your Mac mini, you're in luck. The following section shows you how to save some bucks when you order your mini.

Saving money by adding options yourself

Buying a Mac mini is a little like buying a car. The basic model has an affordable sticker price. But as soon as you start adding options — power windows, sunroof, and cruise control — the price begins to climb like Lance Armstrong ascending the Pyrenees.

While you probably can't add your own sunroof to your new car, you *can* save substantial bucks by buying the basic Mac mini and adding some extras or options yourself. For instance:

✔ **RAM:** Depending on when you bought your Mac mini, you either have 256MB, 512MB, or 1GB. When you order a Mac mini, Apple offers to up your RAM memory from the basic configuration for a fee. It may seem tempting until you find out that you can find an upgrade RAM module for at least $15 cheaper than what Apple charges at purchase time. If you hunt around, you can find a 1GB RAM model for the mini for about $85. Chapter 7 shows you how to install RAM yourself.

For the best prices for RAM memory, check out www.ramseeker.com. This site isn't a seller of RAM. Instead, it finds the cheapest prices at the moment from different sellers and displays links to those sellers' Web sites. You don't need to know the tech specs of the type of RAM that fits in the mini. Just choose Mac mini from the menu on the RamSeeker home page, and you get a list of Mac mini RAM prices from several different RAM sellers. The price of RAM can change daily, so make sure you check back before you place your order.

✔ **Keyboard and mouse:** If you have a box of keyboards and mice in your garage from all of the Macs and PCs you've owned, there's no need to buy another set. If you do need a keyboard or mouse, you can find them for less than what Apple charges. Chapter 2 describes what to look for in a keyboard and mouse for your mini.

✔ **Wireless goodies:** If you're going to be adding wireless peripherals to the mini, you'll need Bluetooth. An external Bluetooth adapter generally costs less than Apple's internal Bluetooth upgrade. On the other hand, Apple's price for AirPort wireless networking is on par with other vendors, and its bundle of both AirPort and Bluetooth upgrades is actually a good deal. If you already bought your Mac mini without wireless, read Chapter 6 to install it yourself.

✔ **Hard drive:** Apple can increase the basic 40GB hard drive to 80GB for $50, or to 100GB for $150, which isn't bad. The problem is that 80GB or even 100GB isn't a whole lot of storage if you plan on filling up a 60GB iPod or want to do a bit of video editing with iMovie. Over time, Apple increases the size of the biggest hard drive option, but it is never as big as what's available. If you think you'll need to go beyond 100GB of storage, order your mini with the basic 40GB and put your money toward a big hard drive. Chapter 7 describes replacing the internal drive.

✔ **DVD burners:** One upgrade from Apple that you just can't beat is the SuperDrive DVD burner. You won't be able to come near Apple's price of $100 for the slot-loaded DVD-RW drive, so if you want to put your movies on disc or need over 4GB of storage per disc, the Apple upgrade is the way to go. If you missed out when you bought your mini, check out Chapter 8 to do your own upgrade.

Even if you already own a Mac mini, you may still need to add some of these hardware options. But you may not know what hardware is already inside the mini. Fortunately, all you have to do is ask Mac OS X. Go to the menu and choose About This Mac. A window appears, as shown in Figure 1-2, showing your mini's processor speed and the amount of RAM. To find the amount of free hard disk space, go to the Finder and look at the bottom of a folder window. For instance, Figure 1-3 shows that my hard drive has 24.12GB of free space.

Figure 1-2:
Check out
your
processor
speed and
installed
RAM.

Figure 1-3:
Look at the
bottom of
the window
for the
available
hard disk
space.

To find out if you have internal Bluetooth or AirPort, or to see if your DVD drive can burn DVDs, do the following:

1. **In the About This Mac dialog (refer to Figure 1-2), click the More Info button.**

2. **The System Profiler utility opens, as shown in Figure 1-4.**

Figure 1-4:
Open
System
Profiler to
check the
hardware
options
installed
inside the
mini.

3. **Click Disc Burning to find out if your optical drive can burn DVDs.**

   Figure 1-4 shows that this Mac mini can.

4. **Click Bluetooth or AirPort Card to see if your mini has these wireless options installed.**

New tricks for a not-so-old mini

Saving money is all well and good, but a more fun reason to mod your mini is to make it do something different. If you like to use iTunes to listen to music and watch movies, try a few modifications to have the mini control the entertainment center in your living room, as described in Chapter 9. Or have it control music and video in your car (check out Part V).

Try doing these things with an iMac. And do you really want to spend $1500 to dedicate a PowerBook to your car?

Speaking of going mobile, you can also use the mini in different places. If you don't have a notebook computer to carry to different locations, the Mac mini can be the next best thing. Chapter 3 shows you how to take the mini on the road.

Changing your mini's look

Some modifications have no productivity value at all but are very high on the coolness meter. Making your mini look different is pure indulgence. Do something easy, like turning the mini into one half of a pair of fuzzy dice. Or attempt something harder, like building a clear plastic case reminiscent of some of the older iMacs. Or amaze your friends by putting your modern Mac mini into a 15-year-old Mac Classic.

The chapters in Part VI describe these kinds of modifications and hacks. Part VI also describes the tools and techniques you can use to build your own mod designs.

What's in Store

There are mods and there are mods. Some mods don't require much effort or time to make, while with others, there is "some assembly required." Finally, other mods can fall into the categories of hobbies, or with some people, obsession.

A good place to start out modding is to add peripheral hardware and new software. The next level is cracking open the case and exposing the guts of your mini, something that you'll find yourself doing a lot in this book. When you start replacing parts yourself, you may venture into the realm of voiding your warranty if your mini is less than 90 days old. Part VI includes instructions on how to break out the ultimate hardware hacker's tool: the soldering iron.

The following subsections describe some of the things you can expect to do when mini modding.

Plugging things in

Okay, maybe you don't think that plugging hardware into the Mac mini qualifies as a mod. Fair enough, but you can do some interesting things by plugging hardware into your Mac mini.

Some chapters in this book use the Mac mini's connection abilities to do all kinds of things. I'm not just talking about plugging in external hard drives and scanners, but plugging in things like stereos and TVs. If you're new to the Mac or switching from Windows, read Chapter 2 for the basics. If you've been plugging into Macs for years, skip Chapter 2.

Adding software

Not all modifications are made completely with hardware. Some modifications require you to install new software on the Mac mini. For instance, the description in Chapter 10 of controlling home appliances uses software that you may not have heard of before. It's not difficult to install software, but it's not something you should do blindly, either. The next step up from that is hacking the operating system, described in Chapter 18. Check out the section, "Software Considerations," later in this chapter.

Adding software includes upgrading Mac OS X. Although Apple wants you to upgrade to the latest and greatest, the latest may not actually be the best for your purposes. Always be careful before changing a perfectly good OS installation. For the details, check out the section, "When to upgrade Mac OS X," later in this chapter.

Breaking open the box

Many of the mods and hacks require that you crack open the Mac mini to get to the guts. It's not obvious how to open it, or that it can be opened at all. There are no screws, no visible tabs, and no holes in which to stick implements. The Mac mini looks like it appeared fully formed, just like Athena popping out of the head of Zeus (although without quite the same mythic proportions).

I will be honest with you: The first time you open the mini will be nerve-wracking. Don't worry, though. It's actually not that difficult — as long as you know what you're doing.

Chapter 4 describes how to open the Mac mini.

Replacing parts

Some mods involve taking original parts out of the mini and replacing them with something else, either because you just want something better, or you want to make repairs yourself. Apple sanctions the replacement of a few parts, such as RAM. For other parts, such as the hard drive and the optical driver, you're on your own. It's not a good idea to remove these parts before the 90-day warranty expires, though.

The main thing to remember about replacing internal parts is to make sure you're not carrying a static electricity charge that can damage the Mac's circuitry. Some parts will come with a wrist strap that you attach to a metal appliance, which has the effect of electrically grounding you. If you don't have a wrist strap, just be sure that before you touch any of the Mac mini's internal parts, you touch a metal lamp or other metal object to discharge static electricity you may be holding.

Planning Your Mod

The most basic goal of any project is to finish it. Doing some planning before you start can prevent you from running out of money, time, parts, technical skill, or enthusiasm in the middle of a project. Planning is knowing what you're getting into and how to get out of it.

The more complex a project is, the more planning will be helpful. Some mods, such as installing more RAM, require a minimum of planning. For others, such as installing a Mac mini in your car, you want to spend the time to do thorough planning before you touch or buy anything.

Here are the basic steps to take to plan for a complex modding project:

1. Estimate the scope of the project.
2. Estimate the time it will take.
3. Estimate the cost.
4. Locate potential suppliers of parts and tools.
5. Set realistic expectations.

Sizing up the job

The first step in planning a project is to estimate how big a job it will be and how much work you'll need to put into it.

List all major steps involved in the project. Check to see if you're missing anything. It's easy to overlook something when you're reading about it. I find that the act of writing things down gives me a better understanding of what's involved. This makes it less likely that I'll skip a step or hit a brick wall in the middle.

After you make your list, review each of the steps. Identify any steps that might stick out as particularly labor-intensive or that might require additional research or understanding. You need to know what you're doing at each step of the way.

Estimating time

Estimating how long it will take to complete a project is one of the more difficult aspects of planning, but it is important to know if you want to finish the project. You can think of time estimation as the second, more detailed part of the estimating process you started in the preceding section.

Here's a trick. Before you start your time estimation, decide how much time you want to spend on the project. You'll find this handy to compare it to the estimate you come up with.

Look at the list of steps you created in the preceding section and assign a time estimate to each step. If the project requires a technique that you've never used before, try out some sample tasks to see how long it will take.

Now add up the time estimates for each step. Then increase the sum by 25 percent. Like a lot of home improvement projects, a complex modification will almost always take longer than you initially thought it would.

Finally, compare this final number to the amount of time you were willing to spend on the project. I'm guessing that it will be larger. You'll now need to reevaluate how much time you are willing to put into the project.

Estimating costs

Cost estimation is one of the easier planning tasks. That's because it's objective: You find numbers and add them up. This doesn't mean you can't underestimate costs, so it pays to be methodical.

- ✔ **Create a parts list.** Go through your list of steps again and list the parts that you'll need. Don't forget the smaller items. The cost of items such as cables can quickly add up when you aren't looking.

- ✔ **Create a tools list.** First, list the tools that the project will require. Then inventory your own tools and note which tools you'll need to buy.

- ✔ **Use the Internet to estimate cost.** Whether it's cables, drives, or tools, you can use Google to search for what you need and come up with pricing information. If these are big-ticket items, include estimates for shipping and sales tax.

It's annoying as all heck when Google returns 600,000 items that are mostly relevant to Windows PCs. To restrict Google to Mac items, try searching `www.google.com/mac`. This will separate the Macs from the chaff.

Now add up the costs. If the total exceeds the amount you wanted to spend for the project, you may want to rethink your plan. But it's better finding this out now than after you started to invest.

Locating suppliers

For some particularly adventurous modifications, be sure you can actually get the parts or tools you need before you start your modifications. You don't want to get halfway through a project only to be stopped because you can't find a particular and necessary item. If you have to rethink your plan, it's best to do it before you start so you don't waste your efforts.

Throughout this book, I give you suggestions as to where you will find parts. These are only jumping-off places, as are some of the mods described in this book. When you branch off on your own mods, you may need to find your own vendors. Of course, the Internet, and Google in particular, is a great way to find suppliers, no matter where they are located.

Setting realistic expectations

The final bit of planning is to estimate your own abilities and endurance. Before you start a modding project, make sure that you have a realistic idea of what you can accomplish. Part of this is knowing what kind of commitment you're willing to give to the project.

Ask yourself some questions and see if you can give yourself some honest answers:

> What do I really want out of this project?
>
> Do I have the time and energy to devote to my goal?
>
> If I don't reach my goal, what would I be willing to settle for?

What you don't want is to get stuck halfway through a project, with a partially assembled Mac mini gathering dust.

Software Considerations

Some Mac mini mods call for adding software or upgrading Mac OS X. Installing software may seem like an easy aspect of modding, but before you buy the new software, you first need to find out if your Mac mini is up to snuff.

When to upgrade Mac OS X

Don't be a Mac OS X pioneer when it comes to upgrading to major new "cat" versions of Mac OS X (Jaguar, Panther, Tiger, Leopard, and so on). A *Mac OS X pioneer* is someone who races out to buy the newest version of Mac OS X while the shrink-wrap on the box is still warm.

Bad idea.

The first ".0" releases of Jaguar, Panther, and Tiger contained bugs and incompatibilities with existing software and even with some hardware. It takes a little while for manufacturers to catch up to Mac OS X, and it takes Apple some time to create backwards compatibility with some software.

The best practice is to hold off changing cats until Apple issues one or two ".1" upgrades. That's a version such as 10.4.1 or 10.4.2 (or 10.5.1 or 10.5.2) that you can install using the Software Update utility in System Preferences.

Let other people find the problems with brand new versions of Mac OS X for you. Read the problem reports at Web sites such as `macintouch.com` and `macfixit.com`.

Researching your software's needs

Before putting out any money for software, do a little research. If you don't plan, your brand new software may run slowly, or it may not run at all.

Read the requirements

Before you install software, and even some hardware, read the requirements that the manufacturer recommends for a minimum Mac system. This will be the amount of RAM memory, the amount of free hard disk space, and the type of processor the software needs to run.

If you're buying software in a retail store, the requirements section is listed on the box in ultra-small type. The manufacturer's Web site should also list the software's requirements.

Check for Intel processors

Starting in 2006, Apple will begin shipping certain Mac models with Intel Pentium processors (the same processors that Windows PCs use). Eventually, Apple will retire the PowerPC, and all Macs will run Intel processors. (Perhaps Apple will change the name from Macintosh to Macintel, but I wouldn't bet on it.) We don't know when the Mac mini, or any other Mac model, will make the switch.

As far as requirements go, a lot of software will run on both Intel and PowerPC processors. Most of the software you already have (which is written for PowerPC software) will also run on Intel-based Macs. So if the processor requirement says "1 GHz G4," it will likely run on an Intel Mac of some gigahertz rating. Newer software may only run on Intel Macs, so you will need to check your software carefully before purchasing.

The switch to Intel processors could also affect hardware. Most peripherals use driver software, sometimes built into Mac OS X, and sometimes provided by the manufacturer. Chances are good that some hardware just won't work on the newer Macintel boxes, at least for a while.

At this point, it's difficult to say whether PowerPC or Intel processors are faster. When comparing different processors, the gigahertz ratings of each don't reflect the same performance measures. The main reason Apple is switching to Intel is that IBM is not moving fast enough in producing new versions of PowerPC processors. At some point, the fastest Intel processors will be faster than IBM processors, not because of gigahertz ratings, but because Intel is advancing faster than IBM. This will translate into faster Macs.

Don't squeak by

Software manufacturers always list the bare minimum hardware required to run their software. This is kind of like watching a big blockbuster movie on a tiny black and white TV with a 1-inch speaker. Yes, you can do it, but you'd be happier with beefier hardware.

So if the manufacturer says its software requires 256MB of RAM memory and you have 256MB, go out and buy some more RAM. Otherwise, you're likely to get slower performance than you'd like.

If the requirement for free hard disk space is 3GB and you have 3.1GB, the software will install, but you aren't going to have much space to do much else.

If the required processor is a 1.2 GHz PowerPC and your Mac mini has a 1.2 GHz PowerPC processor, you're squeaking by. (Chapter 19 describes how to use a soldering iron to push that 1.2 GHz to 1.4 GHz.)

Chapter 2

Completing Your Mac mini

. . . .

. . . .

*T*he expansion ports are the easiest way to expand the Mac mini's functionality, so this is a good place to begin your mods. In this chapter, I start with a tour of the Mac mini's ports, and then go on to describe the options for making your Mac mini complete and what you need to accomplish this. I even show you how to mod a Windows keyboard to act like a Mac keyboard with the mini. This chapter is not just for newbies and switchers, however, because I tell you about some tricks you may not have thought about even if you're a mini modding master. If you are going to do something unusual with the ports, I direct you to other chapters that contain more detail.

The Back Panel

The image of the Mac mini as a solid, sleek monolith falls away when you turn it around to face the back. The small package sports a full complement of connector ports, as shown in Figure 2-1. These are

- ✔ Audio out
- ✔ FireWire 400
- ✔ Two USB 2.0 ports
- ✔ Video output
- ✔ Modem
- ✔ Ethernet
- ✔ Power

Note the handy dandy icons above each port to help you remember which is which.

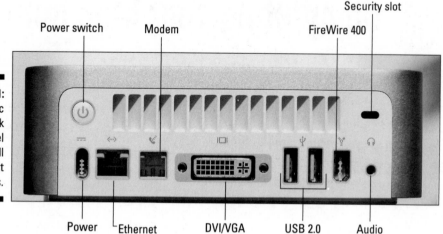

Figure 2-1: The Mac mini's back panel has a full complement of ports.

Power switch   Modem   FireWire 400
                                        Security slot

Power Ethernet   DVI/VGA   USB 2.0   Audio

Audio

Use the audio-out port to plug in headphones or speakers. The port uses a ⅛-inch mini stereo jack with a type of signal called audio line out, the same type used by iPods and portable CD players. This means you can connect your iPod earbuds into this port.

You can also use adapters to connect other sizes of cables and other types of audio devices.

FireWire

FireWire and USB are all-purpose ports. Older iPods, some printers, and certain other devices can be plugged into either. Generally, FireWire is the better port to use when you are moving a lot of data in or out of the Mac.

Apple uses two types of FireWire ports in Macs, the 400 Mbps (megabits per second) port and the 800 Mbps. The Mac mini contains only the FireWire 400. Still, if FireWire 800 is the gold standard of connection ports, FireWire 400 is the silver.

Although the Mac mini has only one FireWire port, you can use multiple FireWire devices on your Mac by adding a FireWire hub or by stringing devices together in a chain. To string up a FireWire chain, the devices must have two FireWire ports.

FireWire provides power to devices, so that iPods and hard drives don't need their own power supplies. Some devices may not get all the power they need when used in a chain or in a hub. If that's the case, plug the devices directly into the Mac mini's FireWire port.

Common uses of FireWire

As an all-purpose port, FireWire can connect almost any device to your Mac mini. Here are the more common uses:

- ✔ **External storage:** FireWire is the best way to connect external hard drives, optical drives, and other storage devices. The performance is good and you can boot from a FireWire hard drive, which makes it a good backup medium.

- ✔ **iPods:** Older iPods *only* connect to a Mac using FireWire. More recent iPods work with both USB 2.0 and FireWire, or just USB 2.0 but no longer come with a FireWire cable. You can buy a FireWire cable for your iPod from Apple or other vendors.

- ✔ **Digital movie camcorders:** Sony refers to FireWire as "iLink" on its camcorders. Sony's version doesn't accept power from the Mac to the camera, but is otherwise the same standard as FireWire.

- ✔ **Internet movie cameras:** Some cameras that you use for Internet video conferencing, such as Apple's iSight, use FireWire for the connection to the Mac and for power.

Less frequent uses of FireWire

I haven't yet seen a FireWire-enabled toaster, but you can find other types of devices with FireWire ports. The high-end models of some devices use FireWire. FireWire enabled devices include

- ✔ **Printers:** Higher-end models include a FireWire port as well as a USB 2.0 port.

- ✔ **Scanners:** Some of these devices include both FireWire and USB ports. There's no particular reason to choose one or the other here.

- ✔ **Digital still cameras:** Some high-end digital still cameras use FireWire instead of USB.

- ✔ **Professional audio capture/output:** Want to build your own recording studio? Many of the high-end, pro audio interfaces use FireWire instead of USB.

- ✔ **Video capture:** A video capture device enables you to use iMovie to edit video from analog sources, including VCRs and analog camcorders. This is possible because these devices convert the analog video into digital signals.

✔ **TV tuners:** Watch and record TV on your Mac. Check out Chapter 9 for more information.

Using FireWire to move data between two Macs

FireWire offers a feature not found in USB 2.0: *target disk mode*. This feature enables the mini to appear as a hard drive from another Mac when the two are connected together with a cable in their FireWire ports. (The other Mac needs to have been built in the year 2000 or later.) If you need to move a lot of data between the mini and another Mac, target disk mode is significantly faster than using Ethernet.

You can also use target disk mode to try to repair your mini's hard drive if the mini isn't booting properly. Just run Disk Utility from the other Mac with the mini in target disk mode.

To put the Mac mini into target disk mode, do the following:

1. **Turn the Mac mini off.**

   The other Mac can stay on.

2. **Connect a FireWire cable in the ports of the two Macs.**

3. **Start up the Mac mini while holding down the *T* key until the FireWire icon appears.**

   With Mac OS X 10.4 Tiger, an alternative method is to open System Preferences, click Startup Disk, click Target Disk Mode, and then restart.

   The Mac mini's hard drive appears on the desktop of the other Mac.

4. **When you're done with it, drag the Mac mini's icon to the Trash and press the mini's power button to turn it off.**

5. **Unplug the FireWire cable from both Macs.**

USB 2.0

USB 2.0 is similar to FireWire in several ways. Running at 480 Mbps, USB 2.0 sounds like it is similar to FireWire 400. However, for moving large amounts of data, USB 2.0 can be slower because of the way it sends information. USB 2.0 sends data in discrete bundles, while FireWire transmits data in continuous streams.

Like FireWire, USB 2.0 supplies power to devices. You can also use USB hubs to add more devices, though you can't create chains of devices. You can also use older USB 1.1 devices in the Mac mini's USB 2.0 ports.

Common uses of USB 2.0

More devices use USB 2.0 than use FireWire, which is why the mini has two USB ports. Here are the most common uses of USB:

- ✔ **Input devices:** These include your basic keyboard and mouse, as well as joysticks and game pads.

- ✔ **Printers:** Most inkjet printers connect via USB.

- ✔ **Scanners:** USB has long been a common interface on scanners.

- ✔ **Digital still cameras:** Most of these use USB to connect to computers.

- ✔ **iPods:** iPods sold today use USB to connect to computers. Older models had FireWire ports.

- ✔ **Audio interfaces:** Devices that add audio input or output ports often connect to USB ports. Audio interfaces are another way to add speakers.

- ✔ **Bluetooth adapters:** These small transmitters connect wireless peripherals such as keyboards and handheld phones.

Less frequent uses of USB 2.0

Although less common, these two uses are possible with USB 2.0 as well:

- ✔ **Storage:** You can find USB storage devices, such as hard drives. I don't recommend them because FireWire is a faster way to connect to drives. USB can be slowed by all of the other things going on over the USB bus.

- ✔ **Graphics:** Believe it or not, you can actually add a second monitor to the Mac mini through a special USB adapter. This is one unusual use of USB that I can recommend. To see how, read the "Adding a second monitor via USB" section, later in this chapter.

DVI video

The video port on the Mac mini is a type called *digital video interface* (DVI), which is found on Apple's displays and on many displays made today. You also find DVI on some HDTVs, set top boxes, DVD players, and projectors. The Mac mini DVI port can display resolutions of up to 1920 x 1200 pixels.

The Mac mini's DVI port is of a type known as DVI-I, which has an analog component to it: 4 of the 29 pins are devoted to VGA video. This means that you can use a fairly simple converter cable to connect the Mac mini video port to analog displays, such as VGA and televisions. I describe this further in the "Adding a Display" section, later in this chapter.

Modem

 These days, the modem port is used mostly for creating dialup Internet connections. Otherwise, the modem port is as archaic a method for connecting to the Internet as floppy disks are for storing data.

Ethernet

 Use the Ethernet port to connect the Mac mini to a local network or to the Internet. You can also connect the Ethernet port to an AirPort Base Station to get your Mac on a wireless network if you don't have a built-in AirPort.

You can also connect the Ethernet port directly to a DSL modem or cable modem (which really aren't modems at all, but the old name stuck when the new technology became available).

Power

 Of course, this port is where you plug in the power adapter brick that comes with the mini. The power brick (also known as a *transformer*) takes AC current from the wall socket and turns it into DC current.

 If you want to replace the power brick because you're locating the mini in an unusual location — such as in a car or in a PC case — the main thing to remember is that you need to provide 18.5 volt and 4.5 amps DC (85 watts max) to this port.

Most generic power bricks provide 12-volt DC, which won't work to power a mini. The power port on the Mac mini is a non-standard shape to prevent you from accidentally plugging in the wrong brick.

What, No Keyboard?

A Mac mini without a keyboard and mouse is, well, a paperweight. It's up to you to turn it into a computer. But there's more to the keyboard and mouse story than plugging in a couple of cables. This section describes some of the keyboard and mouse options available to you, including how to mod a Windows keyboard for use with your Mac. I also show you how to make the Mac mini share a keyboard with your other Mac or even with a PC.

USB keyboards

If you already have a USB keyboard, plug it into your Mac mini. If you're looking for something new, you have a wide range to choose from. At $29, the Apple Keyboard is near the bottom of the price range. You can find USB keyboards for $15, but at that price you don't find the main two features of the Apple Keyboard: the audio volume keys and a built-in USB hub that gives you two more USB ports. Not all $30 keyboards have the built-in USB hub, and I wouldn't buy a keyboard without it. The Apple Keyboard's Achilles' heel is the arctic white color of the keys, which can get dirty after some use.

When you start going up the price hill, the ergonomic features emerge. First there's the built-in wrist rest, one of technology's greatest achievements. (Movable type wasn't bad, either.) You also encounter the split keyboard, where the left and right halves are at angles to each other. Science says that split keyboards are better for your wrists, but you really need to get a split keyboard under your fingers before you commit to one. Having been typing on straight keyboards (and typewriters) since the 7th grade, I can barely type my name on the ergonomically correct split variety. But you may think it's the best thing since wrist wrests after you try one.

Increasing the price tag further gets you into the keyboard-as-control-panel school of keyboard design. These models have programmable buttons to activate common functions and built-in scroll wheels like those found on higher-end mice.

If you're going to spend a lot of time typing, get yourself into a real, non-virtual store to get a feel for it. Check out the Where to Buy section of your favorite keyboard manufacturer's Web site to find a store. But if you're just using the keyboard to enter a few commands for your hacked mini, go ahead and order the $15 special.

Using a Windows keyboard with the mini

One of the selling points of the Mac mini is the opportunity to plug your old PC Windows USB keyboard into the USB port, just as you would a Mac keyboard. If your PC Windows keyboard uses a PS/2 connector instead of USB, just get an inexpensive converter cable. For instance, the Keyspan ($19, www.keyspan.com) lets you plug both a PS/2 keyboard and PS/2 mouse into a single USB port.

While you're typing text, a Windows keyboard seems pretty much the same as the Mac variety. But as soon as you try using key commands, you'll notice that some of your most trusted Mac keys have been replaced with strange, new keys. If you're a Windows user switching to the Mac, you'll find that your familiar keys are acting strangely. In the next few sections, I describe how to deal with the differences. First the easy stuff.

The Eject key

You'll notice that the Eject key that Apple places in the upper-right corner of its keyboard is missing on Windows keyboards. No problem; just press the F12 key and hold it to eject a CD or DVD. (This also works on any Mac keyboard.)

Control versus Ctrl

As you can see in Figure 2-2, the Ctrl key in the lower-left of the Windows keyboard is in the same position as the Mac Control key. Fortunately, the two are the *same* key; Ctrl does everything that Control does.

Figure 2-2:
The
Windows
keyboard
(left) has
different
keys than a
Mac
keyboard
(right).

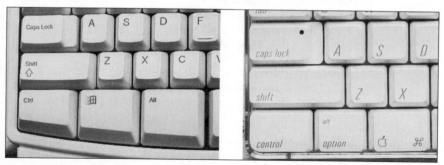

Windows, Alt, Option, and ⌘

The most perturbing difference between Windows and Mac keyboards is that the Windows keyboard has no Option or ⌘ (Command) keys. Instead, there's an Alt key that works like the Mac Option key, and a Windows key that acts like the Mac ⌘ key.

Not only that, but the layout is backwards. As you can see in Figure 2-2, the Windows key (with ⌘ functionality) is in the location of the Mac Option key, and the Alt key (with Option functionality) is in the location of the Mac ⌘ key.

To put the things back where you expect them, you need to swap the functionality of the Windows and Alt keys. This is easy, although not obvious, with Mac OS X v.4, Tiger. With earlier versions of Mac OS X, you need to install a piece of software that adds the ability to remap the key functions.

If you have Tiger, follow these steps to remap the Windows and Alt keys on a PC keyboard:

1. **Open System Preferences and click the Keyboard & Mouse icon.**

2. **On the Keyboard tab, click the Modifier Keys button.**

3. **Select Command from the Option Key menu, as shown in Figure 2-3.**

4. **Select Option from the Command Key menu.**

The effect is immediate — the Alt key now acts like the ⌘ and the Windows key now acts like the Option key.

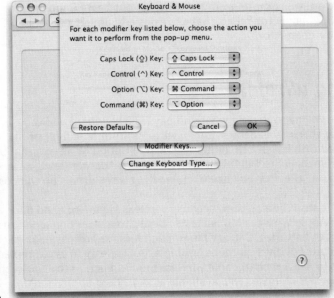

Figure 2-3:
Switch the functions of the Option and Command keys.

If you're running Mac OS X 10.3 Panther, you must install a piece of free software in order to remap the Windows and Alt keys. Two such freebees are uControl (http://gnufoo.org) and DoubleCommand (http://doublecommand. sourceforge.net). These utilities provide a settings window to do the same type of remapping that Tiger provides. (Apple doesn't get the credit here. This is another case where other developers came up with an idea that Apple later decided to build into Mac OS X.)

Mousing around

Apple's plain-Jane, one-button mouse gets bashed a lot. It has no second right button and no scroll wheel. Trained Windows users will probably find the idea of using a one-button mouse as absurd as driving a three-wheeled car. But for those who like the simplicity of a one-buttoner, the Apple mouse has a pleasant feel to it, keeping your hand in a natural position while moving and clicking.

If you want something with more features, Mac OS X supports two-button and three-button mice, as well as mice with scroll wheels. Apple's Mighty Mouse is a two-button version. You can even use *five*-button mice, such as several offered by Logitech (www.logitech.com).

PC mice are welcome as well. Just plug in your USB PC mouse. If your mouse has a PS/2 connector, all you have to do is add an inexpensive PS/2-to-USB converter connector.

Going wireless

If you're willing to double what you pay for a keyboard and mouse, you can shed the shackles of cables and go wireless. Your Mac mini needs to be equipped with Bluetooth, either the built-in option or an external USB adapter such as the $40 D-Link USB Bluetooth Adapter (www.dlink.com). As you can see, the convenience of eliminating wires drives up the cost.

It doesn't stop there, either, because wireless keyboards and mice eat batteries. The Apple Wireless Mouse lasts about three weeks on a pair of expensive Lithium AA batteries. Battery life is much less for ordinary batteries, and is only a matter of days on rechargeable AAs. One way to avoid replacing batteries is to use a rechargeable wireless mouse, such as the Logitech MX 1000 Laser Cordless Mouse ($80, available at www.logitech.com).

Despite the cost, a wireless keyboard and mouse can be very useful or even mandatory for some of the modding projects covered in this book. For instance, wireless input is very handy when carting your Mac mini around with you, as described in Chapter 3.

Sharing your keyboard/monitor with another Mac or PC

For many, the Mac mini is a second computer, perhaps a special-purpose computer. The mini itself doesn't take much desktop space, but two sets of keyboards and displays do. With keyboards and monitors, one's company, two's a crowd.

You can easily share a single keyboard, mouse, and display between another Mac and a mini, or even between a PC and a mini. All you need is a *KVM switch,* which stands for "keyboard, video, mouse." (I never knew why video was in the middle and why it wasn't a "KMV switch." For some reason, the inventors didn't ask me.) Here's how to set up and use a KVM switch:

1. **Connect the video ports of each computer to the KVM switch.**

   The necessary cables usually come with the KVM switch.

2. **Plug the monitor into the KVM switch.**

3. **Run a USB cable from a USB port on the Mac mini to a USB port on the KVM switch. Do the same for the other computer.**

4. **Plug the keyboard and mouse into the KVM switch.**

5. **Connect any other USB peripherals you want to share to the KVM switch, or to a USB hub connected to the KVM switch.**

After you set this up, one position of the switch makes the keyboard, monitor, and mouse work with the Mac mini. Turn the switch the other way, and your devices work with the other computer.

The knob on the KVM switch shown in Figure 2-4 controls which computer the monitor and keyboard connect to. This particular KVM switch from Dr. Bott (www.drbott.com) supports up to four computers, labeled A, B, C, and D. Dr. Bott also offers a 2-computer version, the MoniSwitch 2 USB ($139). The MoniSwitch uses VGA video ports, so you need to use the Mac mini's DVI-to-VGA converter on the Mac mini, as described in the next section. You can also find KVM switches that support DVI, such as the Gefen 2x1 DVI KVM Switch ($200).

Figure 2-4:
A KVM
switch
lets you
share one
keyboard
and monitor
between
two Macs.

Adding a Display

The Mac mini isn't fussy when it comes to connecting a display. It can run the shiny new digital flat screen that you just bought or that old CRT monitor that came with your old PC. In fact, there's no such thing as a PC monitor. It all comes down to the type of connector on the monitor and the type of video signal it accepts, and the types of converter cables you use. You can even use a television as a display, as you might if your mini is part of a home theater system.

It doesn't end there, either. After you connect a display, you can even add a second display.

Types of video: Digital and analog

The DVI video port in the back of the Mac mini sends out digital video signals, but also has the ability to send analog signals if you use the right type of connector. Digital signals consist of two types of discrete pieces of electronic pulses representing a 1 and a 0. Analog signals are a continuous, constantly fluctuating stream of voltages.

Digital video produces sharp, bright images on a digital display. That's because digital data are exact, reproducing exact replicas of the images. A digital video signal does not degrade as it travels through the cables that are a few feet in length.

Analog video produces images that are not as sharp. Analog signals can degrade as they move through the cables, causing problems with the display image. Analog signals are also prone to degradation from interference.

Just because a monitor has a DVI port doesn't mean it's a digital display. If you have to connect the Mac mini DVI port to an analog display, the image quality won't be as good as when the same port is connected to a digital display.

Other types of video ports, such as VGA and SVGA, are always analog. VGA is the older version, supporting only 640 x 480 pixels. SVGA is the modern version, kind of a VGA 2.0. Because SVGA has been around so long, it's often referred to as VGA. Before the rise of DVI in popularity, VGA/SVGA was the most common video port, and is still widely used.

ADC is an Apple-only digital interface that Cupertino only used for a few years. (See the later section, "ADC adapters.")

Televisions in North and South America use a type of analog video signal called NTSC. It's a lower quality, lower resolution standard than VGA/SVGA. NTSC uses several different connector types, including S-Video and composite video. See Chapter 9 for a more complete description.

Choosing a type of video adapter

You may need a video adapter to connect a particular display to the Mac mini. You might be able to use the adapter that comes with the Mac mini, or you may need to buy a new adapter. Here are your choices.

The easy way: DVI

You may not need any adapter at all. A display with a built-in DVI port is the easiest monitor to connect to the Mac mini. You can find monitors with a DVI port for under $300.

The Mac mini DVI-VGA adapter

Connecting the Mac mini to a VGA monitor is almost as easy as connecting to a DVI monitor. Just use the DVI-to-VGA adapter that came with your Mac mini.

If your monitor has both, use DVI. The fewer connectors you use, the less potential for trouble.

ADC adapters

Here's a little story. Once upon a time, Apple introduced its first flat-panel LCD displays using a standard DVI port. This made the people happy. Then the grand poobahs at Apple decided to switch to something called ADC, the Apple Desktop Connector, invented by the people working for the poobahs. It was a versatile video connector that included USB inside the cable. A definite gee whiz, if it weren't for the fact that no one else on the planet used ADC. This caused Apple to switch back to DVI on its displays and on its Macs. And they lived happily ever after.

Except, that is, if you happen to be an owner of one of the older ADC displays that you once paid a pretty penny for. The good news is that you can buy a DVI-to-ADC converter cable to connect your ADC display to the Mac mini. The bad news is that you have to pay another pretty penny for it. Apple can sell you one for $100. Dr. Bott's DVIator ($95, www.drbott.com) does the same thing, and Addlogix (www.addlogix.com) has one for $90.

Don't confuse DVI-to-ADC converters with Apple's $29 ADC-to-DVI connector. The latter enables you to use DVI displays with older Macs with ADC video ports, and won't help you at all.

TV adapters

In some of the modding projects, you attach the mini to a TV. For instance, there is usually no room for a monitor in your home entertainment center. Or you might be using the mini for a presentation.

Apple's DVI to Video Adapter connects to a TV that has a composite video connector (shown on the left in Figure 2-5) or an S-Video connector (shown on the right in Figure 2-5). Using this adapter, the Mac mini provides a resolution of 856 x 480 pixels on a TV.

Chapter 9 has more in depth descriptions of connecting the Mac mini to television systems.

Figure 2-5:
Connect
to a TV via
S-Video or
composite
video with
the Apple
DVI to Video
Adapter.

Adding a second monitor via USB

PowerBooks, Power Macs, and iMac G5s have the ability to support a second monitor, but Apple didn't include this feature in the Mac mini. If you've never thought about what you're missing, consider these two uses of a second monitor:

- ✔ Use both displays as a single continuous desktop, dragging files, windows, and tool palettes from one to the other. This expands your desktop space so that you can see multiple windows and documents at the same time.

- ✔ Use both displays for mirroring, so that the second display produces exactly what is on the first. This is handy when giving a presentation, where the second display can be a large projection system.

You might put this one in the category of "who'd a thunk it," but you can add a second, third, or fourth display to the Mac mini using an *external* video card that plugs into your USB port. The $99 SEE2 from Tritton Technologies (www. trittontechnologies.com) is a USB 2.0-to-SVGA adapter, as shown in Figure 2-6.

Figure 2-6:
The SEE2 enables you to add a second monitor to the Mac Mini.

Don't expect a high-performance graphics accelerator, because the SEE2 is a slower graphics card than what is already in the Mac mini. The speed of USB 2.0 limits the display resolution to 1280 x 768 pixels in full color, or 1280 x 1024 pixels at 16-bit color, which are thousands of colors rather than millions.

To get up and running, you install some driver software from Tritton, plug the SEE2 into your USB port, and plug your second monitor into the SEE2. Next, go to System Preferences and click Displays. You see settings for both monitors. You can set the display resolution of the monitor and the arrangement of the two. For instance, if the monitors sit side by side, you set the cursor to be able to move from the right side of the left monitor into the left side of the right monitor. This enables you to drag windows and other items between the two monitors.

Chapter 3

The mini as a Portable Computer

*Y*ou can take it with you — the Mac mini, that is. It's the first desktop computer you can easily move between two places without worrying about throwing out your back. The two places can be the bedroom and rec room, home and college, or home and office. Forget all the remote-control-over-the-Internet jazz for keeping in touch with your Mac from a distance. Just take it with you.

Just keep in mind that the Mac mini is never going to be a replacement for a notebook computer. It doesn't have a battery, so you can't use it on an airplane. On the other hand, a notebook computer costs more than a mini and a monitor, so if you don't need to operate on a battery, there's no reason to pay for it.

Building a Mac mini Travel Kit

If you're a multimodel kind of person, taking your Mac mini with you can be a cost-effective alternative to owning multiple computers at different locations. But what should you schlep around and what should you leave behind? This chapter looks at three scenarios:

✔ **Carry only the Mac mini by itself.** This is easiest on your back and great if you already have computer setups waiting for you.

✔ **Carry the Mac mini and keyboard and mouse.** This is a reasonable compromise between the other two extremes.

✔ **Carry everything: mini, keyboard, mouse, and monitor.** This is the cheapest scenario because you only have to buy one set of hardware.

This chapter describes what you need for each of these alternatives, what they cost, and what they weigh.

Oh Solo mini

If you're carrying a mini by itself, you're using it as kind of a plug-in module. You can plug it into a preexisting setup when you go to visit a relative. Or, you can use the Mac mini to plug into your own setups. You have a desk at home all set up with a monitor, keyboard, printer, scanner, and maybe an iPod dock and a FireWire drive. The only thing missing is the computer. Then, you have another desk with a similar setup in another location — at work, in a dorm room, or at a vacation house. Instead of buying a computer for each location, you can plug in the same $500 Mac mini.

Power adapter: To carry or not to carry

Because the Mac mini doesn't run on batteries, you need to use the power adapter brick whenever you run the mini. At this point, no battery solutions are available to you, unless you've outfitted your car to power your Mini (see Chapter 13).

When carrying the power adapter, unplug the removable cable and coil it up. This prevents it from crimping, which, over time, can cause the cord to break.

If you're leaving everything except the mini at your different locations, it would be convenient to have a power brick at each location so that you don't have to carry it. This is an attractive option considering that the power adapter is a third of the size and weight of the Mac mini, not including the cords.

Apple doesn't sell the Mac mini power supply brick separately, but other vendors do. You can find mini power bricks at online stores that sell Mac parts, such as Mac-Pro Systems (www.mac-pro.com) and We Love Macs (www.welovemacs.com). The official name is the Mac Mini Power Adapter, and the part number is 661-3463.

There is a catch. The Mac mini power bricks sell for a whopping $110 or more, almost a quarter of the cost of the mini itself. (This could be why Apple doesn't sell the bricks at its online store.) This price could come down over time, so keep checking the Web. The Apple adapter is the only game in town; at least it was at publishing time. Should an alternative become available, it would need to have these power specifications:

- **Rating:** 85 watts AC, 110/230V
- **Output:** 18.5 VDC, 4.6 amps

Remember that a third-party power supply would have to use the proper power connector that plugs into the mini.

Cables

If you're leaving everything on the desktop, you don't need to bring many cables with you besides the power adapter. You may need the DVI-VGA adapter that comes with the Mac mini, though. If you're afraid of losing it, keep the adapter plugged into the mini's video port while you're on the road.

It doesn't hurt to also throw FireWire and USB cables in your bag, just in case.

Carrying a mini

If you aren't carrying a keyboard or monitor, a separate travel bag isn't necessary. You can easily slip the 6.5-x-6.5-x-2–inch Mac mini and the power adapter in a briefcase or backpack. An old laptop carrying case also works well for a Mac mini and the power adapter.

If you're throwing the mini in a bag with other stuff, consider using a cloth sack or slipcase to prevent scratches. An old ski cap does the job, though it may be embarrassing to show in public (see Figure 3-1).

Figure 3-1:
Mac ski hat hack: hip protection from scratches in a backpack, or just plain dumb?

A more upscale way to go is to use a carry bag that's designed to fit the Mac mini. These bags typically run about $40 and are approximately 7 to 7½ inches square. These include the Mac Mini SleeveCase, from Waterfield Designs (www.sfbags.com), which is shown in Figure 3-2. It protects the mini while keeping the size small enough to place in another bag. Another option is the eM², from Tom Bihn (www.tombihn.com). You can easily fit these cases inside a briefcase, larger carry bag, or backpack. Should you want a slightly wider, heavier bag that can fit a bit more inside it, consider the Sportfolio Mac Mini from Marware (www.marware.com).

Figure 3-2:
Waterfield's
Mac Mini
SleeveCase
fits inside
other bags.

Weighing in

Add up the weight of the Oh Solo mini travel option, and you get a good result. I'm not counting the weight of any bags or cases. But the smaller the bag, the less it weighs.

Mac mini	2.9 pounds
Power brick, cable	1.25 pounds
Total	**4.15 pounds**

For the sake of comparison, this is almost a half-pound lighter than the smallest PowerBook, which makes the mini and components a breeze to carry on airplanes and subways.

Toting the Keyboard with Your mini

BYOKM — bring your own keyboard and mouse — makes sense when you're traveling to places unknown, or to places known to not have keyboards. Or maybe you just don't want to buy a separate keyboard for each of your desks. If you get a keyboard that's maximized for traveling, you won't add much weight. You add some length, however, and you need a bigger bag.

Mobile keyboards

You *could* carry a full-size keyboard with you, if you must have all 109 keys. Or, a smaller, lighter keyboard could suffice. The following sections describe your options, including smaller, lighter keyboard variations.

Some of these keyboards are oriented toward PCs instead of Macs. Chapter 2 describes the differences and how to get around them.

Slightly smaller keyboards

When you're looking for a smaller keyboard, the first thing you can ditch is the area in between the alphabet keys and the numeric keypad. This area includes the full-size Home, Page Up, and Page Down keys and the full-size arrow keys. Keyboards without this area usually shrink these directional keys and fit them around the alphabet keys.

Apple used to provide this type of keyboard with Macs in the late 1990s. Figure 3-3 shows one of these older models (on top) next to a current Apple keyboard.

Figure 3-3:
The top keyboard is missing the middle section, which makes it shorter and lighter.

A good example of a smaller keyboard is the Kensington SlimType Keyboard ($40, www.kensington.com). It includes Mac-specific keys and a Mac-like look. For another $10, the SlimType Ultra has a built-in USB port. So-called slim keyboards are lighter because they use less plastic.

It's scandalous to say this among power users, but I prefer the shorter keyboards, even on desktop Macs. The mouse is closer to the center than with a standard-size keyboard, and I have more desk space.

Mini keyboards

An even smaller class of keyboards is known as *mini keyboards.* No, they're not named after the Mac mini. They're the same size as keyboards used in notebook computers. Mini keyboards, such as the one shown in Figure 3-4, do away with the numeric keypad as well as that middle area that I describe in the preceding section. As on notebook keyboards, some of the alphabet keys on mini keyboards double as numeric keys.

Figure 3-4: A mini keyboard is similar to that of a notebook computer.

Eliminating the middle area and the numeric keypad shrinks mini keyboards to under a foot in length — five or six inches shorter than full-size keyboards. This means that you don't need a big bag to carry one.

The alphanumeric keys are usually full-size, as in the PowerBook or iBook keys. Mini keyboards shrink the keys that you don't often use, such as the function keys.

Ergonomic Resources (www.ergonomickeyboard.biz) and Fentek Industries (www.fentek-ind.com) offer a variety of mini keyboards. None are Mac-specific, but the USB keyboards work with your Mac mini.

The main drawback to mini keyboards is that it's difficult to find a Mac-specific model. Chapter 2 shows you how to get around that. Just make sure that you buy a USB keyboard, not one that uses some other type of interface.

Cables

Don't forget to bring a USB cable if the keyboard doesn't have one or if you aren't using a wireless keyboard. It's a good idea to include an extra USB cable and a FireWire cable in your mini travel kit. It's also wise to bring the DVI-VGA adapter that comes with the Mac mini if you're not sure what type of monitor awaits you at your destination.

Carrying the mini with a keyboard

One option is to carry the Mac mini in a slipcase (as described in the section "Carrying a mini," earlier in this chapter) and carry the keyboard in a separate case. Waterfield Designs (www.sfbags.com) has a keyboard carrying case for $29. It's designed to hold Apple's USB and wireless keyboards, but it also fits smaller keyboards.

To put everything in one bag, the bag needs to be big enough for the keyboard. Waterfield Designs' Large Vertigo ($89) can fit a mini keyboard and a Mac mini and power adapter. The company offers a bundle of the Large Vertigo with the Mac Mini SleeveCase for $119.

You can find similar large bags, as well as bags that fit large keyboards, at Tom Bihn (www.tombihn.com) and Marware (www.marware.com).

Bags designed to carry 17" notebook computers can fit a keyboard and a Mac mini. Plenty of these are available. eBags (www.ebags.com) offers a good selection from different manufacturers.

Weighing in

Keyboard weight varies from just over a pound for a mini keyboard to more than 2½ pounds for a full-size keyboard. I use a mini (12") keyboard weight to calculate the following total. I didn't include the weight of a carrying case because they can vary a great deal.

Mac mini	2.9 pounds
Power brick, cable	1.25 pounds
Keyboard (mini)	1.2 pounds
Mouse	0.2 pounds
Total	**5.55 pounds**

By comparison, this is the same weight as the mid-size, 15-inch PowerBook. This is still a reasonable amount to carry around town and across the country.

Taking a Display with You

Carrying around a monitor with your Mac mini isn't as crazy as it might sound, as long as we're talking *flat-screen* monitor. You can place it in a bag with the mini and a keyboard and actually lift it.

Of course, people will tell you to go buy an iBook — and you might consider doing that. But if you just want to move your computer between desks at different locations, and you don't need to run on battery power, you can save hundreds of dollars with a Mac mini and an LCD screen. A Mac mini and a monitor are also significantly lighter than an iMac.

What you mainly need is a small, lightweight display and a bag in which to carry it.

Displays you can carry

Don't look to Apple for lightweight flat-panel monitors. Apple's smallest is now a 20-inch display, and it ain't cheap.

You can buy a lightweight, 15-inch display for less than $300 (and sometimes less than $200). Everyone wants a 17-inch or larger monitor, so the 15-inchers have become a bargain. This is also a good size to use for regularly moving among home, office, or school. It's the same size as the most popular notebook format (and bigger than the biggest iBook). So unless you're a professional graphics designer, you aren't really giving up much by using a 15-inch monitor.

You have a lot of 15-inch monitors to choose from. Searching Tom's Hardware Guide (www.tomshardware.com) and clicking "less than 17-inch" brings up 131 15-inchers. Here are a few of them:

- ✔ **15-inch Hitachi CML152:** Weighs 6.6 lb. and sells for about $290
- ✔ **15-inch NEC AccuSync LCD52V:** Weighs 7.1 lb. and sells for about $230
- ✔ **15-inch Samsung SyncMaster 153T:** Weighs 7.1 lb. and sells for about $180

You get the idea. For reviews of 15-inch displays, check the big hardware review sites, such as PCWorld.com, PCMag.com, and CNET.com. Macworld.com is good, too, but remember, nothing is Mac-specific about a display. A monitor is a monitor.

A transportable flat-panel monitor doesn't have a big stand that isn't removable. Most stands are removable or can fold. Apple's older "picture frame"–style stands were ideal for carrying because the stand folded flat on the unit. Look for this option on other flat panels.

Carrying cases

Some travel bags marketed for big laptops can hold flat-screen displays as well. You often have pockets into which you can slip the Mac mini and a keyboard. Manufacturers include Timbuktu (www.timbuk2.com), Trager, Columbia Sportsware, and many others. eBags (www.ebags.com) is a shopping site that has bags from a few different vendors that can fit flat-panel displays. To find them, search for "monitor" in the search field on the home page.

A complete, full-size portable workstation

Perhaps you're not interested in small monitors and tiny keyboards. You're also not interested in unplugging and plugging in a bunch of USB, FireWire, and video cables every time you move the Mac mini. But you're still interested in throwing it all in the car to move it around.

Take a look at iMove, an extreme carrying case that's designed and sold by Rivo Cortonesi. iMove isn't actually a case; it's a transportable rack that holds the Mac mini and the power brick, a full-size 19- or 20-inch flat-panel monitor, and a full-size keyboard. To move the rack, unplug the power cord from the wall socket, attach the cover, pick up the rack, and put it in your car. Everything, including the power brick and the cables, is fixed to the frame. You don't have to unplug cables, nor do you have to compromise on keyboard and monitor size. There's no setup, either, when you get to your destination. Remove the cover, plug in the power, pull out the keyboard, and you're ready to boot. Look for the iMove at Cortonesi's Web page, http://homepage.mac.com/rcortonesi/iMove/

Make sure that you measure your monitor and check the size that the bag holds, not just the external dimensions of the bag. Monitors tend to have a bigger border around the screen than those on laptops. A bag designed for a 17-inch notebook computer should fit a 15-inch flat-panel display.

If you are flying regularly and want to check your monitor, you can find rigid shipping cases specifically designed to hold monitors. The cost is more than that for carry bags; cases for 15-inch flat-panel monitors start at about $250. Cases for bigger monitors cost more. Some even have wheels. To get a feel for what's available, visit JustCases.com (www.justcases.com).

Weighing in

Of course, if you don't care about weight, you can always use a bigger carrying case for a full-size monitor and keyboard.

But if you do care about what you're lifting, here's what you can expect. The estimated weight here assumes a mini-size (12-inch) keyboard and a 15-inch flat-panel display. Even 15-inchers vary in weight, so I've taken a bit of a conservative estimate, using a weight that is greater than two of the monitors I mention earlier in this chapter. I don't include the weight of the carry bag in the estimate.

Mac mini	2.9 pounds
Power brick, cable	1.25 pounds
Keyboard (mini)	1.2 pounds
Mouse	0.2 pounds
15-inch LCD	7.5 pounds
Assorted cables	1 pound
Total	**14.5 pounds**

This is 4 pounds lighter than a 17-inch iMac without its keyboard, or 6 pounds lighter than an iMac with its keyboard. The heavier iMac has its advantages — a bigger screen and full-size keyboard, and it's all in one piece. The Mac mini–based mobile setup wins on price, however, costing about $500 less than the iMac. It's also about $500 less than the cost of a 14-inch iBook. This is $500 that you can spend on something else, such as another Mac mini.

Part II
Cracking Open the mini

The 5th Wave   By Rich Tennant

"Kevin! I'm looking at the bottom of your Mac mini, and I don't think you're going to need a putty knife to get into this thing."

In this part . . .

You can accomplish a lot by plugging innovative hardware into your Mac mini. But when you crack open the case, you open up whole new worlds — or a whole new can of worms if you go in blindly. That's where this Part comes in.

Although the term "crack open" sounds a little drastic, it describes the feeling you get while you're gaining access to the guts of the mini. In this Part, I share the tools and techniques you need to open your mini. You also discover the wonders packed inside this tiny little box.

Chapter 4

Opening the Mac mini

In This Chapter

▶ Keeping your warranty intact

▶ Choosing the right tool

▶ Eliminating static electricity

▶ Removing the outer casing

▶ Closing up the Mac mini

Opening up the Mac mini lies somewhere in between challenging and nerve wracking. It's not difficult, but it's not exactly easy, either. The first time you open it you may experience apprehension, anxiety, befuddlement, and anxiety. Most of this is gone the second time you crack open your Mac mini, though you still need to take care not to do any damage.

You need to open the Mac mini in order to do many of the mods in this book. So take a deep breath, collect the right tools, and think before you act. If you do, you'll find yourself marveling at the insides of an amazingly well engineered computer — one that you haven't broken.

Anyone who needs to open the mini should read this chapter.

Going Where Apple Doesn't Want You

The principles of opening Mac mini are similar to those of opening an iPod. There are no screws. Invisible tabs hold it together. To get inside, you have to pry it open by sticking something where you'd least expect it. In short, it looks like Apple designed the Mac mini to keep you out.

In a sense, this is true. The primary design goal for engineers in Cupertino was to squeeze as much hardware into as small a space as possible. Because of this, taking the Mac mini apart is not as easy as it is in more spacious Macs such as the Power Mac or even the iMac G5.

To prevent people from dangerously poking around the mini's guts just for fun, Apple discourages mini owners from performing their own internal upgrades. It does this with a case that appears to be impenetrable. Of course, the key word here is *appears,* because you can open the case without any special tools.

Another key word here is *discouragement.* Apple doesn't *forbid* you from opening your Mac mini. The first hint of this is buried in the warranty.

Keeping the warranty intact

I don't know about you, but the warranty isn't the first thing I tear into when I eagerly open the stylish packaging of a brand new Mac. Filled with impenetrable, 100-word sentences of gobbledygook, warranties are written by attorneys for other attorneys.

Yet, for Mac mini modders, it's important to be aware of what's in the warranty. If your Mac mini is less than a year old, you don't want to unintentionally void the warranty. Now, you may want to *intentionally* void the warranty with a radical modification. If not, here's an English translation of the Mac mini warranty.

For one year after you buy your Mac mini, Apple will either replace defective parts or give you a new or rebuilt mini. If you damage anything while you have the mini open, Apple won't replace the part you broke. So if you break or bend a plastic or metal part, or damage your memory card while removing it, you're stuck with that part.

Fortunately, Apple doesn't say you can't open the Mac mini yourself. Opening and disassembling the Mac mini does not void the warranty.

Another piece of good news is that any damage you cause doesn't void the entire warranty. If you break a tab off and the hard drive dies, Apple will still replace the hard drive.

But there's another line of warranty interpretation that grows out of this. If Apple thinks that the broken tab led to the dead hard drive, it won't warranty the hard drive. This means you need to think about a chain of causality. If you need to break something, or intentionally cut, bend, or otherwise modify a part, you may unknowingly affect the viability of another part, thus voiding the warranty for that other part. The more radical the mod, the less likely Apple will replace damaged parts.

If you can't get to sleep at night and want to read the warranty, don't fret because you've thrown it away with the mini's packing material. You can read it at Apple's Web site: www.apple.com/support/macmini.

Minding your AppleCare contract

For $150, you can buy the AppleCare Protection Plan, which is a contract that extends your mini's warranty to three years. The extended warranty will also cover certain Apple peripherals you buy with your Mac mini, such as a display or an AirPort Extreme transmitter. It also extends phone support from 90 days to three years.

Not a bad deal for a heavily used Mac and a user who doesn't want to futz with it. It's less of a deal for modders, because the extended warranty has the same exclusions as the standard warranty I describe in the preceding section. It doesn't forbid mods, but the more physical hacking you do, the less likely Apple is to replace broken parts.

The bottom line is if you're going to do a lot of hardware hacking, don't buy the AppleCare Protection Plan extended warranty.

The Putty Knife: The Official mini-Cracking Tool

There's no need to buy an expensive new tool set to get inside the Mac mini. The official tool for cracking open the mini is an inexpensive putty knife, available in any hardware store. You do, however, need to modify the putty knife slightly using some sandpaper in order to get it ready for mini-cracking duty.

Okay, my editors want me to tell you that the technical word for a properly prepared putty knife is *disassembling tool.* A real "cracking tool" would be a hammer, which I don't recommend for this particular job.

The best putty knife for the job

Apple recommends that you open a Mac mini with a 1½-inch-wide putty knife, shown in Figure 4-1. A small putty knife lets you cleanly get in, pop the inner tabs, and get out. Some say that it's easier to open the Mac mini using a wider putty knife, one that's several inches in width. The tradeoff is that a wider knife is more difficult to insert and more work to modify with sandpaper.

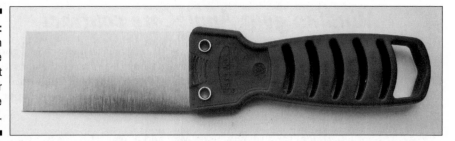

Figure 4-1:
A 1½-inch
putty knife
is the best
tool for
opening the
Mac mini.

A metal cooking spatula also works, as long as you modify it with a bevel, as described in the next section. I find a spatula to be awkward to work with because the handle is so far away from the blade.

You may be tempted to use a plastic tool in an effort to avoid scraping the aluminum case or denting the plastic housing. A good thought, but plastic won't work. Plastic tools are too thick for the job. Think thin for cracking open your Mac mini.

Modding your knife for cracking duty

Modifying the putty knife is important to opening the Mac mini. You will have a harder time if you don't, and you risk damaging the mini's case.

The idea of this mod is to create a bevel on the edge of the blade, which is visible in Figure 4-1. You bevel only one side of the putty knife's blade. This one-sided bevel enables the knife to slip into a narrow crack in the Mac mini's outer cover.

If a friend points out that a cutting knife is already tapered and might be a better option, don't let him near your mini. A knife's point and sharp edge will take a toll on the Mac mini's case.

The putty knife is a better choice, and beveling one side of the edge is quick and easy:

1. **Place a sheet of 120 or 150 grit sandpaper flat on a table or workbench.**

2. **Holding the putty knife at a 45 degree angle with the blade down, move it up and down the sandpaper for two or three minutes.**

3. **Check the edge periodically to see if your bevel is coming out even.**

Bevel only one side of the putty knife edge. You need the other side to remain straight in order for the putty knife to be effective.

A Quick Reconnaissance

Before you attempt opening the Mac mini, take a look at how it's put together. This section helps you visualize what you're doing while you're opening the mini.

Figure 4-2 is a view of the Mac mini in the position in which you disassemble it, upside-down. You can see the port panel on the left. Here, the cover is removed, exposing six white plastic tabs. Six more are on the other side. The ends of these tabs hold the Mac mini together.

Figure 4-2:
You open the Mac mini by pressing the white tabs inward.

Your job is to use your modified putty knife to push these tabs inward. This causes the tabs to slip out of a slot, which in turn, releases the cover.

Three plastic tabs are on the side opposite the port panel, as shown in Figure 4-3. This is the front side of the Mac mini. Unlike the side tabs, these front tabs don't need any attention from you while you're opening the Mac mini. You need to be aware of them when you replace the cover, though.

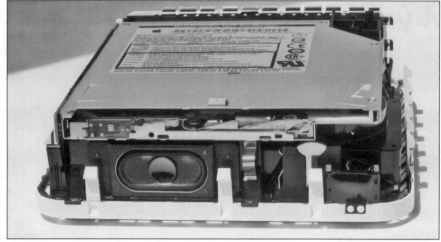

Figure 4-3:
Three
plastic tabs
hold the
front of the
Mac mini
together.

Removing the Outer Casing

To open up the Mac mini, you first discharge static electricity. This is the same phenomenon that causes the little zap you experience as you walk across a carpet and touch a metal lamp. This zap can damage the electronics inside the Mac mini. To prevent this damage, neutralize your body's static charge. Then wield your modified putty knife and dig in.

In this section, you discover how to accomplish both of these steps.

Discharging static electricity

Here's how to safely discharge static electricity from your body:

1. **Turn off the Mac mini and unplug all cables except the power cable.**

   Keep the power cable plugged into the wall to draw away any static electricity.

2. **Touch the metal part of the Mac mini.**

   This discharges the static electricity you may be carrying.

After you discharge, try to remain seated until after you finish closing up the Mac mini. If you get up to walk around, you can build up another static charge. If you need to get up, make sure you discharge yourself again by performing Steps 1 and 2 before touching any parts inside the Mac mini.

3. Unplug the power cord.

At this point, if you have an electrostatic discharge strap, attach it to your wrist. This will ground static electricity in your body while you work. A wrist strap isn't mandatory; it's an extra precaution. Manufacturers of RAM memory or other internal parts sometimes provide one. You can also pick one up at an electronics supply store.

Popping the top

After you have discharged static electricity, you are ready to open up this puppy. This is a tricky maneuver the first time you do it. The basic procedure is to use the modified putty knife to widen the gap between the outer casing and the inner plastic housing. This gap isn't apparent. It looks more like a thin line than a gap, but the bevel in the putty knife forces the gap open. (I describe how to bevel the putty knife in the previous section, "Modding your knife for cracking duty.") You then use the putty knife to release the tabs.

Here's how to open the mini:

1. **Place the Mac mini upside-down on a soft cloth with the rear port panel facing you.**

2. **Place the edge of the modified putty knife on the place where the aluminum outer casing meets the inner plastic housing.**

   Make sure the straight side of the putty knife faces the outer aluminum case and the beveled side faces the interior plastic of the Mac mini.

3. **Press the putty knife straight down into the narrow space between the outer aluminum casing and the inner plastic housing.**

   You may find it easier to start with a corner of the putty knife. You need to use some force when you press down. Don't be timid about it.

   To avoid scratching the aluminum case or gouging the plastic, press the putty knife down vertically, and not at an angle. Also, take care not to slip with the putty knife.

4. **Stop pushing when the putty knife suddenly slips down about a half inch or when you feel it stop.**

5. **Push the handle of the putty knife outward and down, as shown in Figure 4-4, to release the tabs inside.**

Don't use a lot of force here.

Clicking sounds indicate that the tabs are releasing. Keep pushing with the putty knife until the base of the Mac mini rises slightly above the outer case.

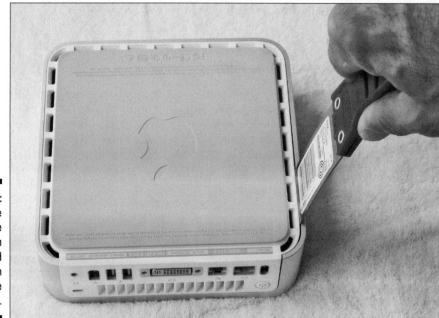

Figure 4-4:
Insert the
putty knife
and push
outward
and down
to release
the tabs.

6. **Repeat Steps 1 through 5 on the opposite side to lift that side.**

You may find that the first side of the mini has slipped down again. This means that you didn't lift the side far enough and the tabs have reengaged. If this is the case, go back and repeat the procedure.

After you complete this step, you should find that most of the tabs on the sides are disengaged and the port panel is lifted up slightly, as shown in Figure 4-5.

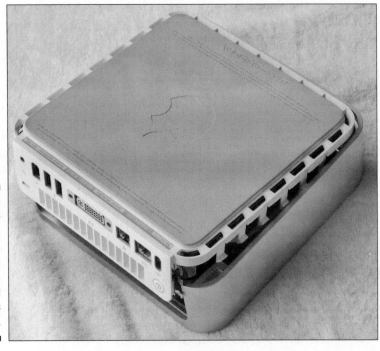

Figure 4-5:
After disengaging most of the tabs on both sides, the rear panel appears lifted.

7. **To release the remaining side tabs and the three tabs on the far side, lift the rear port panel and tilt the housing back.**

   You hear more clicking sounds as you do this.

8. **Continue pushing the port panel up and back until the Mac mini clears the outer casing.**

9. **Remove the body of the Mac mini from the outer casing and set it on its rubber bottom, as shown in Figure 4-6.**

You're now ready to start disassembling the guts of the Mac mini. Chapter 5 shows you how to locate the components and to begin disassembling the interior of the mini.

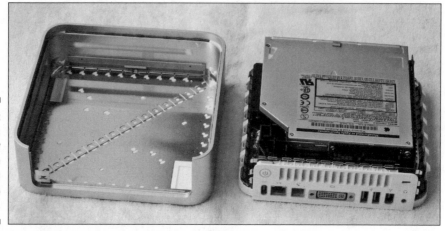

Figure 4-6:
Lift the Mac mini body out of the outer casing and set it on its bottom.

Closing Up the Mac mini

Just because you've opened the Mac mini doesn't mean you know how to close it. That's because the procedure for closing the Mac mini is *not* the reverse of removing it. There are two differences:

✔ You open the Mac mini when it is upside down; you close it in its upright position.

✔ When opening the Mac mini, you lift at an angle; when closing it, you move the case straight down. This is important.

Here's how to replace the outer casing:

1. **With the Mac mini sitting on its bottom, place the outer casing loosely on top of the Mac mini so that it is parallel to the table.**

   It is important that the downward motion of the outer casing is vertical at all times. Tilting the case can bend the metal tabs and guides.

2. **Align the plastic tabs so that they'll slip inside the outer casing as you move it down, as shown in Figure 4-7.**

   Don't forget the three white tabs on the side opposite the port panel. You need to align these as well.

3. **Align the metal tab above the right side of the port panel, also visible in Figure 4-7, so that it isn't forced to the outside of the mini.**

   You may need to push this tab in slightly as you close the mini.

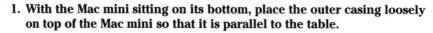

Figure 4-7:
Align all of
the tabs
before
pressing
down
vertically.

4. **Push the outer case down slightly.**

5. **Pick up the Mac mini with both hands with the port panel facing you.**

6. **Press the two sides with both hands while using your thumbs to apply pressure to the back.**

   Make sure the Mac mini goes down evenly on all sides.

7. **Just before you finish, make sure the row of metal tabs above the port panel is aligned with the top.**

   These metal tabs are visible in Figure 4-7. The danger here is that these metal tabs can easily bend outward as you press the casing down. If this happens, use a small pair of pliers to bend the tabs back.

8. **Slowly squeeze the Mac mini until it snaps together.**

If you finish one mod and plan to do another, you might want to leave the Mac mini open for a while. This will cut down on the wear and tear on the aluminum casing and plastic housing that repeated opening and closing could cause. Just be sure you discharge any static before you touch any part in the interior of the Mac mini. I describe how in the earlier section, "Discharging static electricity."

Chapter 5

First Mods Inside the Mac mini

After you crack open the Mac mini (which I show you how to do in Chapter 4), take it apart and explore the innards. The layout of the internal parts is not one that is easy to figure out, even if you've been inside a computer before. The Mac also has some unusual components that keep it all together.

If you are going to remove *any* parts inside the Mac mini, you need to read this chapter. Here, you discover where the parts are, what they look like, and what it takes to remove them.

This chapter also shows you how to remove the internal frame and the wireless antennas. You must remove these to access most of the mini's components that I describe in later chapters. This chapter also describes how to replace the battery.

Amazing, Isn't It?

I've peeked inside many a Mac since I cracked open my first 128K Macintosh back in 1984. But even to an old hardware hacker, disassembling the Mac mini is a remarkable experience. Inside this pint-sized package are all the parts of a full-sized computer, fitted together like a three-dimensional jigsaw puzzle. You have no space to move around in and no obvious place to begin disassembly. Buried deep within this mass are several expansion slots, though not in the traditional sense of the term.

A single, quiet fan cools the entire system, including the graphics processor. Although the internal Mac mini looks like a nearly solid amalgam of metal and plastic, it includes paths that route cooling air to where it is needed. Using

Keeping track of the screws

If you're planning to remove parts from the interior of the Mac mini after you open it, you'll be removing tiny screws. Not only are these screws easy to lose, but they are also of different sizes, so you need to keep track of which screws go where. One way to keep the screws separate (and to prevent loss) is to use small baby food or spice jars to hold them. Drop each set of screws into a different jar and immediately screw the cover on. Use masking tape to label the holders to identify which part the screws came from — hard drive, DVD drive, and so forth. This way, you can keep all the screws from accidentally spilling and know where to put them when reassembling your mini.

this effective system, the mini stays cooler than the PowerBook, which is known to sizzle.

Fortunately, after you remove the cover, you no longer need a putty knife. All the components are held together with screws — itsy, bitsy, tiny, and weenie, but without yellow polka dots. (Now *that* would be even more remarkable.)

Anatomy of a Mac mini

It may not look like it, but the Mac mini is modular in design, more so than other Macs. It consists of three major components, two of which hold all the parts. To access most of the parts, you separate the Mac mini into the following three modules:

- ✔ **Top housing:** This is the official name for the outer (or top) casing. Chapter 4 describes how to remove it.

- ✔ **Internal frame:** Made of black plastic, the internal frame holds the DVD drive and hard drive, the fan, and the speaker. This chapter describes how to remove the internal frame, which is the first step to gaining access to many of the parts.

- ✔ **Bottom housing:** This consists of the bottom and the backside port panel of the Mac mini. The bottom housing holds the motherboard, RAM, wireless cards, and ports.

Figure 5-1 shows the internal frame and the bottom housing separated.

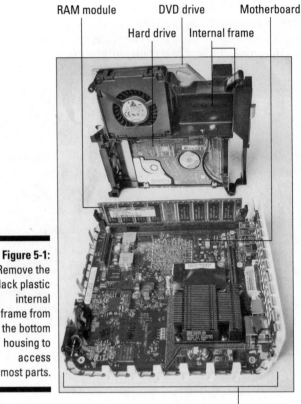

RAM module   DVD drive   Motherboard

Hard drive | Internal frame

Figure 5-1:
Remove the
black plastic
internal
frame from
the bottom
housing to
access
most parts.

Bottom housing

The first step in getting inside the Mac mini is to remove the outer casing.
The second step for accessing most parts is to remove the internal frame.
This chapter describes how to remove and replace the internal frame.

First, here's an overview of what the major Mac mini parts are and where
they are located in the internal frame or the bottom housing.

Interconnect board

The *interconnect board* is a 1-½-x-2-½–inch circuit board located on the rear of
the internal frame. It connects the hard drive and DVD drive to the motherboard. Both drives plug directly into the interconnect board without using
cables. The interconnect board provides the power and data signals to the
drives.

Figure 5-2 shows the interconnect board in place in the internal frame. The hard drive is visible at the bottom of the figure. The two screws in the top corners of the board hold the DVD drive in place. The fingers at the bottom of the interconnect board fit into a connector on the motherboard.

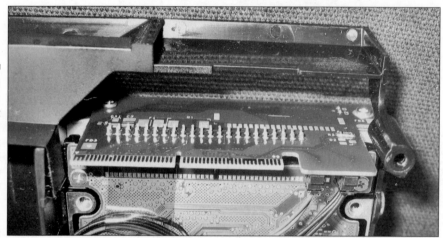

Figure 5-2: The interconnect board connects the DVD and hard drives to the motherboard.

The interconnect board also has two small cables plugged into it (visible on the lower right in Figure 5-2). One powers the fan, and the other provides audio to the built-in speaker.

AirPort, Bluetooth, and mezzanine board

The job of the mezzanine board is to hold the AirPort and Bluetooth cards and connect them to the motherboard. The AirPort and Bluetooth antennas are also connected to the mezzanine board. If you don't have either of these internal wireless options, your Mac mini doesn't have a mezzanine board.

Unlike iBooks, PowerBooks, iMacs, and Power Macs, getting to the AirPort slot in the Mac mini is not easy. Not only is the mezzanine board located in the bottom housing *under* the internal frame, but the AirPort and Bluetooth cards are also located on the *bottom* side of the mezzanine board. (The phrase "pain in the assembly" comes to mind.) Fortunately, if you already have these cards installed, you have no reason to get to them.

If you don't have AirPort and Bluetooth in your Mac mini, Chapter 6 describes how to add these features.

The DVD drive

The DVD drive is the first thing you see when you remove the cover, as I describe in Chapter 4. It sits on the top of the Mac mini stack in the internal frame. The Mac mini looks like it's all DVD drive, but the drive is actually only a half-inch thick.

You'll have either a "combo" DVD-R (read only) or a "superdrive" DVD-RW (read and write) drive. Both drives look the same, but Apple identifies which type you have on the yellow sticker near the bar code.

Compared to the AirPort card, or even the hard drive, removing and replacing the DVD drive is a breeze. You don't have to remove the internal frame — you just remove six screws. Chapter 8 describes how to remove the DVD drive. Unless you are replacing the drive, the DVD drive can stay put, because you don't need to remove it to get to anything else.

The hard drive

The hard drive is a small-form-factor drive, the same type found in iBooks and PowerBooks. It rests on the bottom of the internal frame and is not visible until you remove the internal frame. The hard drive sits next to the fan, which you must remove to remove the hard drive.

I show you how to remove and replace the hard drive in Chapter 7.

RAM

The RAM module sits in the Mac mini's single memory slot, which is located on the motherboard on the bottom housing. You can see the module in Figures 5-1 and 5-3. Replacing the RAM module with a higher-capacity version is easier than removing any other part, because you don't have to remove the internal frame or unscrew anything. But because of the cramped quarters inside the mini, removing RAM is not quite as straightforward as it is in other Macs.

Chapter 7 describes how to upgrade your RAM.

The mother of all boards

When you remove the internal frame, you reveal the motherboard in the bottom housing. Apple calls it a *logic board,* but the rest of the world calls it a motherboard. The terms are interchangeable.

The motherboard, shown in Figure 5-3, is actually a two-sided circuit board, with chips and circuitry on the top and bottom. In one sense, the motherboard *is* the computer, because it contains the circuitry that does all the thinking. The ports (on the right side of Figure 5-3) are soldered onto the motherboard, as are the processor, graphics chip, and RAM slot. The modem card (for telephone dialup) sits on top of the motherboard. The two slots visible in the figure are for the mezzanine board (left) and the interconnect board (right).

Connector for mezzanine board   Connector for interconnect board

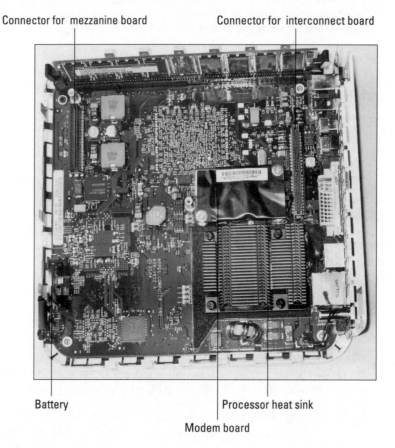

Figure 5-3:
The mother-
board sits in
the bottom
housing.

Battery   Processor heat sink

Modem board

The brains of the outfit

The processor does the number crunching in any computer. You don't see the processor because it sits under the heat sink. The fan in the internal frame draws hot air from the heat sink and pushes it away through the conduits built into the internal frame.

Because the processor is soldered to the motherboard, you can't upgrade the Mac mini with a faster processor. You can, however, bump the speed of a slower processor through a hack called *overclocking*. This procedure is described in Chapter 20.

Graphics and video memory

The answer to the question "Where's the video card?" is "There ain't one" — at least, not as a card. The first-generation Mac mini has an ATI Radeon 9200 graphics processor chip located on the back of the motherboard. The Mac mini also has 32MB of graphics memory. Like the processor, the graphics processor and graphics memory are soldered onto the motherboard, which means you can't upgrade the video. This is a trade-off of the Mac mini's low price tag.

Battery

Every Mac has a long-lasting lithium battery to help it boot and to remember the date and time. The battery in the Mac mini is a ¾-inch disk positioned on its side at the edge of the motherboard.

When your Mac mini gets to be a few years old, you may find that it no longer keeps the correct date and time after you turn it off. If this happens, you need to replace the battery. The section "Changing the Battery," later in this chapter, describes how to do this.

Removing and Replacing the Internal Frame

Many of the mods described in the following chapters begin by removing the internal frame. These chapters refer to this section for the procedure.

The RAM module and DVD drive are the only major parts that you can remove without detaching the internal frame. Replacing RAM is described in Chapter 7. DVD drive removal is described in Chapter 8.

If your Mac mini includes the built-in AirPort or Bluetooth options, you need to move the antennas out of the way to remove the internal frame, as I describe in the next section. If you don't have internal wireless, skip to the section "Removing the internal frame," later in this chapter.

Removing the antennas

The AirPort and Bluetooth antennas sit on top of the internal frame, with cables connected to the mezzanine board under the internal frame. If you have either feature, you have to remove its antenna to remove the internal frame.

Each antenna consists of a metal rectangle and a stiff wire (see Figure 5-4).

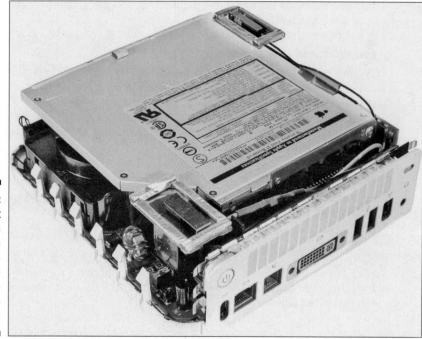

Figure 5-4:
The AirPort
antenna
is in
the fore-
ground; the
Bluetooth
antenna is
in the rear.

Removing the Bluetooth antenna

The Bluetooth antenna is located on the upper-left side of the Mac mini. It's shown in the background of Figure 5-4. Follow these steps to remove the antenna:

1. **Loosen the yellow tape that holds the antenna to the DVD drive.**

2. **Grab the rectangular portion of the antenna and pull it up and out. Place the antenna off to the side of the Mac mini.**

   The antenna remains connected to the Mac mini at the rear.

   Try not to bend the long, straight portion of the antenna. Doing so could degrade the Bluetooth connectivity.

Removing the AirPort antenna

The AirPort antenna is located at the rear of the Mac mini, as shown in the foreground of Figure 5-4. Unlike the Bluetooth antenna, the rectangular part of the AirPort antenna has a black latch that locks it down.

To remove the AirPort antenna, follow these steps:

1. **Loosen the yellow tape that holds the antenna to the back panel of the Mac mini.**

2. **Use a plastic implement (such as the handle of a plastic fork) to move the black latch toward the rear of the Mac mini.**

3. **Grab the rectangular portion of the antenna and pull it up and out. Place the antenna off to the rear of the Mac mini.**

You can now remove the internal frame, as I describe in the next sections.

Tools for removing the internal frame

The screws that hold down the internal frame are some of the smallest you'll see outside of a pair of eyeglasses. To remove them, you need a jeweler's #0 Phillips screwdriver. You can pick one up at an electronics supply store, such as Radio Shack, or at most hardware stores. Figure 5-5 shows one sitting next to a quarter.

Figure 5-5:
A jeweler's #0 Phillips and a pair of bent nose forceps.

If you can find one, I highly recommend using a pair of special tweezers, sometimes called *bent nose forceps*, shown in Figure 5-5. They're great for lifting the screws out of the wells that they sit in, and even more useful for holding the tiny screws as you replace them. You can find bent nose forceps in electronics and hobby stores.

Removing the internal frame

Three screws hold down the internal frame, making it fairly easy to remove. You need a jeweler's #0 Phillips screwdriver to remove these screws.

Follow these steps to remove the Mac mini's internal frame after the top cover is off (as I describe in Chapter 4) and any antennas are set aside (see the previous section):

1. **Pull back the yellow transparent tape on the right rear of the unit to release the power button cable, as shown in Figure 5-6.**

   Should you need to buy some more of this type of tape, look for *kapton tape.*

Figure 5-6: Peel back this bit of tape to detach this small cable from the internal frame.

2. **Remove the two screws near each corner at the rear port panel of the Mac mini, as shown in Figure 5-7.**

   These screws sit in wells, so it's best to remove one screw at a time. If you have a pair of forceps, use them to pick each screw out of the well that it sits in. If you don't have forceps, turn the Mac mini upside down so that the screw falls in your hand.

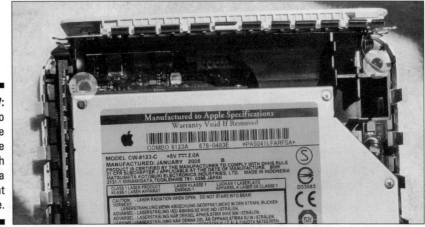

Figure 5-7:
These two wells at the rear of the mini each contain a screw that you remove.

3. **Remove the screw in the right-front corner of the Mac mini, as shown in Figure 5-8.**

Figure 5-8:
Remove the screw in the right-front corner of the Mac mini.

4. **Lift the internal frame straight up, unplugging the interconnect board from the motherboard as you do.**

    The interconnect board is located at the rear end of the DVD drive. If you look closely at Figure 5-7, you can see the edge of the board.

If you have Bluetooth or AirPort, guide the antenna cables down through the opening in the internal frame as you lift the frame.

Replacing the internal frame

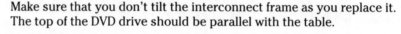

After you're finished with your mod, reinstall the internal frame by following these steps:

1. **Line up the interconnect board with the connector on the motherboard.**

2. **Press the interconnect board into the connector, and lower the internal frame onto the Mac mini.**

   Make sure that you don't tilt the interconnect frame as you replace it. The top of the DVD drive should be parallel with the table.

3. **Drop the screws into the wells and fasten them with a jeweler's #0 Phillips screwdriver.**

   Bent-nose forceps work well for placing the screws into the well.

4. **Retape the power button wire to the internal frame using the yellow tape.**

5. **If you have Bluetooth or AirPort, replace the antennas and refasten with the yellow tape (refer to Figure 5-6). For AirPort, use a plastic tool to slide the black tab on the rectangular portion of the antenna to lock it down.**

Changing the Battery

With the internal frame removed, you can replace the battery if it has exhausted its charge. The battery, located at the front edge of the motherboard, is shown in Figure 5-9.

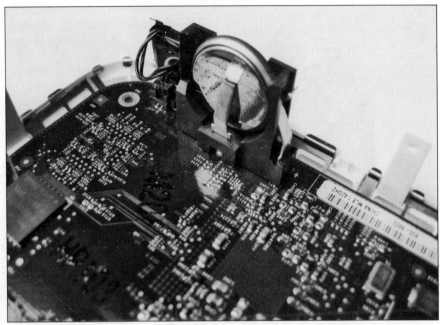

Figure 5-9:
Pull up on
the battery
to remove it.

There's a little bit more to changing the battery than just sticking a new battery in the slot.

1. **Pull the old battery up out of the slot.**

2. **Push the new battery down into the slot.**

3. **Wait at least 10 seconds.**

4. **Reset the Power Management Unit (PMU) by pressing the PMU switch located near the ports at the rear of the motherboard, as shown in Figure 5-10.**

Use a plastic tool to press the switch. The back of a plastic fork works, but don't use a metal tool. You can use your finger if it fits, but you won't have much control.

Don't press the PMU more than once. Pressing it multiple times could damage the PMU circuits.

Figure 5-10:
After changing the battery, press the PMU switch on the motherboard.

Resetting the PMU also resets the parameter RAM, which erases the date and time stored in the Mac mini. After you replace the internal frame and the outer cover, reconnect the outer cables, boot the Mac mini, and then reset the date and time in System Preferences.

Part III
Upgrading the mini Yourself

The 5th Wave   By Rich Tennant

AFTER INSTALLING OSX 10.2, NED AND LORETTA SELECT THE COMPUTER'S BACKGROUND

"Oh—I like this background _much_ better than the basement."

In this part . . .

Conventional wisdom says that the Mac mini isn't upgradeable. But conventional wisdom isn't always so wise when it comes to mods. Or Macs.

Sure, you *could* pay someone to add more memory, or you *could* send your mini out to get AirPort installed. But since you bought this book, I'm guessing that you don't want to.

Once you get inside, the thing to realize is that it's tough to guess how the Mac mini's mass of pint-size parts come apart (without breaking, that is). Reassembling isn't straightforward, either, unless you don't mind ending up with extra parts.

In this Part, I show you how to mod a wireless mini to include internal AirPort and Bluetooth. You'll also discover how to upgrade the RAM and the hard drive, and how to replace a DVD read-only drive with a DVD burner. And how to put it all back together again.

Chapter 6

String Your Own Wireless

Part of a Mac's appeal is the clean lines of Apple's eye-catching designs. What a shame you have to muck it up with tangles of cables for peripherals and networking — unless, that is, you go wireless. You also get the practical effects, of course.

Apple offers two wireless options for the Mac mini: wireless networking, known in Macs as AirPort, and wireless peripherals, known as Bluetooth. If you didn't order one or both of these options when you bought your mini, you can add them for about the same cost as ordering them in a new mini. This chapter shows you what to buy and how to install it.

What's in a Name

Although Apple refers to wireless networking as AirPort, the Windows world refers to it by its engineering name, IEEE 802.11. (Kind of rolls off the tongue, doesn't it?) Sometimes the PC world refers to it as *wireless Ethernet,* which is a bit of an oxymoron that means "wireless wired networking."

The type of AirPort that Apple uses in the Mac mini is called *AirPort Extreme,* which can operate at two different speeds: 11 Mbps (known as 802.11b) and the faster 54 Mbps (called 802.11g). The main point to remember is that they are all compatible — AirPort, wireless Ethernet, and 802.11 — whether they are on other Macs or on Windows PCs.

Windows users sensibly refer to Bluetooth as "Bluetooth," the code name that stuck when the technology went to market. The name comes from the 10th-century Viking King Harald Blatand, who was known as Bluetooth. The standard explanation for using the name is that Bluetooth (the king) united Denmark and Norway, just as Bluetooth (the technology) unites devices. But knowing how engineers think, I'd guess that the naming had something to do with the standard's co-creation by the mobile-phone company Ericsson, as in Leif Ericsson, the 10th-century Viking explorer. Engineers are funny that way.

Buying and Installing Internal Wireless

In the Mac mini, AirPort and Bluetooth are tied at the hip. Both sit on the same daughter card, called the *mezzanine board*. Both use radio frequencies over the air, and both have antennas that plug into the mezzanine board.

This results in two different approaches on adding wireless, depending on what you already have:

- ✔ **You have neither wireless option.** You have to buy and install a mezzanine board, as well as the wireless card or cards and antennas.

- ✔ **You have one wireless option, either AirPort or Bluetooth.** Your Mac mini already has a mezzanine board. To add the second wireless option, you just need to buy the wireless card (AirPort or Bluetooth) and the appropriate antenna.

The installation procedures for each situation differ as well. With the first situation, you install a new mezzanine board that contains the wireless cards. With the second, you remove the existing mezzanine board to install the wireless card.

The next section describes the first situation, installing wireless where no wireless has gone before.

Installing if you don't have wireless

If you have neither AirPort nor Bluetooth, I recommend adding both at the same time, along with the mezzanine board. You can save money over adding only one wireless option, and the installation is easier.

If all you need is Bluetooth, you can spend a lot less money by plugging in a small external USB Bluetooth adapter. For more information, see the section "The USB Approach to Wireless," later in this chapter.

Buying what you need

The best way to add wireless to your Mac mini is to buy a kit that includes everything for both AirPort and Bluetooth. You can find the kit for under $100, which is cheaper than if you bought all the parts separately.

The kit is called the Apple Mac Mini AirPort Extreme and Bluetooth Upgrade Kit. It contains the following parts:

✔ Mezzanine board.

✔ AirPort Extreme card. This is the standard AirPort Extreme card that can go in any Mac sold today.

✔ AirPort antenna.

✔ Bluetooth card.

✔ Bluetooth antenna.

✔ Two #0 Phillips-head screws.

The kit isn't available at many of the ordinary online Mac stores, but there are a few specialty outlets that carry them. Check out these:

✔ PC SuperStore (www.pcsuperstore.com/)

✔ Cost Central (www.costcentral.com/)

✔ ExperCom (www.expercom.com/)

✔ Adorama (www.adorama.com/)

Prices can vary a lot, so I recommend that you shop around.

At the time of publication, Apple didn't sell kits on its Web site. Apple retail stores do sell the kits but require that you let them install it — you have to bring your Mac mini into the store. The Apple retail stores don't have the best price, but they don't charge for installation either.

Tools for installation

The only installation tool you need is a jeweler's #0 Phillips screwdriver for the three screws that hold the internal frame and for the two screws that secure the mezzanine board.

Sometimes the kit comes with yellow kapton tape to secure the antenna wire to the DVD drive. If your kit didn't come with any, pick some up at an electronics store such as Radio Shack.

Installing the wireless kit or mezzanine board

When you buy a kit, the AirPort Extreme and Bluetooth cards are already installed on the mezzanine board, with the antennas already connected to the board.

Figure 6-1 shows the mezzanine board with the two wireless cards installed, as they come in the wireless kit. The AirPort Extreme card is the one with the yellow tape. The Bluetooth card is the small card at the top. You can also see that the antennas are connected to the cards.

Figure 6-1:
The preinstalled AirPort and Bluetooth cards on the mezzanine board.

Figure 6-1 shows the bottom side of the card, the side that faces the motherboard when you install it. The lower portion of the photo shows the connector.

Follow these steps to install the kit:

1. **Remove the Mac mini's outer cover, as I describe in Chapter 4.**

2. **Remove the internal frame, as Chapter 5 describes.**

3. **Locate the place on the motherboard where you will plug in the mezzanine board.**

   There are two connectors on the motherboard, as shown in Figure 6-2. You plug the mezzanine board into the connector that's closer to the RAM module. The other connector (closer to the processor heat sink) is for the interconnect board.

Figure 6-2:
Plug the mezzanine board into the connector at the upper left.

4. **Turn the mezzanine board so the AirPort Extreme and Bluetooth cards are facing the motherboard.**

5. **Plug the mezzanine board into the connector on the logic board.**

6. **Install the two screws at opposite corners of the mezzanine board using a jeweler's #0 Phillips screwdriver.**

   Figure 6-3 shows what the installed mezzanine board should look like.

Figure 6-3:
The installed mezzanine board and the Bluetooth and AirPort antennas.

7. **Make sure that the antenna cables are firmly seated in the mezzanine board.**

8. **Pass the antenna cables through the gap at the rear of the internal frame.**

9. **Carefully lower the internal frame down onto the motherboard.**

   Make sure that the wires are routed to the right of the interconnect board.

10. **Replace the three screws in the internal frame to secure it to the bottom housing.**

11. **Snap the AirPort antenna onto the black plastic column (as shown in Figure 6-4) next to the rear port panel.**

   The AirPort antenna is the larger of the two.

Figure 6-4:
Snap the
AirPort
antenna
onto this
black
column.

12. **Secure the power button cable to the black plastic column using the yellow kapton tape.**

    Figure 6-4 shows the location of the tape on the column, with the wire cable still loose just below it.

13. **Tape the AirPort antenna wire to the edge of the DVD drive.**

14. **Clip the Bluetooth antenna into the black plastic slot at the edge of the DVD drive, near the RAM module.**

15. **Tape the Bluetooth antenna wire to the edge of the DVD drive.**

    The installed antennas should look like those shown in Figure 6-5.

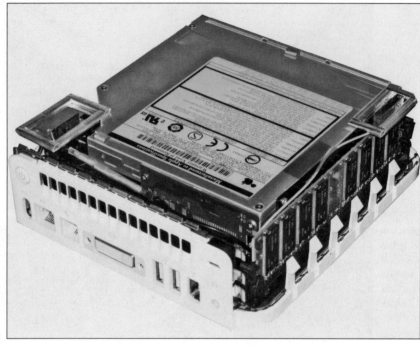

Figure 6-5:
The
installed
antennas
look like
this.

16. **Replace the outer cover of the Mac mini, taking care not to bend any of the metal tabs.**

    Chapter 4 has some tips for getting the cover on without bending anything.

Installing if you already have Bluetooth or AirPort

If you already have either AirPort or Bluetooth and want to install the other wireless option, your Mac mini already has a mezzanine board installed. All you need to buy is the appropriate card and antenna. The AirPort and Bluetooth cards are of a type used in other Macs, but the antennas are specific to the Mac mini.

Shopping for individual wireless parts

Individual Mac mini wireless parts are harder to come by than the Apple Mac Mini AirPort Extreme and Bluetooth Upgrade Kit. One Web site that does carry individual parts is Computer Graphics and Network USA (http://cgnusa.com).

You may not, however, save any money. A single card and antenna can cost just as much as the entire kit, containing both sets of wireless options and the mezzanine board.

You *will* save money if you already have an AirPort Extreme Card. The Mac mini uses the standard Apple AirPort Extreme Card (shown in Figure 6-6), which is used in all Macs. In this case, you just need to buy the Mac mini AirPort antenna and an inexpensive role of kapton tape, the translucent yellow tape used in various places inside the Mac mini.

Figure 6-6:
A standard
AirPort
Extreme
card fits
in the
Mac mini.

Kapton tape is heat resistant, with adhesive that doesn't go all gooey on you inside of a warm Mac mini. You can find kapton tape at electronic supply stores or on Web sites, including, strangely enough, KaptonTape.com (www.kaptontape.com/).

TIP

The Mac mini uses the same Bluetooth cards found in most other modern Macs, but these cards aren't sold as widely as AirPort Extreme Cards. For instance, Apple doesn't sell them at its online store. In fact, if you already have AirPort and only need Bluetooth, I recommend going with a 1-inch external USB Bluetooth adapter instead. This can save you as much as $70 and is much simpler to install. You can find more information on external wireless options in the section "The USB Approach to Wireless," later in this chapter.

Installing Bluetooth or AirPort in a preinstalled mezzanine board

When you already have either Bluetooth or AirPort, installing the other is quite easy; just follow these steps:

1. **Remove the Mac mini's outer cover, as I describe in Chapter 4.**

2. **Remove the Bluetooth or AirPort antenna and internal frame, as detailed in Chapter 5.**

3. **Use a jeweler's #0 Phillips screwdriver to remove the two screws in the opposite corners of the mezzanine board (which you can see in Figure 6-3).**

4. **Remove the mezzanine board by pulling it straight up.**

5. **Insert the AirPort Extreme or Bluetooth card in the slot on the mezzanine board.**

   You can see the location of the cards in Figure 6-1.

6. **Fasten the wireless board to the mezzanine board using one of these methods:**

   • *AirPort card:* Place kapton tape on two sides of the AirPort card–mezzanine board assembly, as shown in Figure 6-1.

   • *Bluetooth card:* Screw in two #0 Phillips screws in opposite sides of the card, as shown in Figure 6-1.

7. **Plug the AirPort or Bluetooth antenna into the appropriate card.**

8. **Install the mezzanine board and reassemble the Mac mini, as described in Steps 3 through 16 in the section "Installing the wireless kit or mezzanine board," earlier in this chapter.**

The USB Approach to Wireless

If you don't care to crack open your Mac mini, you can use a good ol' USB port to add wireless Bluetooth and AirPort. External adapters are not quite as clean as having it all inside, and you'll spend more money on the external approach if you want both Bluetooth and AirPort. If you want to add only Bluetooth, however, an external adapter is less expensive than an internal card and antenna.

USB Bluetooth

One of the main reasons to go wireless is to get rid of cables. A Bluetooth USB adapter fulfills this goal. It plugs right into a USB port, extending out about 1¼ inches, as shown in Figure 6-7. Unless your Mac mini is in a very tight space, an external Bluetooth adapter can be as invisible as internal Bluetooth.

Figure 6-7: The tiny D-Link USB Bluetooth adapter is cheaper than internal Bluetooth.

The D-Link USB Bluetooth adapter (www.dlink.com) is a popular device that you can find for under $30. You don't have to install any software; just plug it in and it works.

External AirPort

At this point, the external AirPort solutions are not as attractive as external Bluetooth. You can find small AirPort USB adapters that are slower than the internal AirPort or adapters that are just as fast, but are large.

For small and slow, you can use D-Link's $49 DWL-122, which is an 11-Mbps (802.11b) device. Now, *slow* is a relative term. A rate of 11 Mbps is faster than a typical DSL Internet connection can handle, but it's slow if you're moving big files around between computers.

For fast and big, try the 54-Mbps Macsense AeroPad Mini 802.11g ($90, www.macsense.com). *Big* is also a relative term; the AeroPad Mini is 3⅛-inches long × 2⅜-inches wide × ¾ inch thick. But unlike the DWL-122 and the Bluetooth adapter, the AeroPad Mini requires cables, two of them to be exact. A USB cable delivers power to the adapter and an Ethernet cable transmits the data signals. This is similar to Apple's AirPort Express, but the latter plugs into a wall outlet for its power, which ties you down.

Several small 54-Mbps USB 802.11g adapters (the Belkin Wireless G USB adapter, for instance) are available, but at this time, they don't work with Mac OS X. The hardware is fine, but they don't have Mac driver software. This could change at any time, so keep checking.

Chapter 7

Upgrading the Hard Drive and RAM

. . . .

In This Chapter

▶ Buying and replacing RAM

▶ Buying a new hard drive

▶ Removing and replacing the internal hard drive

▶ Restoring software, files, and settings

. . . .

*I*f you want to make your Mac mini faster, upgrading RAM and your internal hard drive is the way to do it. Installing RAM is easy; replacing the hard drive takes a bit more work.

RAM is short for *random-access memory,* often referred to as just *memory.* You may have heard some people refer to a hard drive as *memory* as well, but the correct term is really *storage.* Hard drive storage is permanent, but RAM is erased every time you shut down the Mac. RAM is a solid state, which means that it has no moving parts. A hard drive has spinning disks as well as some electronic components.

Upgrading RAM means getting bigger RAM that can hold more data, which, in turn, makes the system faster. Upgrading the hard drive means getting a drive that can hold more data *and* that spins at a faster rate.

This chapter describes what you need to buy and how to install what you buy to replace these internal components. Of course, you can always plug in an external drive, but an external drive cuts down on portability and is slower than an internal drive.

If you haven't already opened your Mac mini, you may want to read Chapters 4 and 5, which describe how to remove the cover and disassemble the internal frame.

Chapter 19 describes hacking the Mac mini to attach a bigger hard drive than usually fits inside the mini.

Upgrading RAM

Upgrading RAM is a pretty simple procedure. Crack open the Mac, press a couple of tabs, and add the new RAM. You have no screws to remove and no other parts that you need to remove first. If you're thinking of paying someone to upgrade your Mac mini's RAM, keep in mind that the installer isn't going to work very hard to earn your money.

When replacing RAM, you have to buy the correct amount and type.

Mac OS X performance and RAM

RAM is tied to performance in a negative way. Too little RAM leads to slow performance and frequent appearances of the dreaded spinning beach ball. Adding RAM can fix this, but only to a point, and it depends on what you're doing. Microsoft Word, for example, is not going to run faster with 1GB RAM than with 512MB. iMovie, though, runs faster.

How much is enough?

During the first seven months of the Mac mini's existence, it came with 256MB RAM. Apple realized that this wasn't enough and upped the minimum configuration to 512MB.

If you're dedicating the Mac mini to playing DVD movies in your car, you probably don't need more RAM. But if you're editing movies, photos, or audio, you need more.

If you are going to upgrade, I encourage you to consider going for the maximum of 1GB RAM. Consider that the Mac mini has a single RAM slot. When you upgrade RAM, you take out the old RAM module and replace it with a new one. The old RAM module might make a good coffee stirrer, but it isn't good for much else. That means that you should upgrade once and buy as much RAM as you think you'll ever need.

Buying the right RAM

Different computers have different types of RAM. You can often just ask for RAM that works with the Mac mini. But if you're shopping around, it's good to know what you're looking for.

The Mac mini comes with a type of RAM called PC2700 (333-MHz) DDR SDRAM with 184 pins — quite a mouthful. It can also use PC3200 (400-MHz) DDR SDRAM, which is the same size. The latter is faster RAM, but the Mac mini runs it at the same (slower) speed as the PC2700 DDR SDRAM. There's no point in paying more for the PC3200 type.

I like to find the best RAM prices at www.RAMseeker.com. This site doesn't sell RAM but instead lists the cheapest prices for your specific Mac from multiple RAM vendors. RAM prices fluctuate daily, so check just before you decide to buy.

Installing a new RAM module

In this section, I describe how you remove the old RAM module and add the new module. First is removing the old RAM module:

1. **Remove the outer casing (as I describe in Chapter 4).**

2. **If you have internal Bluetooth, remove the Bluetooth antenna by following these steps:**

    a. *Loosen the yellow tape that holds the antenna to the DVD drive.*

    b. *Grab the rectangular portion of the antenna and pull it up and out. Place the antenna off to the side of the Mac mini.*

The antenna remains connected to the Mac mini at the rear.

Try not to bend the long, straight portion of the antenna. Doing so could degrade the Bluetooth connectivity.

3. **Locate the RAM module on the left side of the Mac mini.**

4. **Push down on the black plastic latches on both sides of the RAM module.**

The left latch hits the metal shielding and doesn't go as far down as the right latch, as shown in Figure 7-1. This is normal. Don't force it or you can damage the shielding.

Because the right latch can go down farther, the right side of the RAM module pops up slightly, as Figure 7-1 shows.

Figure 7-1:
The latch on the left side of the RAM module doesn't go down as far as the right latch.

5. **Carefully grab the top of the right side of the RAM module and lift it out of the slot, right side first, as shown in Figure 7-2. Then pull out the left side.**

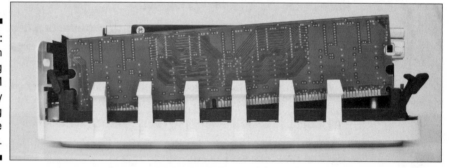

Figure 7-2:
Begin removing the RAM module by pulling up on the right side.

Now you can install the new RAM module.

Your new RAM module looks something like the one shown in Figure 7-3. Notice the two sets of gold-plated fingers at the bottom. (No kidding, this is real gold.)

Figure 7-3:
A RAM module has two sets of fingers of different sizes.

You're not imagining things if the module looks lopsided. One side of the fingers is bigger than the other side. This guarantees that the RAM module fits in only one way. If it's not going in, you have it oriented the wrong way.

To install the module, push it straight into the RAM slot. Don't put it in at an angle. Keep pushing until the two latches automatically pop up into the locked position.

Buying a Replacement Hard Drive

Let's face the facts: The Mac mini comes with a slow hard drive that isn't particularly big. This gives you two reasons to replace the internal hard drive: to get a drive that can store more data and that is faster than your current drive. (Okay, there's a third reason — to replace a dead hard drive. But if the hardware gods aren't angered, a hard drive should last many, many years.)

You can buy a drive that has a larger capacity, one that is faster, or one that is both bigger *and* faster. You'll pay more for the latter, so you should think about what you need.

There is no such thing as a "Macintosh hard drive" or a "PC hard drive." A hard drive is a hard drive. You do need a drive with an IDE interface, however, not a serial ATA interface.

Buying a faster drive

You probably know that capacity is measured in gigabytes (GB). Hard drive performance is indicated by the rotational speed of the disks inside. Apple has shipped hard drives in the Mac mini that turn at 4,200 or at 5,400 revolutions per minute (rpm). If you have the former, you can easily find 5,400-rpm hard drives, which can boost the performance of your mini. For the fastest drive, look for a 7,200-rpm unit. While 5,400-rpm drives are common, 7,200-rpm drives that fit in the mini first appeared in 2004, so they are more difficult to find, particularly in larger capacities.

Buying the right form factor

One thing you don't have a choice of is form factor. The *form factor* is measured by the size of the disk that spins inside the drive. The Mac mini uses a 2.5-inch-diameter drive, as shown in Figure 7-4, next to two bits (as in 25 cents, not part of a byte). A 2.5-inch drive is sometimes called a *notebook drive* because it's the form factor that fits into notebook computers, including PowerBooks.

Figure 7-4:
The Mac
mini uses a
2.5-inch
hard drive,
shown here
next to
two bits.

Be sure you buy an *internal* drive, not a FireWire or USB drive.

Replacing the Hard Drive

Unlike replacing RAM or the DVD drive, removing the hard drive requires you
to dig deep inside your Mac mini. It's also complicated by the fact that you
need to install software.

Replacing the hard drive includes four basic steps:

1. (Optional) Back up your software and settings.
2. Remove the old drive.
3. Install the new drive.
4. Install Mac OS X and the software on your new drive.

Steps 2 and 3 are straightforward; just follow the step-by-step directions. But
you have several options with Steps 1 and 4, depending on what software you
want to save and how you would like to handle it. I describe the options for
Steps 1 and 4 in the next section of this chapter.

Throughout the rest of the chapter, I go through these four basic steps in detail — and in order. I start with the different options for Step 1, saving your software.

Saving your software and settings

You can choose one of several strategies to get your software, files, and settings from your old hard drive to the new one. Here are the best scenarios:

- ✔ **Don't save anything.** If you don't have any settings or files on the Mac mini that you need, you don't have to back them up. The Mac mini Install DVD that came with your mini can create a new installation of Mac OS X exactly as you found it when you started up your mini for the first time. The original applications that came with your Mac mini are also installed.

- ✔ **Install your old drive in a FireWire enclosure.** You can place the old drive in an inexpensive enclosure, which turns your old internal drive into a handy external hard drive. Neat, isn't it? You then use Migration Assistant to automatically migrate your files, applications, and settings to the new internal drive.

- ✔ **Manually copy files and settings to discs.** You copy preference files, documents, and applications that didn't come with the Mac mini to CDs or DVDs. After you install the new hard drive, you use the Mac mini Install DVD to restore Mac OS X and the Apple applications. Then you manually add the other files you copied.

To discover how each of these scenarios work, keep reading.

Don't save anything

If you don't need to save anything, you don't have to do anything here. It's a piece of cake, the absolute easiest option. If this is you, move on to yanking out the old hard drive, described in the section "Tools for removing the hard drive," later in this chapter.

Installing your old drive in a FireWire enclosure

This is the best option if you have a lot of settings, a mess of documents, and a lot of applications that you've installed. It saves you from having to reinstall your applications from the installation CDs and from reconfiguring all the settings, or from manually copying preference files.

But wait, there's more! This option lets you use your old hard drive as an external drive, which is a very useful thing to have no matter what you are doing with your Mac mini.

If you want to go this way, you don't need to copy anything because everything you need is already on the old hard drive. You can proceed to the "Tools for removing the hard drive" section. For more on reusing your old hard drive, see the "Turning Your Old Drive into an External Drive" section, later in this chapter.

Manually copying files and settings to discs

This option is the most time-consuming way to move your files and settings to your new drive. Here, you selectively copy files and settings to CDs or DVDs. The problem is, there are hundreds of files with weird names in dozens of folders. In the next few sections, I show you which folders to move to your new hard drive.

Saving settings: the Preferences and Application Support folders

To save the settings from your old hard drive, copy the Preferences folder and the Application Support folder onto one or more CDs. A typical Preferences folder is 20MB or so in size. The Application Support folder can be up to several hundred megabytes, depending on how many applications you have.

The Preferences folder is where Mac OS X keeps your settings for AirPort, networking, Internet, QuickTime, keychain, printing, and other features of your Mac. Application Support contains settings for applications as well as certain related files. Some Web browsers store bookmarks here.

If you are using Safari and want to save bookmarks, you should also copy the Safari folder.

All three of these folders reside inside the Preferences folder, which is located in the Library folder in your home folder. In the language of paths, the locations are described as follows:

- ✔ /Users/(*your user name*)/Library/Preferences
- ✔ /Users/(*your user name*)/Library/Application Support
- ✔ /Users/(*your user name*)/Library/Safari

Saving applications

You don't need to back up the applications that came with your Mac mini. The Mac mini Install DVD installs them onto the new drive for you.

For other applications, you may need to copy them from the old hard drive to CDs or DVDs. Many applications work when you drag and drop them to the new hard drive. However, some may not be functional with a simple drag and drop. For these, you have to install them from their original CDs. You also have to download and install any upgrades that you may have added.

Saving documents

If you have data on the old hard drive that you want to keep, copy your files to one or more CDs or DVDs.

If you have a lot of data on the Mac mini, the Documents, Music, Movies, and Pictures folders could each be quite large, depending on what you have in them. If you don't have a DVD burner and have a lot of data, some of your files may be too big to fit on a CD. If this is the case, or if you have more data than can fit on a reasonable number of optical discs, consider the option of placing your old hard drive in an external hard drive enclosure to turn your old hard drive into an external drive. (See the section "Turning Your Old Drive into an External Drive," later in this chapter.)

Back-up software

By "manually copy," I was thinking of the good ol' drag 'n drop procedure. But you can also use back-up software to copy files from the old hard drive to optical media. If you have back-up software, go for it. If you don't, here are a couple of suggestions.

If you happen to subscribe to Apple's .Mac service (www.mac.com), you can download a copy of Backup, Apple's back-up software available only to members. It backs up keychain passwords, your address book and calendar, and various settings to your online .Mac account or to a CD or DVD. The nice thing about Backup is that you don't have to know where Mac OS X hides these things — you just check them off in a list. You can also select folders of your files.

If you already have an external hard drive handy and want to create an identical copy of what's on your hard drive, Carbon Copy Cloner (www.bombich.com) is the best buy for an amazing $5. Carbon Copy Cloner copies everything, including Mac OS X's invisible files, which enables you to start up from the back-up drive.

As a reminder, though, you don't *need* to copy everything (or anything, for that matter) if you're going to reuse your old hard drive in an external FireWire enclosure.

Tools for removing the hard drive

To remove the internal hard drive from the Mac mini, you need two Phillips screwdrivers. One is a small, jeweler's #0 Phillips screwdriver, and the other is a standard (not "jeweler's") #1 Phillips. You can pick up the jeweler's #0 at an electronics supply store, such as Radio Shack, or at most hardware stores. Figure 7-5 shows the two screwdrivers sitting next to a quarter.

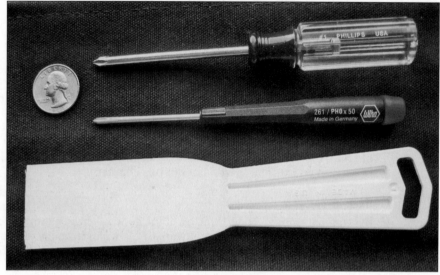

Figure 7-5:
Use these
tools to
replace
the mini's
hard drive.

The third tool that you need is a plastic putty knife or other plastic, thin implement for unplugging the drive connector. I like the putty knife because it's tapered at the edge. The plastic putty knife in Figure 7-5 costs a buck.

You can use another thin plastic implement, but do not use a metal tool, or you risk damaging the Mac mini's interconnect board.

Removing the drive

To remove your Mac mini's internal hard drive, follow these steps:

1. **Remove the outer casing, as I describe in Chapter 4.**

2. **Detach the internal frame from the bottom housing, as described in Chapter 5.**

3. **Turn the internal frame over, as shown in Figure 7-6.**

4. **Use a jeweler's #0 Phillips screwdriver to remove the three screws on the corners of the fan.**

   Note that the lower-right corner of the fan (as shown in Figure 7-6) does not have a screw.

5. **Flip the fan to the left, as shown in Figure 7-7.**

Figure 7-6:
You can see
the hard
drive and
fan with the
internal
frame
flipped over.

Tape to remove

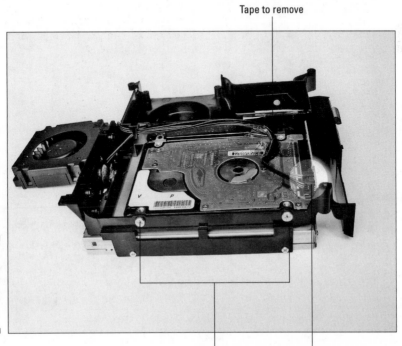

Figure 7-7:
Remove the
fan and
place it to
the side.

Screws   Fan and speaker cables

6. **Unplug the fan and speaker cables from the interconnect board.**

   The spot where the cables plug into the interconnect board is shown in the lower-right corner of Figure 7-7.

7. **Remove the yellow tape (shown in Figure 7-7) that attaches the cables to the hard drive.**

   You may notice another piece of yellow tape that covers a small hole in the black plastic internal frame; you can see this tape near the upper-right corner of Figures 7-6 and 7-7. Do not remove this tape; the hole needs to be covered to direct airflow within the Mac mini.

8. **Using a #1 Phillips screwdriver, remove the two hard drive screws on the black internal frame, as shown in Figure 7-7.**

9. **Remove the remaining two hard drive screws on the opposite side of the hard drive, as shown in Figure 7-8.**

10. **With a nonconductive tool (such as a plastic putty knife), pry the hard drive off the connector of the interconnect board, as shown in Figure 7-9.**

Figure 7-8:
Remove the two screws (center) in the black frame.

Figure 7-9:
Unplug the hard drive from the interconnect board with a plastic tool.

11. **Lift the hard drive out of the internal frame.**

Installing the new drive

Installing the new hard drive is almost, but not exactly, the reverse of removing it. Follow these steps:

1. **With the circuit-board side of the hard drive facing up, align the connector pins of the hard drive to the black connector on the interconnect board, shown in Figure 7-10.**

You can't place the drive on the surface and slide the drive into the connector. If you do, the fingers don't align with the connector. Instead, you need to hold the hard drive above the surface.

Figure 7-10:
The hard drive connector and the fan and speaker connectors.

I find this easiest to plug the drive into the connector if I rotate the whole assembly 90 degrees so that the hard drive is going down into the connector.

Take care not to bend any of the pins on the hard drive.

2. Push the hard drive all the way into the connector.

To avoid stressing the interconnect board, support the back of the connector board with your fingers as you push the drive in.

3. Replace the four screws, two on each side of the hard drive, using a #1 Phillips screwdriver.

These screws are shown in Figures 7-7 and 7-8.

4. Connect the fan and speaker cables to connectors on the interconnect board, as shown in the upper-right corner of Figure 7-10.

5. Fasten the cables to the hard drive with the yellow tape that you previously removed, as shown in Figure 7-7.

6. Place the fan partially into the internal frame, with the cable side touching the internal frame and the rest tilted up at an angle, as shown in Figure 7-11.

Figure 7-11:
It may take
a few
attempts to
route the
fan cable
properly as
you replace
the fan.

7. **Route the fan cables under the bottom clip of the frame and through the slots, as shown in Figure 7-11.**

   The cables don't have much extra space in which to flap around. This routing keeps the cables out of the way and prevents them from getting pinched when you reassemble the internal frame.

8. **Push the fan down all the way into the internal frame.**

9. **Replace the three fan screws using a jeweler's #0 Phillips screwdriver.**

10. **Replace the internal frame as described in Chapter 5.**

11. **Replace the top casing as described in Chapter 4.**

Turning Your Old Drive into an External Drive

After you upgrade your hard drive, your Mac mini is faster or has more storage. But it bugs you that you have a perfectly good hard drive — your old drive, complete with Mac OS X, your applications, and your settings — sitting on a shelf. You *could* use it as a very cool-looking but expensive coaster.

Don't put your coffee cup on it yet, though. For under $40, you can make good use of your old drive by turning it into an external hard drive, which you can use for backup.

To do this, buy an external hard drive enclosure. This is basically an external hard drive without the drive inside. Enclosures come in USB 2.0 and FireWire flavors. You need FireWire to use the Migration Assistant to move your software and settings to the new drive. FireWire drivers are also faster than USB drivers.

 Make sure that you buy an enclosure made for 2.5-inch hard drives, not for 3.5-inch drives. You can find 2.5-inch FireWire hard drive enclosures in stores all over the Web. One good source is PC Pitstop (`www.pc-pitstop.com/external_enclosures/`).

The process of getting the drive into the enclosures depends on the particular enclosure you have. Here's the basic procedure:

1. **Open the enclosure.**

   If you're lucky, there are screws or some other obvious means of getting inside.

2. **Place the drive inside the enclosure and plug the drive into the cable or connector inside.**

3. **Fasten the drive to the enclosure.**

   The enclosure may use screws or clips to hold the drive in place.

4. **Reassemble the enclosure.**

Installing Software

A new hard drive is a blank slate. To make it functional, you need to install Mac OS X, your applications, and your data and settings files.

You have three options for installing software, data, and settings on the new drive. I describe these three options in the section "Saving your software and settings," earlier in this chapter. Here are the methods for installing the software:

✔ **You had nothing to move.** If this is the case, just use the Mac mini Install DVD to install Mac OS X and all the software that came with the Mac mini.

✔ **You placed your old drive in an external enclosure.** Follow these two basic steps:

   1. Use the Mac mini Install DVD to install Mac OS X and all the software that came with the Mac mini.

2. Use Migration Assistant to move your files, settings, and documents from the old drive to the new drive.

✔ **You manually copied files from the old hard drive.** Here, you use the Mac mini Install DVD to install Mac OS X and all the software that came with the Mac mini. Then you manually drag files that you saved from the CDs or DVDs to the new internal hard drive.

The following sections describe these methods. But notice a common thread here: The first step for all three situations is to install Mac OS X and the Mac mini applications onto the new drive. This is described in the next section.

Installing Mac OS X and applications

The Install DVD that came with the Mac mini can install both Mac OS X and the bundled applications. Here's how to run the installation:

1. **Turn on the Mac mini.**

2. **Insert the Mac mini Mac OS X Install DVD that came with the computer in the optical drive slot.**

   The Mac mini now boots from the DVD. The Mac OS X installer appears on-screen.

3. **Click through the dialogs until the installer asks you to select a destination disk.**

4. **Click the Options button.**

5. **Choose Erase and Install.**

6. **Select Mac OS Extended (Journaled) from the Format Disk As pop-up menu.**

   The word *journaled* refers to a log (or a journal) that Mac OS X keeps to continuously record changes to a file. If the hard drive is unexpectedly stopped, such as with a power failure, the journal helps Mac OS X restore the drive so that it can function correctly.

7. **Click the OK button.**

8. **Click through the remaining dialogs, following the instructions.**

When the installation is complete, the Mac mini restarts from the hard drive. A series of screens appear where you create a username and password and enter settings. You're also asked to enter Internet settings. You can enter them now, but you don't need to if you've saved your old settings or if you would just rather do it later.

Installing Mac OS 9 (optional)

If you need to run older Mac OS 9 applications in the Classic environment, you need to install Mac OS 9 separately. You can find the OS on a separate installation disc called the Mac mini Mac OS 9 Install disc. To install Mac OS 9, follow these steps:

1. **Insert the Mac mini OS 9 Install disc.**

2. **Double-click the `Install Mac OS 9 System Support` file.**

3. **Click through the screens until you get to the Select a Destination dialog.**

4. **Select your hard drive and click the Continue button.**

5. **Select the Mac OS 9 (US English) check box and click the Install button.**

You can go have a cup of coffee while the installer does its thing. It won't take as long as the Mac OS X installation, so maybe just a quick espresso.

Using the Migration Assistant with your external drive

If you installed your old hard drive in an external FireWire enclosure, you can use the Mac OS X utility called Migration Assistant to move your settings, applications, and files to the new internal hard drive. (If you moved your files and preferences manually, skip to the next section.)

Follow these steps to move your software from the external drive to the internal drive:

1. **Plug in the external FireWire enclosure that contains your old hard drive.**

2. **If the Mac mini is off, start it by pushing the Power button.**

3. **Launch Migration Assistant.**

   You can find Migration Assistant in the Utilities folder, which is inside the Applications folder.

4. **Click the Continue button on the screen that appears.**

5. **In the Authenticate window that appears, type your Mac OS X password.**

6. **In the Migration Method window that appears, select the From Another Volume in this Mac check box, as shown in Figure 7-12, and click the Continue button.**

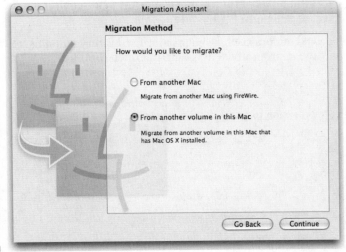

Figure 7-12:
Choose this setting to migrate your software from your older hard drive to the new drive.

7. **Choose the external FireWire hard drive (your old hard drive) and click the Continue button.**

   After you click the Continue button, it may take a few minutes for the Migration Assistant to gather the system information from the external drive.

8. **Select a user to migrate, and click the Continue button.**

   If you never set up multiple users on the Mac mini, you should see only your name, as shown in Figure 7-13.

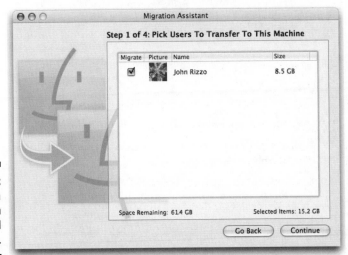

Figure 7-13:
Select a user from your old drive.

9. **Select the types of things that you want to move to the new hard drive, as shown in Figure 7-14.**

   Files and folders contain your data. The Library contains your settings. Only the appropriate settings are migrated (not the entire Library folder).

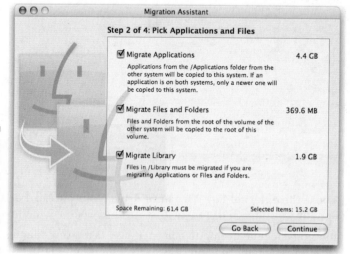

Figure 7-14: Select the items you want to move to the new internal drive.

10. **Click the Continue button until you get to the Machine Settings dialog, as shown in Figure 7-15.**

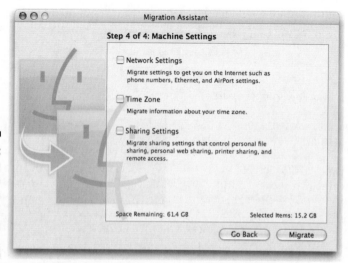

Figure 7-15: Choosing time zone and settings to import in Migration Assistant.

11. **Choose the type of time zone and network-related settings you want to import.**

    If you used the same name for the new account as you did for your old account, the dialog in Figure 7-16 appears.

12. **Choose the Replace the Existing User Account with the One You're Transferring option.**

    This option gives you a single user account on the Mac mini. The first option (Rename the Account) gives you two user accounts, one that has all your old settings and files and a second that is the basic account that the Mac mini first sets up.

Manually adding your files and settings

If you didn't install your old hard drive in an external enclosure, but instead copied your preferences and files, read this section.

At this point, you have a Mac mini with the software set up exactly as it was when you first took it out of its Styrofoam shell. You may have copied several folders to optical discs, including Preferences, Application Support, Documents, Music, Pictures, or Movies. Don't replace the new folders with your old folders, because this can mess up your setup. Instead, selectively choose which files to drag over into the new folders.

In the Preferences folder, you can move all the files with Apple in the file-name, as well as files and folders related to applications you have. The same is true with the Application Support folder.

After you copy the Preferences and Application Support files to the new drive, you can drag over applications from your backup optical discs to the Applications folder on the new internal hard drive. Many applications, such as Microsoft Office, are fully functional. Other applications may be missing files that were stored in other places and won't launch. If you run into any of these, reinstall them from their original installation CDs.

Chapter 8

Installing a DVD Drive

• •

• •

*I*f your Mac mini did not come with a SuperDrive, you have two options for adding the ability to write to DVD discs: plug in an external FireWire DVD burner or replace the internal optical drive with a DVD burner. Fortunately, the optical drive is one of the easier parts to replace inside the Mac mini. This is mainly because you don't need to remove the internal frame.

In this chapter, you discover which optical drives work in the mini and how to install a drive.

But first, I want to set the record straight on optical drives: There is no actual "burning" involved in writing to a CD or a DVD. Yes, lasers are involved, but they bear no relation to light sabers or Federation-issue phaser guns. But because "DVD burning" is the common lingo, I use it throughout this chapter.

Reasons to Replace an Optical Drive

You can find good reasons to have the ability to burn DVDs. You can use the iDVD software that came with your Mac mini to put your home movies on disc and watch them on TV. A DVD's 4.7GB of storage is also an attractive and cost-effect alternative to using CDs for storage and backup.

Of course, this doesn't do you any good if you didn't get a SuperDrive when you ordered your Mac mini. You have a choice between plugging in an external DVD burner drive or replacing your internal optical drive. An external drive is certainly the easiest way to go — all you do is plug it in.

There are good reasons however to go the internal route and to do it yourself:

- ✔ **Getting a faster drive than Apple offers:** Apples offers a 4X DVD burner drive (at least, as of publishing time), but 8X drives are plentiful. This translates into faster burning. (The section "Understanding the X factor: Drive speed," later in this chapter, describes 4X, 8X, and other Xs in more detail.)

- ✔ **Buying an internal DVD burner drive is cheaper than buying an external FireWire drive:** Because an internal drive doesn't come with an external case with a FireWire interface, vendors can sell the internal version for less money.

- ✔ **Saving desk space:** You may have bought a Mac mini to keep your desk free of computer equipment. Adding an external DVD burner is just one more piece of clutter.

- ✔ **Replacing a broken drive yourself to save money:** Of course, this only saves you money if your one-year warranty has expired. If it hasn't, send the broken mini back to Apple. The company owes it to you.

Putting it together, the story looks like this. When you bought your Mac mini, you didn't think you needed DVD burning. Now that you've decided that DVD burning is for you, you can spend under $100 for a new internal DVD burner. That's about the same as Apple would have charged, but you get a faster drive than Apple would have provided.

Buying the Right Drive

Most people find it more than a little annoying to buy a drive that doesn't work in your Mac, doesn't fit, or isn't the best drive for the money. With a confusing variety of standards and types, selecting a DVD burner is more difficult than choosing a hard drive.

The following sections show you what to look for in a DVD burner drive. I describe three main considerations here: form factor, read and write standards, and burning speed. Understanding these areas makes you an informed shopper.

You can find internal DVD drives specifically identified as working in the Mac mini at FastMac (www.fastmac.com) and OWC (www.macsales.com).

Determining what you already have

Your Mac mini came with either a Combo Drive (CD read and write, DVD read-only) or a SuperDrive (CD and DVD read and write). If you aren't sure what kind of drive is in your Mac mini, you can ask it:

1. **Go to the menu and select About This Mac.**

2. **Click the More Info button.**

   The System Profiler utility launches.

3. **Click Disc Burning in the Contents column on the left.**

You now see information about your optical drive. The window in Figure 8-1 says that the drive can read DVDs and can write to CDs, but doesn't mention writing to DVDs. That means this Mac mini has a Combo Drive and can't burn DVDs. If you have a SuperDrive, System Profiler adds a line called "DVD-Write."

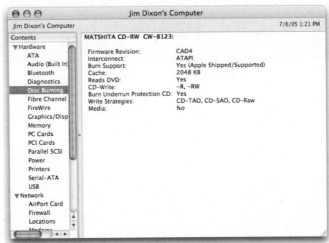

Figure 8-1:
System Profiler tells you what type of optical drive you have.

Form factor

The Mac mini uses the same size optical drives as those used in the PowerBook and other notebook computers. A mere half-inch thick, the drive fits in your hand, as Figure 8-2 demonstrates.

Figure 8-2:
The ultrathin
Mac mini
optical drive
fits in your
hand.

This photo is also informative in that it shows the drive's shape. If a drive isn't shaped like this, it's the wrong drive for the Mac mini.

The mini's optical drive also features *slot loading,* which means it sucks the disc into it, without using a tray.

Many DVD burner drives can fit in the Mac mini. Two examples are the TEAC Slim DV-W28E-793 and the NEC ND-6500A. You can find the latter for under $100. Both are 8X drives, which burn DVDs at twice the speed of Apple's drives.

DVD formats

DVD formats describe the method used to read and write data on an optical disc. The drive and the disc media are identified by these formats.

Apple uses the terms *Combo Drive* and *SuperDrive* to describe the formats that its optical drives support. You may see these terms used by companies that sell Apple products, but the rest of the world mostly ignores them. This is why it's helpful to know what the lingo means. Here's the translation:

- **Combo Drive:** This drive can read DVDs but not write to them. The world at large refers to this particular drive as *DVD-ROM/CD-RW*.

- **SuperDrive:** This drive is a DVD reader and burner. In the Mac mini, the SuperDrive is known as *DVD±RW/CD-RW*. This is what you look for when shopping for an upgrade to replace your mini's Combo Drive.

It doesn't help that Apple's terms are moving targets, because they mean different things at different times. A few years ago, a SuperDrive burner was DVD-RW/CD-RW, which, if you look closely, doesn't have the plus sign after the *DVD*. Next year, Apple may decide that SuperDrive means something else. Apple also applies the term *SuperDrive* to burners of different speeds, as described in the next section.

This is clear as day, unless you don't know what DVD±RW/CD-RW means, in which case it's clear as mud. In today's computerspeak, the terms *DVD±RW/ CD-RW* and *SuperDrive* indicate support of all the following CD formats:

- **CD-ROM** is read only. These are the CDs that come with music or software already on them. All optical drives support CD-ROM, which is why you can listen to *Liberace's Greatest Hits* while you work. Almost no drives sold today are CD-ROM–only drives.

- **CD-R** is write once. Burn something onto the disc, and it's permanent.

- **CD-RW** is erasable. In Mac OS X, after you burn something to the disc, you can erase it and burn it again.

With DVDs, things get more complicated:

- **DVD-ROM** is read-only. These discs come with prerecorded movies or software. This is the only DVD format that the Combo Drive supports.

- **DVD-R** is write once. Burn something onto the disc, and it's permanent.

- **DVD+R** is another write-once standard that competes with DVD-R.

- **DVD-RW** is erasable. In Mac OS X, after you burn something to a DVD-RW disc, you can erase the disc and burn it again.

- **DVD+RW** is a competing erasable standard to DVD-RW.

- **DVD±RW** means that the drive supports both DVD-RW and DVD+RW standards.

To sum up the endings for CDs and DVDs:

- ✔ **-ROM** — read only
- ✔ **-R** — read and write once
- ✔ **+R** — another read and write–once standard, but only on DVDs
- ✔ **-RW** — read, write, and erase
- ✔ **+RW** — another read, write, and erase standard, but only on DVDs
- ✔ **±RW** — a drive that supports both -RW and +RW, but only on DVDs

This information shows you not only which drive to purchase but which media (blank discs) to buy. If you don't need to erase a disc, the -R media is both cheaper to buy and faster to burn. You may also see price differences between the + and - flavors.

The final piece of the optical disc format puzzle is your software. If you're using the iDVD '05 software that came with your Mac mini, you can burn to any of these CD and DVD standards with your SuperDrive, a.k.a. DVD±RW. And that's just super.

Understanding the X factor: Drive speed

The last piece of information you need to know about is the speed of burning, as indicated by Xs, such as 2X, 4X, 8X, and so on. This designation means that if a 1X drive took an hour to burn a DVD, a 4X drive takes 15 minutes to burn the same disc. An 8X burner takes only 7½ minutes.

The speed listed for a DVD burner always refers to the speed for write-once burning using DVD-R or DVD+R media, which are the more common writable formats. The erasable discs (DVD-RW and DVD+RW) take twice as long to burn than what is indicated by the X rating. CDs, on the other hand, burn several times faster than DVD-R and DVD+R discs.

The SuperDrive that Apple currently puts in the Mac mini is a 4X burner. When you replace your Combo Drive with a new burner, there's no reason to buy a 4X burner. You can easily find 8X drives, such as the NEC ND-6500A, and 16X drives are on the horizon.

Blank disc media also have X ratings. You want the media speed rating to be equal to or higher than the drive speed. So, you can use 8X DVD-R media in a 4X drive. Media rated as slower than your drive takes longer to burn.

Replacing the Old with the New

The Mac mini's DVD drive is one of the easier components to replace, because you don't have to remove the mini's internal frame. With the right tools, you can upgrade the mini in 15 minutes.

Tools

For this job, you need three tools:

✔ **A small Phillips screwdriver:** Like the other screws in the Mac mini, the screws that hold the optical drive are tiny. A jeweler's #0 Phillips screwdriver works best. You can pick one up at an electronics supply store, such as Radio Shack, or at most hardware stores. Figure 8-3 shows one sitting next to a quarter.

✔ **Bent-nose forceps:** If you can find one, I highly recommend using a pair of these special tweezers, also shown in Figure 8-3. They're great for lifting the screws out of their holes after you unscrew them, and even more useful for holding the tiny screws as you replace them. You can find bent-nose forceps in electronics and hobby stores.

✔ **Plastic putty knife:** You need one of these for unplugging the drive connector. The one in Figure 8-3 set me back a whole dollar.

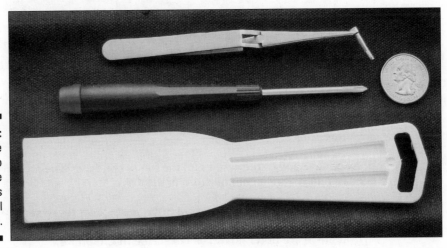

Figure 8-3:
Use these tools to replace the mini's optical drive.

You can use another thin plastic implement (instead of the plastic putty knife), but do not use metal, or you risk damaging the Mac mini's interconnect board.

Removing the old optical drive

The Mac mini's optical drive sits on top of the unit, as you can see in Figure 8-4. This is why you don't need to remove the internal frame, as you do for some of the other parts.

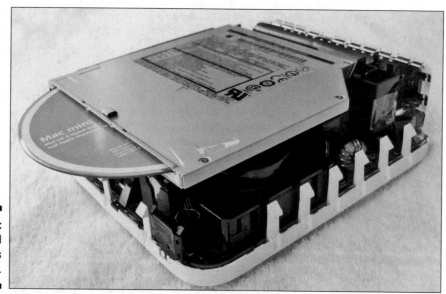

Figure 8-4: The optical drive sits on top.

Before you start, be sure to ground yourself by touching the metal part of the DVD drive while the Mac mini is plugged in. Then unplug the power cord and any other cables.

Don't remove any of the screws on the top of the drive. The six screws you need to remove are all on the sides of the drive.

Now you're ready to remove the old drive. Just follow these steps:

1. **Remove the outer cover, as I describe in Chapter 4.**

2. **If your Mac mini has internal AirPort or Bluetooth installed, remove the antennas, as described in Chapter 5.**

3. **Turn the Mac mini so that the right side is facing up, as shown in Figure 8-5.**

4. **Look under the part of the drive that juts out toward you and remove the two small screws in the black plastic frame, as shown in Figure 8-5.**

Screws

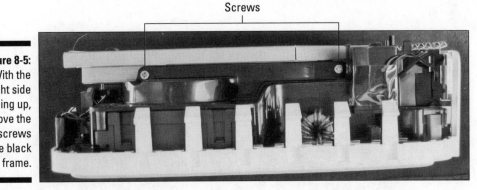

Figure 8-5:
With the right side facing up, remove the two screws in the black frame.

5. **Turn the Mac mini so that the left side is facing up, as shown in Figure 8-6.**

You can see two screws in the black plastic frame.

6. **If a portion of the screws sit behind the RAM, you may find it easier to access the screws if you remove the RAM module. Here's how:**

    a. Pull the two tabs on either side of the module away from the module.

    This releases the RAM module, which pops up slightly.

    b. Pull the RAM module out of the RAM slot.

7. **Remove the two screws shown in Figure 8-6.**

Figure 8-6:
On the left side of the mini, the two screws are located just above the RAM module.

8. **Place the Mac mini on its bottom and turn it so that the rear side is facing you, as shown in Figure 8-7.**

9. **Remove the two screws in the interconnect board, as shown in Figure 8-7.**

Your screwdriver needs to be at an angle to the screws; try not to drop them inside the Mac mini.

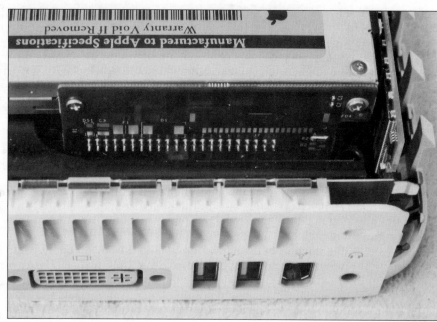

Figure 8-7:
Remove these two screws in the interconnec t board.

10. **Carefully use your plastic putty knife to unplug the optical drive from the interconnect board. Slip the plastic in between the drive and the board and pry them apart.**

Do not use a metal instrument in Step 10, or you could damage the inter-connect board.

11. **Slide the optical drive forward, as shown in Figure 8-8.**

The figure shows the drive's connector, which plugs into the board.

Figure 8-8:
Slide the drive forward; note the connector.

12. **Lift the optical drive out of the Mac mini.**

Installing the new DVD drive

Installing your new optical drive is the reverse of removing it. Just follow these steps:

1. **Slide the drive in place, from the front to the back (refer to Figure 8-8).**

2. **Replace the two screws that attach the interconnect board.**

   The bent-nose forceps really come in handy here to hold the screws in place while you attach them, as shown in Figure 8-9.

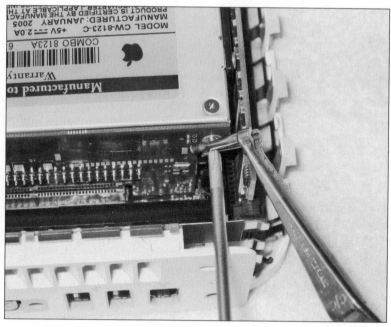

Figure 8-9:
Hold the screw in place with tweezers while you screw it in.

3. **Replace the four screws, two on each side, in the black frame (refer to Figures 8-5 and 8-6).**

4. **If you've removed the RAM module, replace it.**

5. **Place the soft, peel-and-stick *EMI gasket* (shown in Figure 8-10) that came with your new drive on the upper-center edge at the front of the drive. If you didn't get a gasket, remove the gasket from your old drive and place it on the new drive.**

Figure 8-10:
This little piece at the front edge is called an EMI gasket.

6. **If your Mac mini includes AirPort or Bluetooth, replace the antennas.**

Chapter 6 describes how to replace the wireless antennas.

Modding your used combo drive

After you install your new SuperDrive, you're left with a Combo Drive in working order. You could use it as an industrial-style coaster. Or, you could find an external enclosure and turn it into an external drive. You can find slot-loading, slim enclosures that have USB 2.0 or FireWire interfaces — or sometimes both. For $25 to $40, you get a box with a circuit board that converts the drive interface to USB or FireWire, as well as a power cable. If you are searching for FireWire, try using IEEE 1394, which is what the techno-geeks sometimes call FireWire.

Slot-loading enclosures for optical drives are not as common as those for hard drives. You can start your search at www.shentech. com and www.meritline.com.

Part IV
Mods for the Home

The 5th Wave   By Rich Tennant

@RICHTENNANT

"I could tell you more about myself, but I think the playlist on my iPod says more about me than mere words can."

In this part . . .

A lot of people have Macs *in* their home, which means that the Macs sit on a desk. In the chapters in this part, I show you how you can use your mini as an integral part of your home.

First, I show you how you can use the mini in your home theater to play, control, and store audio, movies, TV, and more, and how to connect the computer to the stereo and the boob tube. In his first chapter in this book, Arnold Reinhold tells you how and why you should give your mini kitchen duty. Of course, there's no reason to limit the mini to the living room and kitchen. I show you how to turn your mini into a controller for your house lights and appliances.

Don't let anyone tell you that there's no software for the Mac. There is some very cool software to control your house and to run the various audio and video parts of a home entertainment system. These chapters introduce you to the unusual software and hardware needed to plug your Mac mini into your house.

Chapter 9

The Mac mini Home Theater

*Y*ou may think you already have a hot home theater setup, with a big new TV, a sound system, and assorted peripherals. Yet, install a small Mac mini in your entertainment cabinet and you instantly add the possibilities of a library of music to play as well as video on demand, a TV scheduler and controller, an audio/video recorder, an audio/video downloader, a slideshow player, and more — not to mention that *Nanosaur 2* looks great on big-screen TV.

But you don't actually need the fancy big-screen TV or thundering 5.1 surround sound to get these things. The Mac mini can give you video on demand and all the rest when connected to your regular old TV and old-fashioned stereo.

Planning a Mac mini Media Center

When it comes to toys, it's best to do some planning before you shop. Start out by exploring the possibilities of what you can do with a Mac mini–based home theater. Then decide what you want to do and what you need to do it. After that, it's time for a dose of reality — checking prices and deciding whether to spend the money to do what you want. That is, figuring out if your eyes are bigger than your stomach, so to speak.

I start this section with a list of some of the things that you can do with a Mac mini as the center of your home entertainment system.

What's in a home theater

Using a Mac mini in a home theater gives you flexibility. After you make the basic connections to hook up the Mac mini, you can always add more functionality with new hardware or software.

Listen to the ultimate music jukebox

Using a Mac mini as a music jukebox gives you the convenience of an iPod with the sound quality of CDs. Use iTunes to shuffle through your entire music collection or play your favorite playlists.

If you have a big hard drive, you don't have to worry about file size. Instead of importing CDs as AAC or MP3 files, import them as AIFF or Apple Lossless files to get CD-quality sound.

If your Mac mini is connected to the Internet, you can use iTunes or the RealOne Player to play Internet radio stations through your stereo.

View and store your slide shows

View your vacation pics on your big-screen TV while listening to your favorite tunes. With iPhoto preinstalled on your Mac mini, all you do to get your digital photos onto the Mac mini is plug in your digital camera. You can then use iPhoto to arrange your photos into slideshows while playing music from your iTunes music collection.

Watch video-on-demand DVD movies

Yes, you can pick up a DVD player for the price of a toaster these days.

But if you don't have a DVD player yet, use the Mac mini as your player and spend the money on that Rocky and Bullwinkle collection you've had your eye on.

Watch and store your home movies

Your Mac mini comes loaded with iMovie, which means that any time you plug your digital camcorder into the FireWire port, iMovie launches and asks you whether you want to download your movie to your Mac mini. You never have to edit one second of your movies if you don't want to — you can use iMovie to download and play your home movies.

If you have a new-fangled hi-definition digital camcorder, iMovie supports hi-def in all its wide-screen, crisp-and-colorful splendor.

Record TV and import VCR video with DVR hardware

A device that digitally records TV shows is sometimes called a *DVR* (digital video recorder) or *PVR* (personal video recorder). Neither term is particularly descriptive, but we're stuck with them.

The DVR software that you can run on the Mac mini lets you schedule the recording of shows at any time of the night or day, and lets you record as many shows as your hard drive can hold.

But DVR functionality isn't just using a Mac mini as a digital VCR. You can also play back while still recording so that you can skip the commercials. Here's how it works: You start recording when your show begins, but you start watching about 15 minutes later. Then you can fast-forward through the commercials. It works like TiVo, only without the monthly subscription fee.

Play video games

Because you've hooked up your Mac mini to your big-screen TV, go ahead and play video games on it. *Nanosaur 2*, which comes with the Mac mini, looks great on a big TV. A joystick connected to the USB port can work wonders as well.

There is a caveat here: The Mac mini is *not* the ultimate gaming machine. Mainly, it's limited by its built-in, nonupgradeable graphics hardware. And you can definitely find more games available for Windows-based PCs and a game console such as the Sony PlayStation. But the Mac mini does run games. Think of it as an extra feature of your home theater. After all, a PlayStation can't play your home movies.

 If you're wondering whether a particular game is available for Mac OS X, check out Apple's Macintosh Products Guide Web site (http://guide.apple.com). Click Games in the left column, and you can search or browse an extensive list of games, including free and open source games as well as the big graphic best sellers.

What you need

Creating a home theater that can do all the things that I describe in the previous section takes a bit of hardware and a little software. You don't have to spend a lot of money, though. I realize that "a lot of money" is a relative term. What is expensive to me is a drop in the bucket for Donald Trump. But assuming that you already have your TV and sound system, you can add a complete Mac mini–based home theater system for less than the cost of a PowerBook. Here's what you need:

- **Mac mini:** With a minimum of 512MB RAM. More RAM is even better. Upgrade it yourself, as I describe in Chapter 7.

- **Bigger hard drive:** If you're going to do anything with video, the Mac mini's internal hard drive isn't big enough. You can replace the internal drive with a bigger drive and put the old drive in an external FireWire enclosure, as I describe in Chapter 7. You can also get much more storage capacity with a hard drive that doesn't fit in the mini, namely, a 3.5-inch drive. You can get 250GB for $200 at this point. But you can start with a more modest increase in storage capacity, because you can always add another FireWire drive if you need it.

The Rocstor (www.rocstor.com/) AV series of FireWire hard drives focuses on the high performance that is useful for video and audio applications.

✔ **TV:** Well, obviously. But a new TV is better than an old one, and a bottom-of-the-line, just-fell-off-the-truck model might not have the connectors that give you the picture quality that you want.

✔ **Sound system:** This could be a $5,000, 5.1 surround-sound setup, or it could be the speaker in your TV. I recommend something in between for most people.

✔ **Cables and connectors:** You need to connect the Mac mini video and audio ports to the rest of the system. The Apple DVI to Video Adapter can be useful. I go through these options in the next section.

✔ **Input devices:** After you're connected to your system, you need a way to control the Mac mini. A remote is a good way to go. You can read up on input devices in the next section.

✔ **DVR (also known as PVR) hardware:** A few hundred dollars buys a box and software that turns your Mac mini into a TiVo-type box, recording TV shows for playback later, or just delaying viewing so that you can skip the commercials. The section "Adding DVR Functionality," later in this chapter, describes how to do this.

✔ **Internet connection:** Well, you don't actually *need* an Internet connection. It is handy, though, if you want to use this Mac mini to download music or video directly to your home entertainment system or watch Webcasts on your living room TV.

Instead of giving you a list of software here in this section, I describe the software you need for specific tasks in the rest of this chapter. You don't have to spend a lot of money with software, either — the software costs far less than the hardware. In fact, some of the software is free.

Free, open source software not only does the job but, in some cases, also does a better job than commercial software, and has features that aren't available in commercial software. A good example is VLC, a video and audio player that supports more video formats than the QuickTime Player, and provides video playlists along the lines of iTunes' audio playlists. Some commercial software, such as Roxio Software's Toast, gives you features that Apple's Mac mini software doesn't have.

I get to software in a bit. First, you need to connect all that hardware together.

Connecting the Mac mini

How you connect your Mac mini to your home entertainment center depends on your system. You might be plugging the Mac mini directly into your TV or into a complex system with multiple components.

There are so many different possible configurations of video and audio equipment that can be used in a home theater that it's impossible to give step-by-step directions that cover them all. It's better to consider the types of connections you can expect to find in a home theater as well as how to connect your Mac mini to it.

Audio and video can each come in analog and digital flavors. Some TV and sound equipment provide both analog and digital. Digital gives you higher quality, but analog cables are less expensive. Digital makes the most difference in video, where the improvement can be dramatic. The following sections explore both analog and digital audio and video connections.

Choosing an audio connection

You can get audio out of your Mac mini and to a TV or sound system in three ways: the headphone jack, the USB port, or less commonly, the FireWire port. From these Mac mini ports, you can add various cables and converters to connect with the various different types of audio inputs.

A USB audio interface also adds an audio-in port to the Mac mini. You can use this for importing music from other sources, such as your old vinyl LP collection. You also need software. Garage Band works okay, but if you're doing a lot of LP digitizing, check out BIAS's Peak LE ($129, www.BIAS-inc.com). It gives you a better set of audio-editing tools.

The following sections discuss the most common types of audio connectors that you find on TVs and sound equipment.

The 1/8-inch mini headphone jack

This is the type of connector that the Mac mini uses for the headphone port, providing an analog line-out signal. This type of jack comes in stereo and mono versions. Be sure that you buy the stereo version. The audio-input ports of sound and TV systems don't use the 1/8-inch (or 1/4-inch) jacks, so you usually need some type of converter cable.

A drawback to getting audio directly from the mini headphone jack to an amplifier is that you sometimes get a hum or a buzz. Adding a USB interface can fix that. For instance, Griffin Technology's iMic (www.griffintechnology.com) gives you one input and one output port, both analog 1/8-inch mini connectors. The iMic is small in size, weighing only 2 ounces, and in price: It costs only $40.

Full-sized ¼-inch headphone jack

This is also analog audio. The ¼-inch jack is not as common as the mini head-phone jack for audio-in ports, but if you need to plug into it, you can find ⅛-to-¼-inch converter cables.

RCA connectors, analog

Stereo RCA connectors, one for each channel, are common on TVs and sound systems. To connect to RCA ports, you plug a mini phone jack into the Mac mini's headphone port and use an RCA converter cable, as shown in Figure 9-1. You often find cables with three RCA connectors, two for the audio and a third (usually yellow) for composite video.

S/PDIF (coaxial) RCA, digital

This type of connector provides a digital signal over a coaxial wire cable, using RCA connectors at each end. S/PDIF coaxial is a common type of digital audio connection that can give you cleaner sound than analog.

You need a USB audio interface to connect the Mac mini to an S/PDIF port. However, most devices of this type use S/PDIF optical, which I describe in the next section.

In case you were wondering, S/PDIF stands for Sony/Phillips Digital Interconnect Format. Now you know.

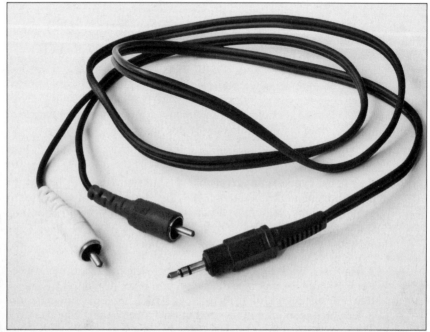

Figure 9-1:
A mini
headphone–
to-RCA
converter
cable.

S/PDIF optical, digital

Also known as TOSlink, optical S/PDIF provides higher-quality digital audio than S/PDIF coaxial RCA. This fiber optic technology transmits data using light with no interference or signal degradation. The TOSlink connector is almost square, with two corners flattened a bit. See Figure 9-2.

If you want to connect your Mac mini to a sound system using digital S/PDIF optical, you need USB computer audio interface that has a TOSlink port. One such device, the $100 Edirol UA-1EX (www.edirol.com) provides digital S/PDIF optical output as well as analog audio RCA input and output. Apple carries these devices at its online store, as do other Web sites.

FireWire audio

You're probably not going to run into much FireWire audio. Professional studio audio-processing equipment often includes FireWire, but the high-speed digital interface is also finding its way onto some consumer sound systems. One lower-end example is the Griffin Technology FireWave (www.griffintechnology.com), a $100 surround-sound FireWire speaker box that's designed to plug into the Mac mini. If you don't have a decent stereo, the FireWave could be a step up in sound quality.

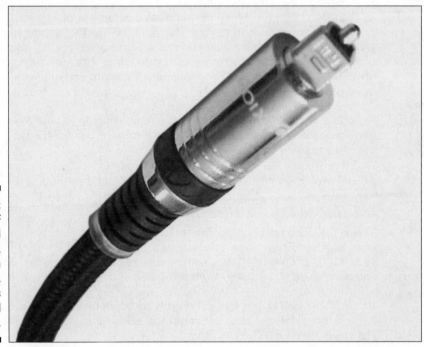

Figure 9-2:
An S/PDIF optical connector, also known as TOSlink, provides digital audio.

If you have some sound equipment with a FireWire port, you may require special driver software for Mac OS X. Check with the device manufacturer to see if such a driver is required or is available.

Wireless tunes with AirPort Express

Apple's AirPort Express probably isn't going to help you much with a Mac mini–based home entertainment center. The Mac mini wirelessly communicates with the AirPort Express, but the Express connects to the sound system with a cable. You might as well just plug the Mac mini directly into the sound system. The AirPort Express is helpful if the Mac mini is in a different room. The AirPort Express works with iTunes but can't move video soundtracks to your sound system.

Choosing a video connection

There's no one way to connect video. You might connect your Mac mini directly to your TV, or you may have other boxes and video equipment in the mix that require a certain connection.

If you have a choice for a video connection, go digital. Now, I'm not one who subscribes to the everything-digital-is-better way of thinking. Give me a good ol' high-resolution hand-held analog book over an e-book any day. But when it comes to moving video from your Mac mini to your TV, keeping it digital gives you a better picture than you can get from analog ports. You notice the boost that digital gives you more with video than with audio, even on a lower-end TV. If you're still shopping for a TV, try to find one with digital input ports.

No matter what TV or video device you're hooking up to your Mac mini, you must plug *something* into the DVI video port in the back. If it's not DVI, you have to use some type of converter.

The following sections describe your video interface options.

DVI (Digital Video Interface)

This is the video port on your Mac mini. Some modern TVs also have a DVI port, which you can connect directly to the Mac mini. A TV with DVI gives you 1920-x-1200–pixel resolution when you use it as your Mac mini's monitor. (TV and movies can still display at the resolution of the TV, which is less than that.)

If your TV or set-top box has a DVI port, it should be your first choice. It's digital and it requires the simplest cable and connectors from your Mac mini. Figure 9-3 shows a DVI connector.

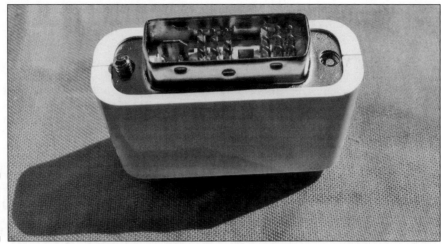

Figure 9-3:
A DVI
connector.

HDMI (High-Definition Multimedia Interface)

This is a fairly new digital format that is appearing on TVs and set-top boxes. HDMI can be less trouble then DVI because it supports a longer cable. You need to find a DVI-to-HDMI converter cable, though. HDMI can carry audio as well as video. But because the Mac mini's DVI port carries video only, you still need to get sound from the Mac mini's headphone port or a USB audio converter.

S-Video

If you can't go digital, S-Video is the best type of analog video interface. S-Video uses a special 4-pin connector. Apple's $20 DVI to Video Adapter (shown in Figure 9-4) does the job. You can find it in Apple retail stores and at the Apple online store.

Figure 9-4:
Apple's DVI
to Video
Adapter
gives you
composite
video (left)
and S-Video
(right).

Because S-Video is not digital, you don't get high resolution when you view Mac OS X on the TV. But S-Video does fine for movies and TV.

Composite video

This is a step down from S-Video in terms of quality. Composite video uses an RCA connector, and it is often a yellow connector in a trio that includes red and white RCA connectors used for audio. Apple's $20 DVI to Video Adapter also works here; it has both S-Video and composite video connectors.

Coaxial cable

Coaxial video (or *coax*) is the same cable that brings cable TV into your house and is the lowest-quality video connection. Coax is also referred to as *RF (radio frequency) cable*. Use coax only for old TV sets that have no other port except the coax connector for cable TV or an antenna. In this case, you need an RF converter box known as an *RF modulator* to connect a Mac mini or DVD player to a coax connector on your TV. (Radio Shack sells inexpensive RF modulators.) You can also use an RF modulator to connect coax to S-Video or composite video, and sometimes digital video.

The coax connection is the weak link in the system, limiting picture quality. A coax connector can give you the same kind of "reception" problems that you can experience with a TV antenna or cable TV, including wavy lines on screen.

Finding a place to plug it all in

Comedian Steven Wright once said, "You can't have everything. Where would you put it?" In the case of a home theater system, you actually can have everything, but where do you plug it all in? Your TV, DVD player, or stereo receiver/amplifier might have some additional ports to connect your Mac mini and other assorted peripherals. If not, you can add one or more of a variety of connection or converter boxes to pull it all together.

Component video

You may have read that another type of video — *component video* — is a good type of video to use in a home system. This is the digital format used to store video on DVDs. Using a component signal yields great quality, but it's not often used on equipment, and DVI-to–component video connectors are not common. You often have to convert component video to analog first and then convert it back to digital. Component video has three connectors. In practice, component video is often down-converted to S-Video.

Mixing digital and analog paths

Many connection strategies involve plugging in both analog and digital video and audio. You want to look at how those connections are made by considering the *path* of a signal from its origin to its destination.

To take advantage of the fidelity of a digital connection, you need to make sure that the audio or video path remains digital from the source (such as the Mac mini) to the hardware that produces the sound (an amplifier or TV, for example). If, at any point in the path, you have to convert to analog, you *will* lose sound or picture quality.

Now, don't get upset if you do have to make an analog-to-digital conversion. Sometimes it's unavoidable. If you need to use a long cable (more than 3 feet), digital signals will withstand signal degradation, and may be preferable even when you have to convert to analog later in the signal path.

Options for connector/converter boxes

If you need a box to connect between different types of cables, the solution that you use depends on what you have and what you want to do with it. You may even need more than one box. Ideally, you want a box that has enough connectors to cover everything. Before you buy one, count the number of analog and video devices you want to add.

Here are a few options for connector/converter boxes, from the cheap and simple to the expensive and sexy:

- **RF modulator (video only), under $50:** Sometimes these devices are *well* under $50. An RF modulator converts coax cables to S-Video or composite video signals. You might have a cable TV coax line coming in but no coax connection on your TV or video-capture device or DVR system. You also use an RF modulator to connect various devices (including the Mac mini) to an old TV that only has a coax input.

- **M-Audio Transit (audio only), $100 (**www.m-audio.com/**):** This versatile little box plugs into your Mac mini's USB port and provides high-quality audio into and out of the Mac mini. The box provides an analog-out port and a port that works with analog-in and S/PDIF digital-in. Another port is TOSlink optical digital-out, which means that you can plug in digital coaxial and convert to optical digital, preserving a digital audio path.

- **Elgato Systems EyeHome (audio and video), $200 (**www.elgato.com/**):** This media player box uses an Ethernet cable to connect to your Mac mini. EyeHome produces video in the form of S-Video, composite video, and component video. It also provides analog audio (using RCA connectors) and TOSlink optical digital.

EyeHome partially solves the "TV as monitor" problem described in the next section by providing its own interface with big, TV-sized text for browsing your Mac mini's multimedia.

- **Video capture or digital video recorder, over $200:** These devices include a TV tuner into which you plug cable TV. They can record TV shows and store them on your Mac mini. Some also digitize analog video from a VCR or analog video camera. You'll also find a set of audio and video connectors. Digital video recorders are described in the "Adding DVR Functionality" section, later in this chapter.

Controlling the Mac mini

With the Mac mini sitting in your home theater cabinet, a traditional monitor, keyboard, and mouse aren't the most practical tools for operating or setting up the Mac mini. You'll be using your TV as the monitor. You have a few options for the keyboard commands and for mousing around.

Using a TV as a monitor

Your big, beautiful TV is the center of your home entertainment center. The potential for greatness is high. The Mac mini has high-quality video output, and many TVs can produce fabulous images. Your movies can look great, and your games will be big.

Now the TV is going to serve as your Mac mini's monitor as well. The problem is that even a big, expensive wide-screen TV has lower resolution than a computer monitor. For instance, Apple's displays give you about 100 pixels per inch. But even an HD big-screen TV has a resolution of less than one-third of Apple's displays at best. For instance, the pixel resolution for a 50-inch, 16:9 wide screen at 1366×768 pixels works out to only 31.9 pixels per inch. With a smaller TV, the resolution could be lower.

This means that normal-sized text you are used to seeing in menus and dialogs may look like illegible blotchy blobs. This makes it difficult to operate the mini — which means that you need to compensate.

Here are a few ways to compensate for blotchy TV screen blobs of text.

Do major setups with a computer monitor

Before you install the Mac mini in your entertainment cabinet, connect it to the monitor and keyboard of another computer in the house. If you need to install more software later, just unplug the mini and move it to your other computer. Remember, the mini is small enough to move around.

Enlarge the text and icons in Finder folders

The Finder lets you enlarge the filename text and file icons, which is handy for browsing through folders while the Mac mini is connected to your TV. You need to use the following procedure for each view (icon, list, or column view) that you want to use. Here's the procedure for list view:

1. **Select a folder and press Control+J to open the View Options window, as shown in Figure 9-5.**

Figure 9-5: Enlarging the text of Finder windows set to list view.

2. **Click the All Windows radio button.**

3. **Choose the Text Size menu and select 16 point.**

4. **Click on the large icon.**

   You may need to widen the Name column of Finder windows.

You can see the before and after results in Figure 9-6. Notice that the name of the window in the title bar is still the same size. Unfortunately, you can't enlarge the text in title bars and menu bars, or in menus and dialogs, and in applications.

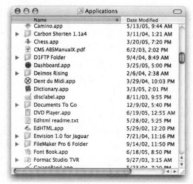 

Figure 9-6:
Before
enlarging
text and
icons (left)
and after
(right),
which is
good for TV
viewing.

Turn on Zoom

If you are going to occasionally use a keyboard with the mini or if you are using a programmable remote, you can take advantage of Mac OS X's Zoom feature to enlarge the whole screen. The default key commands are as follows:

✔ **To zoom in: ⌘+Option++ (hold down the ⌘, Option, and plus keys)**

✔ **To zoom out: ⌘+Option+– (hold down the ⌘, Option, and minus keys)**

These key combinations work in any application, instantly enlarging the text to legible size.

Turning on Zoom is a snap:

1. **Open System Preferences and click the Universal Access icon.**

2. **On the Seeing tab, click the On button in the Zoom section.**

That's it. You can now zoom.

If you are using a programmable remote, such as the Keyspan Express remote, you can map the zoom-in and zoom-out commands to buttons on the remote. For more on programming a Keyspan remote, see the section "Keyboard and mouse versus remote," later in this chapter.

Use a software interface

Some of the DVR boxes include their own software that is suited for viewing on TVs. However, the software that comes with DVR boxes only lets you operate TV viewing and recording.

The Elgato Systems EyeHome ($200, www.elgato.com/) is a digital media player that partially solves the problem of illegible text on a TV. EyeHome takes content from your Mac mini — music, photos, and movies — and displays it on the TV with its own interface. Figure 9-7 depicts browsing movies that have been copied to the Mac mini hard drive. (You can read how to copy movies in the "Ripping DVD movies" section, later in this chapter.)

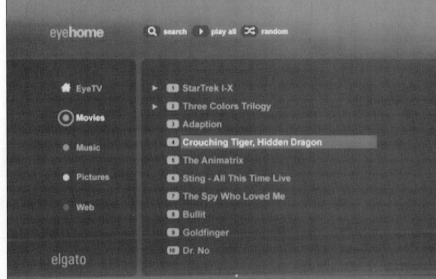

Figure 9-7:
The EyeHome box gives you this interface for playing your Mac mini's content.

EyeHome doesn't actually run iTunes, iPhoto, or DVD Player but instead uses its own software to access the content on your Mac mini. EyeHome also lets you access the Web, not with a Mac mini Web browser, but with its own software that includes a preselected set of Internet radio stations and news sites. It can also read the bookmarks on the Mac mini's copy of Safari and let you access those sites. The software doesn't give you access to files in the Finder, however.

Initial reviews of the user interface were mixed, but the software has been upgraded since EyeHome's first release.

EyeHome is not a DVR box; it doesn't play or record TV. It works with Elgato's EyeTV DVR box, although it doesn't work well with other DVR boxes.

Keyboard and mouse versus remote

A traditional keyboard and mouse are great for working with a Mac mini sitting on a desk, but they aren't the most practical control devices for a home entertainment center.

One way to go is with a wireless keyboard and mouse. You can keep them in a closet when you're not using them or use them on another Mac. Using a wireless keyboard is handy for configuring the Mac mini or browsing the Internet, but it's kind of a clunky way to watch a movie.

The natural tool to control a home entertainment system is, of course, the remote. Here are some remote options for the mini:

- **Bluetooth cell phone with Salling Clicker:** Salling Clicker ($20, `http://homepage.mac.com/jonassalling/Shareware/Clicker/`) is software that lets a Bluetooth-equipped phone control a Bluetooth-equipped Mac mini. It supports several Mac mini applications, including iTunes, DVD Player, and the all-purpose video application, VLC. (Read more about VLC in the next section.) Salling Clicker also supports the EyeTV and EvolutionTV DVR boxes.

- **Griffin Technology's AirClick USB:** The AirClick ($40, `www.griffintechnology.com`) includes a receiver that plugs into the USB port and a remote. The remote uses radio frequencies, so it doesn't need to be in the line of sight with the receiver, as with ordinary remotes. The main drawback is that the remote doesn't have a lot of buttons and is mostly geared toward audio.

- **Keyspan Express Remote:** This unit ($59, `www.keyspan.com`) is probably the best all-purpose remote for a Mac mini. It comes with controls for a number of applications. More importantly, you can program the Keyspan Remote to work with any or all applications, including the Finder, and you can use it to control the cursor. The Keyspan Express Remote communicates with a USB receiver using infrared signals, like your regular TV remote.

The receiver and remote are shown in Figure 9-8. You can see that it's quite a bit smaller than a regular remote. If that bugs you, Keyspan has a solution: You can use a regular TV remote with the Keyspan receiver, as long as the remote is compatible with the JVC remote, which is fairly common.

An older version of the Keyspan Express Remote is called the Keyspan Digital Media Remote. If you have one of these, it will also work.

I describe how to set up the Keyspan Remote in the section "Setting up a remote control," later in this chapter.

Creating a Video Jukebox

Storing music on the Mac mini is a no-brainer. Use iTunes to import your CDs and then play them. Unfortunately, Apple doesn't have a video equivalent of iTunes. Of course, we don't let that stop us.

Figure 9-8:
The
Keyspan
Express
Remote and
receiver.

With a big enough hard drive, you can store tons of video right on the Mac mini, including home movies, DVD movies, and video recorded from TV with your DVR.

I start the following sections by describing *ripping* your DVD movies, which means copying them to the Mac mini's hard drive. I also describe some movies that you can download for free.

To do all this, you need two pieces of open source, free software:

- **MacTheRipper,** for copying DVD movies to your hard drive.
- **VLC,** for playing any type of video format, including digital home movies.

After that, I describe how you can play ripped movies — it isn't as obvious as it might seem. Part of playing movies on your Mac mini is controlling it with a remote. I end these sections by describing how you can configure a remote to do this.

But first, there's a hundred-pound gorilla to deal with: the issue of copyright law and how to stay legal while copying your own DVDs.

Keeping it legal: Copyright issues

There's a certain air of uncertainty surrounding the issue of copying digital contents. You hear about the record industry suing 12-year-olds for sharing music files, and there's talk of increased copy protection on DVD movies.

The owners of copyrights have some valid concerns. Content creators deserve to get paid for what they produce, and should have some protection from bootlegs. But you don't hear much about the legal concept of *fair use.* The idea is that you can enjoy a product that you buy as long as you don't try to rip off the copyright holders. The concepts of fair use and digital rights as applied to DVD movies are similar to those of music files. You can buy a CD and create your own digital copies of the CD contents, move the files onto your iPod, and burn a mix CD of your favorite music, all without breaking the law. However, if you post the files on the Internet or start selling copies of the CD, you are facilitating copyright infringement.

Fair use also applies to movies, but DVDs are more difficult to import into your Mac mini than music CDs. DVDs have extra protection built in, encoding that makes it tougher to make digital copies. DVDs also include encoding that prevents a DVD you bought in North America from being played in another part of the world. This is because movies on videotape had no copy protection and were widely pirated.

You can use software that gets around DVD encoding, enabling you to make a copy of the movie on your hard drive for your Mac mini video-on-demand system. (I describe this software in the next section.) Using your DVDs in this way is fair use.

You cross the line if you copy a movie from a rented DVD. You didn't buy it and you don't own it, which makes it illegal for you to copy it. It's also a no-no to give away copies of movies that you own to your friends, or to trade copies. You can, however, trade store-bought originals. If you want to give your friend a store-bought original DVD of *Citizen Kane* in exchange for a store-bought original DVD of *Animal Crackers,* that's fair use. (Whether it's a fair trade depends on your point of view.)

Bootleggers spoil it for the rest of us. The more illegal copyright infringement that goes on, the harder the movie industry will make it to use our own DVDs.

Ripping DVD movies

When I say *ripping,* I'm talking about copying DVD movies to a hard drive, but *ripping* is a much cooler term. "Copying" also implies dragging some files from one disc to another. It doesn't work that way with DVDs. You have to get around encryption, and you have a mess of files and folders with weird names. The ripping software, however, makes it fairly easy.

Getting ripping software

You can use several programs to rip DVD movies. At this time, the free MacTheRipper is the best. It's available at various places around the Internet at different times. Here are a couple of locations:

✔ www.speedisc.com/downloads/

✔ http://mac.softpedia.com/get/Utilities/
MacTheRipper.shtml

If those don't work, search for MacTheRipper at VersionTracker
(www.versiontracker.com).

Ripping with MacTheRipper

It's pretty easy to use MacTheRipper. The default settings work in most
cases, and the software is smart enough to find everything and put it in the
right place. To rip a DVD movie, follow these steps:

1. **Insert your movie DVD disc into the Mac mini.**

2. **Launch MacTheRipper.**

   The dialog shown in Figure 9-9 appears, displaying the name of the movie.

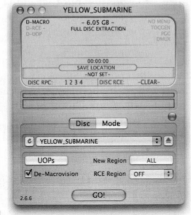

Figure 9-9:
Use MacThe-Ripper to copy DVD movies to your hard drive.

3. **Click the Mode button and make sure that Full Disc Extraction is
   selected.**

   This setting brings in the menus of the DVD and everything else. It is
   also the most trouble-free setting.

4. **Click the Disc button.**

   You can keep the default settings, as shown in Figure 9-9.

5. **Click the Go button to start the ripping.**

When MacTheRipper is finished, you find a folder with the name of your movie.
Inside that is a folder called VIDEO_TS, which has everything you need.

Downloading free movies

One thing you can do with a Mac mini in your home entertainment center is download music and video. If you're interested in free and legal music and video, check out Archive.org (www.archive.org), a project based in the Presidio in San Francisco. Archive.org contains material that is either in the public domain or for which the owners have given permission to share.

You can download several choice films in full-screen, high-definition video. You'll find lots of independent films and documentaries, but for a real treat, look in the Feature Films section. Here, you can find several Cary Grant movies, including Grant and Audrey Hepburn in *Charade,* which is in the public domain due to a copyright flub by the studio. You can also find 50-, 60-, and 70-year-old cartoons, including Bugs Bunny, Popeye, and my favorite — some surreal and risqué Betty Boop from the early 1930s.

For the best quality, download the video in the MPEG-2 format, an uncompressed format that is also the biggest format offered. It took my trusty DSL-connected Mac mini 12 hours to download *Charade,* but that didn't stop me from doing other things on the Mac mini at the same time. (To play MPEG-2, you need to use VLC, which I describe in the next section.)

The audio section of Archive.org is Deadhead heaven. There's close to 3,000 free Grateful Dead concerts and studio-album outtake sessions from 1965 to 1995, many in high-quality soundboard mixes. If you listened to one show a day, it would take you eight years to hear the entire catalog.

Cary Grant, Betty Boop, and Jerry Garcia, all for free. That's quite a resource.

Playing ripped DVD movies

Just as it takes special software to rip a DVD movie, it takes special software to play it. DVD Player works, although it doesn't always get the DVD menus to work correctly, which makes it frustrating to use.

If you want to give DVD Player a try, choose File⇨Open DVD Media and navigate to the folder with your movie title. Then select the VIDEO_TS folder and click the Choose button.

Getting the best software

A better way to go is with the free VLC program from the VideoLAN Project. VLC can play more video and audio formats than the QuickTime Player.

You can download VLC from the VideoLAN Project Web site, www.videolan.org. It's available for a number of different operating systems, so make sure that you get the Mac version.

Playing ripped DVD movies with VLC

There's a bit of a special procedure to play a ripped DVD movie; double-click-ing a file doesn't do it. Follow these steps to play a movie:

1. **Launch VLC.**

2. **Choose File⇨Quick Open File.**

3. **Navigate to the folder that is named after your ripped movie.**

   Try looking in the `Movie` folder if you don't know where your movie is.

4. **Click the** `VIDEO_TS` **folder to select it, and click the Open button.**

The movie appears on-screen. You can use a mouse or remote to work the video menu. If the movie is not covering the entire screen, choose Video⇨Full Screen. VLC will remember this setting. The ⌘+. keyboard command (hold down the ⌘ and period keys) stops the movie. If you have a remote, you can map this and other commands to remote buttons.

To see the on-screen controller, choose Window⇨Controller. Drag the lower-right corner of the controller to expose the playlist, as shown in Figure 9-10. VLC adds a movie to the list every time you open it. You can also drag movie files here from the Finder. After you stop a movie, you can choose to play another movie from this list. Ripped DVD movies are all called VIDEO_TS in VLC, as you can see in Figure 9-10.

Figure 9-10:
The VLC controller creates a playlist of movies.

To save the playlist, choose File⇨Save Playlist.

Setting up a remote control

With a Mac mini connected to your TV, it's convenient to control it using a remote rather than a keyboard. Before you do, you need to set up the remote. Most remotes that work with the Mac mini use a concept called *keyboard mapping* to set certain buttons to activate certain key commands. When you set up keyboard mapping, you have the following two types of settings:

  ✔ **Global action:** This is remote-button behavior that works in every application. One important global action to create is cursor control, where you set the up-, down-, left-, and right-arrows to move the cursor on the screen. You then set up another button to perform a mouse click.

  ✔ **Application-specific mapping:** For instance, if an application uses ⌘+P for Play, you'd map ⌘+P to the remote's Play button.

To give you an idea of how this works, check out how you set up the Keyspan Express Remote. Software controls for other remotes look different, but the concepts are the same.

(For a discussion of the Keyspan and other remote options, see the section "Keyboard and mouse versus remote," earlier in this chapter.)

Most remotes contain a preconfigured set of applications. VLC, however, is not usually among them. In the following steps, you add VLC to the list of applications and configure some of the remote's buttons:

  1. **Launch the keyboard mapping software.**

     Keyspan's software is called KeyspanDMR.

  2. **Turn off iTunes Mode in the window that appears.**

     Other remotes have a DVD Player mode that you should also turn off.

     Special iTunes mode lets you control iTunes even if it is not the front application. The problem is that it prevents you from operating other applications.

  3. **Click the Configure button to open the mapping window, shown in Figure 9-11.**

     Use the Application menu to set button actions for individual applications or global actions. In Figure 9-11, global actions is selected.

     Notice that the Action column has NO ACTION listed. You don't want to set buttons like Stop and Play globally, because the commands for these differ in different applications. You *should* set the arrow buttons (up, down, left, and right) to mouse movements. The Select button is the equivalent to the mouse button. You need to set these actions globally to maneuver around different applications and around the Finder.

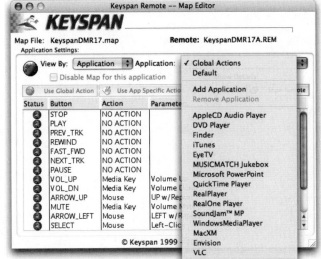

Figure 9-11:
The
Keyspan
Express
Remote
global
settings
work for all
applications.

Figure 9-11 shows VLC already listed in the Application menu. The Keyspan Remote doesn't include it as a default setting, so you have to add it.

4. Choose Application➪Add Application. Browse for VLC.

Figure 9-12 marks the global action set up in the previous section with little globes. It also shows some other commands, but they might not be the right commands for VLC.

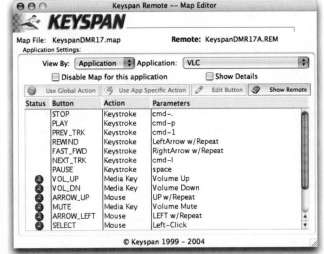

Figure 9-12:
VLC is now
in the list;
commands
set here
work only
in VLC.

5. **To configure a command specifically for VLC, double-click a command, such as Play.**

   A mapping window appears, as shown in Figure 9-13.

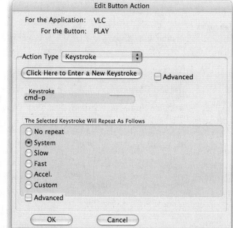

6. **Click the Click Here to Enter a New Keystroke button. Type in the VLC's key command for Play (⌘+P).**

   You can find the key combination for Play and other commands in the menus of VLC. This is true for other applications as well.

7. **Click the OK button.**

Repeat Steps 5 through 7 for other commands.

Adding DVR Functionality

The basic function of DVRs is to record TV digitally on your Mac mini and to schedule taping for later viewing without commercials, without the hassles of tapes. You can also burn video to DVDs for longer-term storage. Some boxes have the "live pausing" feature found in TiVo.

You can also save money with a DVR box that plugs into your Mac compared to the stand-alone variety. Not only are Mac-based DVR boxes less expensive, but you also don't have to pay a subscription fee, as you do with TiVo and other similar devices.

These DVR boxes are easy to install. The hardest part might be shopping for one that best suits you.

The parts of a DVR

To get television or digital video recorder functionality on your Mac mini, a DVR box must have the following elements and functions:

- ✔ **TV tuner:** This accepts a signal from your TV cable or antenna and can distinguish among the channels. Watch out, though. You can find boxes that are *only* TV tuners, which, by themselves, don't give you the ability to record video.

- ✔ **Analog-to-digital converter (analog audio-in port):** This hardware converts the standard TV signals into a digital format that your Mac mini can record. This also lets you plug in analog video sources, such as a VCR.

- ✔ **Digital-to-analog converter (analog video out):** This allows you to view the digital images on an analog TV or send them to a VCR.

- ✔ **Program guide:** The program guide lets you search for and find TV shows that you might want to view or record. Some DVR boxes include Mac mini software that accesses the Internet to get this information. You can also access program guides with a Web browser.

- ✔ **Software:** The software lets you control the system, change channels, pause, and do everything else you need to. All the hardware boxes come with software. The software features differ, however, and they differentiate the models more than anything else.

Comparing DVR boxes

The available DVR solutions vary in price and features. Here are some features that are common to the boxes:

- ✔ The ability to play and record TV in a variety of digital formats.

- ✔ The ability to schedule recording ahead of time.

- ✔ The ability to use TitanTV.com to browse, search, and schedule recordings.

- ✔ The ability to resize TV windows from small to full screen.

Some of the boxes can also pause and "rewind" live TV as you watch it, and let you skip ahead of commercials in live TV. (This is a big feature of the TiVo service, but here you get it without the monthly fee.) The boxes do this by buffering a few minutes of TV on the Mac mini hard drive as the feed comes in.

Some of the boxes also come with a remote to control the device.

The following sections give you a tour of three DVR boxes for the Mac mini: the Miglia EvolutionTV, the Formac Studio TVR, and the Elgato Systems EyeTV 200. Keep in mind that with future upgrades, manufacturers can add features that are not currently included. Check the manufacturers' Web sites before you make a buying decision.

Miglia EvolutionTV

At $279, the Miglia EvolutionTV (www.miglia.com) is the least expensive and nicest-looking box. This is a subjective opinion, so judge for yourself (see Figure 9-14). This figure shows the back of the unit, with coax, S-Video, and composite import ports.

Figure 9-14:
The back
of the
EvolutionTV.

The picture quality tends to be better than that of the EyeTV. Like the others, the EvolutionTV can record in MPEG-2 (DVD-quality) format and MPEG-4 (used by iMovie) format, but it is the only DVR box so far that can record in DivX format.

The software offers the simplest interface of the three DVR boxes described here. This is usually a good thing, but in this case, it isn't always obvious as to how to do something. For instance, you set scheduling from the Preferences dialog. EvolutionTV has the convenient and unique ability to use iCal for scheduling, however.

The biggest deficiency of the EvolutionTV is that it doesn't let you pause live broadcasts.

Formac Studio TVR

Formac Studio TVR ($300, www.formac.com) is a FireWire DVR device. It also includes an extra FireWire port for connection to another FireWire device, such as a digital camcorder. The Studio TVR, as shown in Figure 9-15, doubles as a full-fledged video-capture device for converting your analog videotapes to digital, with a variety of analog video input and output ports, include coax, RCA (composite), and S-Video.

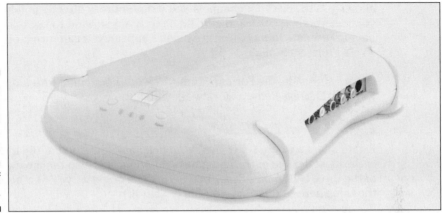

Figure 9-15:
The Formac
Studio TVR
has full-
featured
software
and a lot of
ports.

Images are crisp and sharp, even when displayed at full screen, and the software is full-featured. The Studio TVR software gives you complete flexibility regarding the size of the TV window. You can resize the image to full screen or to predetermined sizes, and you can drag the image to any size you wish. When you minimize the window, the video plays in the Dock icon, with sound. Definitely a cool feature.

Like EyeTV, the Formac Studio TVR software offers a live-pause feature by keeping a buffer of the TV feed; it's called the TimeShift Buffer. You turn it on by pressing the Pause button. You can then press the Backward button to replay items. The Forward button lets you skip commercials. You can set the size of the TimeShift Buffer in the Preferences dialog. The default setting is 15 minutes, which means that after 15 minutes, the early video gets erased. You can change this setting to as long as you want, provided that you have sufficient hard drive space (approximately 13GB per hour).

You can also record shows on the fly or via a schedule. When you record a show, it is stored in a clips drawer. Here, you can play it or edit it to crop out commercials or anything else you don't want.

The Studio TVR software lets you export recorded shows as a QuickTime file. If you want to put the TV show on a DVD, you can export it as MPEG-2, the format used on standard DVD players. (You can even add chapter markers.) The Export to Studio button can feed the video through the Studio TVR's analog output ports.

You can also do a lot of this video editing with iMovie, because the Studio DVR software is integrated with Apple's video editor. The Studio TVR software includes an add-on to iMovie called the iMovie Remote Control, which allows you to select TV channels and video sources directly in iMovie, where you can watch, record, and edit TV directly. If you want to use iMovie without having Formac's Remote Control palette appear, you can turn it off in Studio TVR's Preferences dialog.

On the downside, the Formac Studio TVR does not come with a remote. The Keyspan Express Remote does work with it, however.

Elgato Systems EyeTV 200

Elgato offers a whole set of EyeTV models, but at this point, the EyeTV 200 is the most flexible of the company's offerings. It is also the most expensive of the three DVR boxes described here. (The original EyeTV is the weakest of the three here — trust me, you don't want it.)

Like the Formac box, EyeTV 200 connects to the Mac with FireWire, which means it doesn't need a power cable. It supports coaxial video, composite video, and S-Video-in and comes with a full-sized remote.

The software has a clear user interface and a solid set of features. (Figure 9-16 shows EyeTV's list of recorded video.) Like the Formac, EyeTV 200 can pause live TV, and rewind and fast-forward, through the use of a buffer. The scheduler can wake up the Mac mini from sleep mode to record a program. Unlike the Miglia EvolutionTV, EyeTV 200 doesn't support DivX.

Figure 9-16: EyeTV lets you browse your recorded video.

Capturing video

If you want to edit a video using iMovie, record in MPEG-4 format. You don't have to do any file format conversions. If it's image quality you're after, go with MPEG-2.

Online program guides

Internet-based television program guides, such as TitanTV, are integrated with DVR software, but you can also use them manually with TV tuners to search by show, channel, actor, or other attributes. You must specify where you are, who your cable provider is (or whether you're using an antenna), and what your plan is. You can view schedules for basic cable, digital cable, satellite, or old-fashioned over-the-air TV. You can also read about an episode of a show.

You view most Internet TV program guides with a Web browser. This includes Titan, TVTV.com, TVGuide.com, and Yahoo TV.

TitanTV (www.titantv.com), from Decisionmark Corp., works with a large number of computer and stand-alone DVRs and tuners, and can be used for simple browsing. TitanTV is a free service, but you have to sign up for an account. You must have cookies turned on in your Web browser to sign up for and use the services. (The cookies enable TitanTV to bring up the current TV schedule for your system whenever you go to the Web site.) However, a TitanTV account is not highly personal — you don't even have to add your last name or your e-mail address. You need to add your mailing address.

Once you have an account, you can go and see what's on the tube. TitanTV also lets you configure a favorites table, where you can keep a few of your favorite channels so that you don't have to scroll through listings of dozens of channels that you never watch.

Of course, you don't always want to see what's on right now. Flexible searching lets you search for the name of a show or type of a show, an actor, the time that the show will air, or a combination of these factors.

For a simpler, more convenient method of browsing TV listings, check out TV Tracker from Monkey Business Labs (http://monkeybusinesslabs.com/). TV Tracker is a Dashboard widget that can download listings for broadcast, cable, and satellite programs. TV Tracker doesn't integrate with the DVR boxes, however.

Chapter 10

Automating Your Home

*P*icture your home as a kind of Jetsons' house, but without the robot maid. Moments before you get home, the living room lights turn on, relaxing sounds emanate from the stereo, and the gas fireplace flickers to life. You have to mix your own manhattan and fix dinner, but the kitchen lights dim after dinner, and then the bedroom lights turn on while everything else turns off. The next morning, the coffee maker and the radio turn themselves on and off.

Your Mac mini is the brains that run the automated house, kind of like the computer HAL running the spaceship Discovery in the movie *2001,* but without the homicidal attitude.

You don't need a lot of cash to automate your house. Just install some software on your mini, plug some inexpensive devices into the walls, and tell the mini what to turn on and off and when.

Home automation doesn't require you to dedicate the Mac mini to the task. It uses so little processing power that you can continue to use the mini to surf the Web, read your e-mail, and play *Nanosaur 2*. In fact, you can do the setup on the Mac mini and download the instructions to another device.

This chapter describes what you need to automate your home and how to set up the automation. It comes down to a few basic building blocks that you can expand upon at will. You do it all with a simple bit of technology called X10.

About X10

Although the name sounds like an experimental rocket-fuel formula, X10 is actually a standard for controlling lights and other devices. Nothing is experimental about X10, and it has been around since the 1970s.

X10 uses a network that's already installed in your house or apartment: your in-wall electrical wiring. Your Mac mini transmits low-power digital commands through your building's AC power lines to other X10 devices. The signals transmit a few simple commands: on and off, and dim and brighten.

Some X10 equipment can also send information back to your Mac. For instance, you can use your Mac mini's X10 software to run your sprinkler system. When it starts raining, a rain sensor can send a signal to the Mac mini, telling it to turn off the sprinklers.

The great thing about X10 is that it's a modular system. You can start small and cheap by controlling a few lights. Little by little, you can add devices that control more and more of your house.

What You Can Do

Your X10-enabled Mac mini makes events happen without you having to think about it. You can set up the Mac to react to sensor readings by sending out commands. You can also control multiple actions manually from anywhere in the house, and sometimes from outside the house, from a phone or the Web.

These are some of the areas that you can automate:

- **Lighting:** Lights are a good place to start with X10 automation. You can set the Mac mini to turn lights on and off as you leave for work, when you come home, and when you hit the sack. While you're out of town, have the lights go on and off in different rooms just as if you were still home. You can also automatically dim lights. You can control individual or multiple table lamps, as well as in-wall and ceiling-mounted lights. You can even have the lights react to you with a motion detector: You walk into a room and the lights come on. Neat.

- **Security:** You can save a lot of money on traditional security services by creating your own. Use sensors that detect opening doors and windows, as well as motion sensors, cameras, and alarms. The Mac mini can call you or send you an e-mail if some event is triggered, such as a smoke detector going off. This lets you call the fire department before the fire gets big enough for the neighbors to see it.

- **Sprinkler system:** You may have an automatic sprinkler system that turns on at certain times, whether you need it or not. In the automated house, your sprinklers turn off when it starts raining. And if it already rained, a sensor detects whether the ground is already soaked and prevents the sprinklers from starting. So you water your yard only when it needs it.

✔ **Phone system:** You use a phone as a remote control from within your house or outside of it. You can use the keypad on the phone or use voice recognition to issue voice commands. You can also screen calls so completely that the phone doesn't even ring if the call is from someone not on your list of approved callers. You can also have your home phone call you at different numbers to alert you to various conditions, including a flood in your basement, a fire, a house that's too hot, or maybe the fact that your tropical fish-tank heater is on the fritz.

✔ **Heating and cooling system:** The X10-enabled Mac mini can regulate temperature in different ways. You can have an in-window air conditioner kick in 30 minutes before you get home so that you walk into a cool condo. While you're away, you can have your house contact you if it gets too hot or too cold for your pets. You can then turn on the air conditioning or heating from your remote location.

These are only a few examples of uses for X10 technology. You can come up with many more. There are a few things you need to pick up first.

What You Need

Software that's running on the Mac mini issues X10 commands based on a schedule that you set up, or based on feedback that it receives from X10 devices.

The X10 hardware comes in the form of modules that you plug into wall sockets or, if you want to get fancier, X10-enabled in-wall switches and sockets. The modules are inexpensive, starting at just over $10. You can also buy X10-enabled light switches and wall sockets that include a built-in X10 module. Sensors, such as motion detectors, are also available.

Shopping for X10 hardware

You can find X10 hardware in some retail stores, though you'll probably have to do a lot of legwork to find it. On the other hand, there are some great Web sites that sell X10 products.

Radio Shack is probably the biggest retailer that carries X10 hardware in some of its stores. Call ahead before you make the trip, though. You may end up traveling to a store only to end up ordering a part, which you can do from RadioShack.com without leaving your house.

Here are the best Web sites for buying X10 hardware:

- ✔ **Radio Shack:** The company carries a good selection of X10 products from several manufacturers, and it has its own branded hardware. The problem with Radio Shack's Web site (www.radioshack.com) is that the company sells so many products that it isn't obvious where to look for X10 products.

  Here's a clue: To find Radio Shack's X10 catalog, go to the Security & Home Automation section.

- ✔ **SmartHome:** My favorite online X10 store is SmartHome (www.smarthome.com). In addition to offering its own line of X10 hardware and two different Mac software applications, SmartHome.com has a good deal of information about X10 technology, as well as ideas for home automation projects. SmartHome.com also sells books and videos on home automation topics.

- ✔ **Fun for Geeks:** Fun for Geeks (www.funforgeeks.com/) targets the Mac audience. Keep in mind that the only X10 component that is specific to Macs or Windows PCs is the software. Macs and PCs use the same X10 hardware. However, Fun for Geeks offers bundles of hardware with Mac software. Like a lot of other sites, it also sells non-X10 automation products, which you can often use in an X10 system.

- ✔ **X10, Ltd.:** Another good online company is X10, Ltd. (www.X10.com), the company that first created X10 technology in the 1970s. X10.com doesn't offer much in the way of Mac software but does have a large assortment of every type of X10 module and peripheral that you could think of. Like SmartHome, X10, Ltd. offers its own brand of X10 hardware.

- ✔ **Marrick Ltd.:** Marrick Ltd. (www.marrickltd.com) is another manufacturer of X10 and other electronic equipment, which is for sale at the company's Web site as well as other places. Marrick doesn't sell Mac software but has links to a few software sites.

- ✔ **Home Automation:** Home Automation (www.homeautomationnet.com) isn't an X10 manufacturer but instead carries hardware from other manufacturers, including SmartHome.

Basic X10 hardware types

When you go to an X10 online store, you often find a confusing array of hundreds of devices. Fortunately, most X10 devices fall into one of three categories:

- ✔ **Computer interface modules:** These devices connect the Mac mini to the X10 system.

- ✔ **Receivers:** These devices turn your lights and appliances on and off. They receive a command and act on it.

✔ **Transmitters:** These devices can send commands back to the Mac mini or directly to receivers. I'm lumping hand-held controllers and remotes into this category.

Some X10 modules can both transmit and receive signals. The Mac mini acts as a transmitter, connected through a USB port to an X10 computer interface box. The mini can also be a receiver, reacting to input from other X10 devices.

X10 computer interface modules

The Mac mini transmits X10 signals through the USB port, but X10 devices transmit commands through your house's in-wall wiring. To connect the Mac mini to the X10 system, you need a way to plug a USB cable into a wall socket. This is what an X10 computer interface module enables you to do.

SmartHome has two models: a basic and inexpensive unit (the PowerLinc USB), and a more expensive unit (the PowerLinc Controller) that can free your Mac mini for other tasks.

You can also find wireless radio-frequency (RF) computer interface receivers that enable your Mac mini from wireless X10 devices.

SmartHome PowerLinc USB

The SmartHome PowerLinc USB ($38, www.smarthome.com/1132U.html) is an X10 computer interface with a USB port. As you can see in Figure 10-1, the USB port is at the bottom.

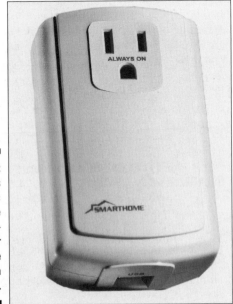

Figure 10-1: SmartHome's PowerLinc USB is the first X10-computer interface with a USB port.

The PowerLinc USB plugs into an AC wall socket, but it preserves an AC outlet by providing a *pass-through* AC plug, which is labeled "Always On." You can use this for any electrical device, including the Mac mini.

Some X10 aficionados recommend that you not plug your computer's power cable into the PowerLinc's pass-through AC plug, however. They say that this can cause noise that interferes with the X10 signals. The recommendation here is to plug the Mac mini's power cable directly into a wall outlet instead of the pass-through plug.

The PowerLinc USB sometimes comes bundled with software for Windows — ignore it.

SmartHome PowerLinc Controller

The PowerLinc Controller ($70) is like the PowerLinc USB, except that it includes computer memory that can store commands and macros that you download from the Mac mini. This lets you shut off the Mac mini or unplug its USB cable and use it for something else. The PowerLinc Controller's memory isn't erased during a power failure because the Controller contains a back-up battery.

To take advantage of the PowerLinc Controller, you need to be running Indigo software ($90) from Perceptive Automation (www.perceptiveautomation. com/). You can find information about Indigo in the section "Setting Up Indigo X10 Software," later in this chapter.

You can also buy the PowerLinc USB bundled with Indigo (try www.funfor geeks.com, for instance). The bundle can save you some money.

Don't buy SmartHome's $120 bundle of the PowerLinc Controller with SmartHome Manager software. This is Windows software, not Mac OS X software. It won't run on your Mac mini.

Wireless computer interfaces

The ActiveHome CM15A from X10, Ltd. (www.x10.com) is like the PowerLinc USB, but it can also receive commands from RF X10 transmitters and hand-held controllers.

WGL Designs (www.wgldesigns.com/) has two RF computer interfaces that work with Indigo software: the MR26a and the W800RF32.

X10 receivers

An X10 receiver accepts commands and responds by turning on or off or dimming or brightening. A receiver module contains a switch that opens when the module receives an On command, providing juice to a lamp that's plugged into it. You can also find receivers for more heavy-duty appliances, like clothes dryers.

The common X10 receivers plug into an AC socket, but there is a wide variety of devices, including modules that screw into light bulb sockets and in-wall switches and plugs.

Plug-in receivers: Light modules versus appliance modules

Receivers that plug into a wall socket (such as the one in Figure 10-2 from X10, Ltd.) are the best way to start with X10. They are inexpensive and you can move them around.

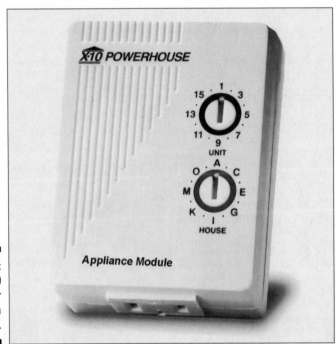

Figure 10-2: This X10 receiver plugs into a wall socket.

Two types of plug-in receivers are available: lamp modules and appliance modules. Lamp modules can dim and brighten; appliance modules can only turn on and off. Don't use a lamp module for an appliance. The lower voltage of dimming can damage an appliance.

Lamp modules and appliance modules look the same. The only difference is the label that identifies the module. Some plug-in modules look like the one in Figure 10-2. Others include a pass-though outlet labeled "Always On." This allows you to plug in something that you don't need to control. With both types, the X10-controlled outlet is usually at the bottom.

Wall- or ceiling-mounted lighting: Screw-in socket modules

For wall-mounted light fixtures or ceiling lights, you can use X10 modules that screw into a light bulb socket. You can also use a screw-in module in a table lamp with a shade if you don't like the look of (or don't have room for) a plug-in module.

The standard screw-in socket is fairly large, but it can respond to all the commands that a plug-in module can.

You can also find shorter compact versions that may fit in ceiling fixtures. These versions can only turn on and off and cannot be dimmed.

X10 light switch

If you're a home handyperson and know how to wire an in-wall switch, an in-wall X10 receiver switch works well for controlling ceiling lights and fans and outdoor lights. It replaces your normal light switch and, as you can see in Figure 10-3, looks a lot like it. You can find 2-way and 3-way switches.

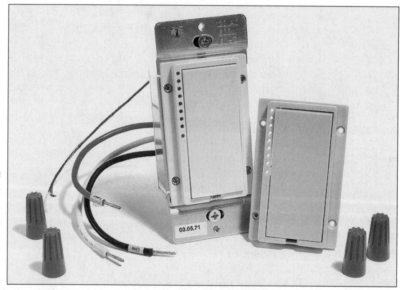

Figure 10-3:
An in-wall
X10 switch
looks like an
ordinary
light switch.

As with plug-in modules, you can control in-wall X10 switches with your Mac mini and X10 software to turn lights on and off and to dim and brighten them.

To control a ceiling fan, find an in-wall X10 switch that has only on and off functions. Don't use an in-wall dimmer module with a ceiling fan. The reduced voltage of a dimmer can damage a fan.

In-wall socket module

You can also replace your in-wall AC outlets with X10 versions to control appliances or lights. The advantage is that you don't have to see an X10 receiver module plugged into a wall socket.

X10 transmitters

A transmitter sends X10 commands to X10 receivers or to the Mac mini. Your Mac mini acts as a receiver when it accepts input and a transmitter when it issues commands.

A transmitter can also be a sensor, such as a thermostat or a motion detector, sending a signal back to the Mac mini or directly to receivers. Some transmitters are devices to which you connect sensors, such as thermostats.

The PowerFlash is a versatile transmitter that is sold by many X10 providers. It can issue different types of X10 commands based on its setting. Because the PowerFlash measures a change in voltage, you can connect a wide variety of devices to each other. For instance, security devices such as motion detectors and magnetic window switches can trigger lights. You can also use it to turn off the vacuum cleaner when someone rings the doorbell. Connect it to the telephone to shut off a radio when the phone rings.

Another type of transmitter is a button-operated controller, which you can use to manually set combinations of lights on, off, or dimmed — or appliances on and off. If your Mac mini has set the lighting according to schedule and you decide you're in the mood for different lighting, the manual controller lets you make the change. You can find controllers as hand-held wireless remotes, plug-in panels like the one in Figure 10-4, and in-wall panels.

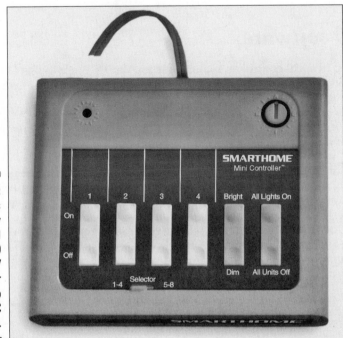

Figure 10-4:
This manually operated X10 transmitter/controller plugs into an AC outlet.

Starter kits

One way to begin automating your house is with one of the "starter kits" that most X10 vendors offer. These kits bundle together an X10 computer interface, some X10 appliance modules, and sometimes the software. You can find starter kits focused in different areas, such as lighting or security, as well as general-purpose kits. In addition to the convenience of getting everything you need to begin, the starter kits are usually pretty good deals, offering a discount over the cost of buying the components separately. If you're paying for software as part of a bundle, just make sure that you get Mac software. You can also buy software and software/hardware starter kits directly from some software manufacturers.

Problem-solving devices

Because X10 signals depend on the electrical characteristics of your home's wiring, electrical interference and other issues can cause problems with communications between devices. Fortunately, these problems are well known and easily fixed by plugging inexpensive devices into a wall socket. The most common devices are filters and phase couplers. The section "Installing problem-solving devices," later in this chapter, describes how to use these problem-fixing X10 modules.

X10 software

The top two X10 controller applications for Mac OS X are Indigo ($90) from Perceptive Automation (www.perceptiveautomation.com/) and XTension ($150) from Sand Hill Engineering (www.shed.com).

Indigo is the better X10 application. With Indigo, it's easier to create complex control situations.

XTension has many supporters who like its ability to let you tweak every detail of a complex setup. Like Indigo, XTension can generate X10 commands based on input from sensors and other X10 devices. But setting up XTension to generate X10 commands is quite a bit more difficult than doing so in Indigo, because XTension requires you to create scripts using AppleScript syntax and special AppleScript verbs from XTension. You don't exactly need to be a programmer, though it's more trouble than choosing items from menus, as in Indigo.

Indigo also supports AppleScripts, but you can do much more in the way of scripting using Indigo's menus and buttons. You don't have to write AppleScript code to come up with some advanced triggering and control mechanisms.

Here are some of the things you can do with Indigo to turn your Mac mini into an X10 maxi:

- ✔ **Download commands to SmartHome's PowerLinc Controller computer interface module:** This lets you shut off the Mac mini and use it for something else. But you may not want to, because Indigo can do things that the controller module can't.

- ✔ **Have Indigo send you e-mail:** You can have a Mac mini running Indigo send you an e-mail message when certain events occur, such as a power failure. This is one of those things that the PowerLinc Controller can't do.

- ✔ **Send Indigo an e-mail message:** For instance, you can set Indigo to start the hot tub just by sending it an e-mail message.

- ✔ **Use a Bluetooth-equipped Sony Ericsson phone as a remote control:** Indigo uses the Salling Clicker application (`http://homepage.mac.com/jonassalling`). Salling Clicker lets you run your Mac from the phone or a Palm hand-held to control Indigo — and therefore your house.

- ✔ **Display almost anything:** Indigo displays the current status of devices, including how much a light is dimmed.

- ✔ **Provide seasonal awareness:** Another powerful feature of Indigo is that you can set an action to occur at sunrise or sunset instead of at a specific time. As you know, the time at which sunrise or sunset occurs changes with the changing of the seasons; because Indigo is aware of this, you don't have to think about it.

Setting Up Hardware

X10 equipment is easy to install. In many cases, you just plug a module into an AC socket and then plug your lamp or appliance into the module. Before you do, you may need to set X10 addresses for your devices.

Configuring X10 addresses

To enable the Mac mini to turn on specific lights or appliances, each X10 device identifies itself with a unique address. When the Mac mini sends out an On command to a particular address, all the other lights with different addresses ignore the command.

An X10 address consists of a number and a letter. The number can be from 1 through 16; the letter is from A through P (the first 16 letters of the alphabet). The range of possible addresses then looks like this:

1A, 1B, 1C . . . 16N, 16O, 16P

There are 256 possible addresses (16 numbers times 16 letters), which means that you can have up to 256 devices in your house. The letters are called *house codes;* the numbers are the *unit codes.*

You can use three different X10 addressing strategies in different parts of your home.

Using the same address on multiple devices

If you use the same X10 address for several devices, you can control all of them together. One command turns on all the lights with the same address, or dims them to the same degree. You probably wouldn't set all the lights and appliances in an entire house with the same address, but you might use the same address for all the lights in a room.

You *could* have a single command work multiple devices that have different addresses, but it is more work to set up the software that way.

Using a unique address for each device

If every device has a unique address, with a different house code and unit code, each device acts individually. As an example, you might use A1, B2, and C10 to control three devices.

This is a good strategy for a room where you never want to control the lights as a group.

Using the same house code for multiple devices

In this strategy, all the addresses have the same letter (house code) but different numbers (unit codes), as in A1, A2, A3, and A4 — up to A16. Using the same house code in a house or room gives you the most flexibility, because it allows you to control each device individually or as a group.

Using the same house code on a group of devices allows you to use an X10 transmitter (such as a motion detector). Transmitters can often send out a command that affects a house code, but they can't send out commands to multiple devices with different unit-code addresses.

This strategy also makes it easier for you to configure the Mac mini to send a single command to multiple devices.

If you want to use a house code to control multiple devices this way, don't use receivers that automatically set their own addresses. Use receivers that let you manually set the address, such as the device shown in Figure 10-5.

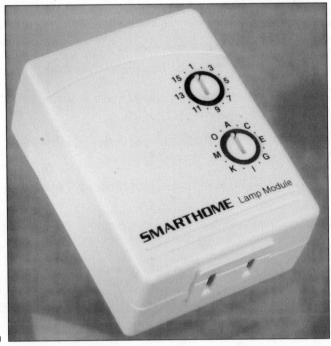

Setting the address

For many X10 devices, you set the address manually. This is often in the form of two dials — one for the letter and one for the number. To set the address, turn each dial with a screwdriver, as you would with the receiver shown in Figure 10-5. Other receivers have dials that you can turn with your fingers.

You can also buy X10 devices that are self-addressing. These devices communicate with the other devices that are plugged into the house to make sure that they have a unique address.

Connecting the X10 network

Figure 10-6 shows a basic X10 setup. To create it, follow these steps:

1. **Set the address of your X10 receiver module or modules, as described in the previous section.**

2. **Plug the X10 computer interface into a wall socket.**

3. **Use a USB cable to connect a Mac mini USB port to the X10 computer interface's USB port.**

4. **Plug an X10 receiver into a wall socket.**

5. **Plug a lamp or other appliance into the X10 receiver.**

You can add additional receivers anywhere in your home, as long as you don't use more than 256 devices.

More-complicated hardware, such as in-wall switches, follow the same basic procedure, although they may be self-addressing.

Don't plug appliances into light modules. Only use appliance modules for appliances.

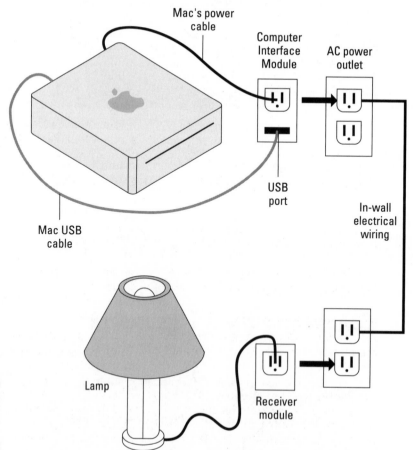

Mac's power cable

Computer Interface Module

AC power outlet

USB port

In-wall electrical wiring

Mac USB cable

Lamp

Receiver module

Figure 10-6:
A basic
X10 setup.

Installing problem-solving devices

The X10 system operates as a guest on your building's AC power lines. As such, it is subject to the electrical characteristics of your electrical system. Several common problems are easily overcome by adding special X10 modules. Typical symptoms include devices that don't respond to commands.

Installing filters for interference and attenuation

If you're having problems with devices not turning on or off when they are supposed to — or working intermittently — you may have one of two problems caused by appliances: noise and device attenuation. Fortunately, both problems have the same fix.

Plug the appliance that is causing the problem into a *signal filter,* and plug the signal filter into the wall socket. The SmartHome FilterLinc ($25) is one such device.

Before you can add a signal filter, you need to find out which appliance is causing the problem.

Identifying interference

Interference occurs when an appliance adds electrical noise on the in-wall power lines. This noise can confuse X10 receivers. Noise-inducing appliances include refrigerators, devices with motors (such as plug-in fans, hair dryers, blenders, or vacuum cleaners), and some fluorescent lights.

To find which appliance is causing the problem, turn off each suspected appliance one at a time.

It's helpful to set your X10 software (such as Indigo) to continually turn a light on and off while you look for the problem appliance.

If you can't locate the appliance, you may have more than one noisy appliance. You can try turning all appliances off and then turn them on one by one.

Identifying attenuation

Attenuation is when an appliance filters out your X10 signals because it thinks the signals are noise. The effect is the same as a noise-producing appliance in that the X10 receivers stop responding or respond intermittently.

Appliances that can attenuate X10 signals include some big-screen televisions, cable and satellite receivers, and some stereo equipment. Equipment related to your Mac can also attenuate X10 signals. This equipment includes printers, power supplies for notebook computers and cell phones, universal power supplies, surge protectors, and higher-end power strips. (Cheaper power strips don't attenuate X10 signals.)

Troubleshooting for attenuation is a bit more complicated than it is for interference. To locate the device causing the problem, it isn't enough to turn off the devices. You have to unplug them to remove their effect on the power system. Plugging offending devices into a signal filter can fix the problem because the filter isolates the troublemakers from the system.

Using phase couplers

Another common problem with X10 systems occurs in houses wired as two-phase, 240- (or 220-) volt systems, as are many homes built in the last 30 years. The symptoms are that X10 devices in one section of the house don't seem to respond to devices in another section. Within each half, or *phase*, everything seems fine. When this problem occurs, you probably have a lack of communication between devices on different phases of a two-phase system. Each phase provides 120 (or 110) volts.

The fix is a $20 device called a *phase coupler* (sometimes called a *coupling capacitor* or *signal bridge*). The device joins the two phases, allowing X10 signals to cross between them. (SmartHome's SignalLinc, as shown in Figure 10-7, is such a device.)

Figure 10-7:
An X10 phase coupler.

One way to test for this problem is to look for a 240-volt appliance, such as an air conditioner, electric oven, range, stovetop, or electric dryer (not a gas dryer) — basically, appliances that use a lot of juice. Now turn on your 240-volt appliance. If your X10 system suddenly works, you need a phase coupler. Turning on a 240-volt appliance joins the two 120-volt phases, accomplishing the same thing as a phase coupler.

To install the phase coupler, plug the coupler into the 240-volt receptacle. Then plug the appliance into the coupler.

If you don't have a 240-volt outlet in your house (perhaps because your major appliances run on natural gas), you can use a hardware phase coupler. This type of coupler sits just outside your home's breaker box, and it is connected to two circuit breakers in the breaker box. If you've ever wired circuit breakers, it's not too difficult to install. If not, get an electrician to install the coupler.

Installing signal amplifiers

Big houses may be too big for the X10 signals to travel from one end to another. The X10 signals degrade over the distance. If you've tried turning on your 240-volt appliances and still can't get X10 devices at opposite sides of a house to communicate, you probably have this problem.

You can solve this problem by installing an X10 signal amplifier, which boosts the signals that X10 transmitters are sending. As with other X10 devices, you plug a signal amplifier into a power outlet.

Unfortunately, signal amplifiers run about $100, quite a bit more expensive than signal filters and phase couplers.

A pragmatic fix that doesn't cost anything is to locate the X10 computer interface in a power outlet that is close to the circuit breaker (or fuse) box. This transmits signals that are close to the power source for the house's wiring system. If you have a controller that lets you download commands, such as the PowerLinc Controller, you can download the commands from your mini to the interface, unplug it from the Mac, and move the interface to the outlet near the breaker box.

You may have to locate your Mac mini near the breaker box if your X10 computer interface is a simple receiver/transmitter like the PowerLinc USB, or if you're using the Mac mini to respond to input from X10 devices.

This approach doesn't work for everyone, particularly if your breaker box isn't in your living space. If this is you, then go for the signal amplifier.

Setting Up Indigo X10 Software

You can do many different things with Indigo installed on your Mac mini and X10 devices in your house. Yet, Indigo is so simple and modular that you use the same techniques to create vastly different home control setups.

To install Indigo, drag the Indigo application from the mounted disk image to the Applications folder. Then run the installer for drivers. You need to install the driver software that comes with Indigo to communicate with an X10 computer USB interface box.

The following sections first describe the Indigo interface and what you do with each major piece. I then give you a specific example to set up — applied knowledge, so to speak.

The Preferences dialog

The Preferences dialog (accessible from the Indigo menu) ties the X10 network to the Mac mini and to e-mail and remotes. As you can see in Figure 10-8, Indigo Preferences has four tabs:

✔ **Interface:** Here, you select the X10 computer interface that connects the Mac mini to the X10 network. These are your main choices:

- *Interface Communication Online:* Check this to establish communications with the X10 network.

- *Interface Type:* This pop-up menu lets you select your X10 computer interface box, including the PowerLinc and ActiveHome models.

- *Enable RF Receiver Interface:* This setting lets you choose a wireless computer interface, the WGL Designs MR26, or the W800RF32 model.

✔ **Email:** This tab lets you enable Indigo's ability to scan incoming e-mail. You can use an e-mail message to trigger an action.

✔ **Sunset & Sunrise:** Indigo knows what time the sun rises and sets from your longitude and latitude settings and the time of the year. These values are set automatically, but you can manually change them here.

✔ **General:** This panel lets you change settings for the log of events that Indigo keeps.

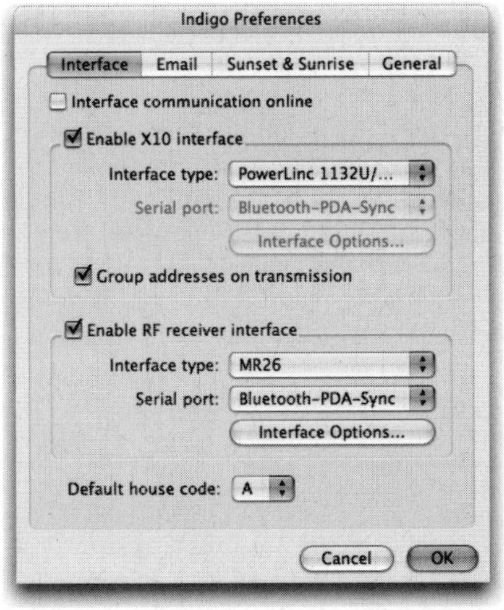

Figure 10-8:
Connect to
the X10
computer
interface in
Indigo's
Preferences
dialog.

The main Indigo window

The main window in Indigo has four buttons on the left side that change the windows to the right (see Figure 10-9).This is what they do:

- **Devices:** This is where you configure the X10 devices, such as lamps and appliances, motion detectors, and thermostats. You add new devices by clicking the New button. You also set addresses and give them names (such as Bedroom Lamp). You can also manually control each device by selecting it and using the controls at the bottom. The bottom of Figure 10-9 shows the lamp-dimming controls.

- **Trigger Actions:** You can create trigger actions, which are automated responses to X10 commands, to e-mails, and to remote-control devices. For example, a motion detector can trigger some lights to come on. If your Mac mini is on an uninterruptible power supply, you could set up Indigo so that a power failure triggers Indigo to send you an e-mail.

  The Trigger Actions pane includes the most complicated of Indigo's settings, so I discuss these controls in more detail in the next section.

- **Time/Date Actions:** This is where you schedule regular events, such as turning on the fish-tank light at 9:00 a.m. or dimming the living room lights at 9:00 p.m. You can also set conditions to schedule so that they occur (or don't occur) unless certain actions happen. For example, you can tell Indigo to start your sprinklers at 3:00 p.m. unless your outdoor rain sensor tells Indigo that it is raining.

✔ **Action Groups:** A group action is a combination of trigger or scheduled actions grouped together to create a complex series of events. For instance, you could set up a group action that responds to a door or window opening. This could turn on lights in different rooms and send an e-mail to your office and mobile phone. You might create another action group called "Dinner Party" that turns on certain lights in multiple rooms and dims to preset levels, and that disables some of your other scheduled actions.

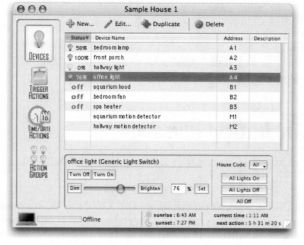

Figure 10-9: Indigo lets you send X10 commands manually through the Devices pane.

Trigger Actions

The Trigger Actions button of Indigo's main window lets you create actions that are responses to events. A trigger action can be to send you an e-mail when a power failure occurs or to turn some lights on when a motion detector is activated.

Click the New button (or double-click an existing trigger in the list), and you get a dialog with three tabs: Trigger, Condition, and Action, as shown in Figure 10-10.

✔ **Trigger:** This tab lets you define what causes the action. The Type pop-up menu lets you select different types of triggers, such as an X10 command from another device, a change in a device's state (such as a light going off), an application starting up, as well as others.

When you select one of these triggers, Indigo displays circumstances that you can set for the trigger, and from which device it came. For instance, if you select X10/RF Command Received, you can set the triggering event for a device as brighten. This means that if the specified X10 device sends a brightening command, your trigger action is activated.

- ✔ **Condition:** This tab is where you add further limitations to the trigger. You can specify that the trigger can only act after sunset and whether various variables are true or false.

- ✔ **Action:** On the Action tab, you tell Indigo what to do in response to the trigger. You can have the trigger turn a device on or off, enable another trigger, run an AppleScript on the Mac mini, or enable a group action, as well as other actions.

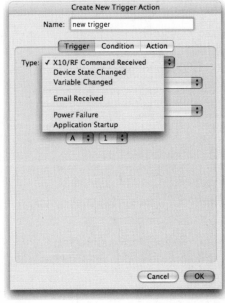

Figure 10-10:
You can specify exactly what causes a trigger and what happens as a result.

An example: Motion-triggered light

Setting up a light to turn on when motion is detected is a good way to show off Indigo's features. You can use this setup to turn on multiple lights inside and outside the house for backyard security, or to have the lights go on automatically when you enter a room. In this example, I describe how to set up Indigo to automatically turn on the front hall light when I come home from work.

First, you create the devices (the motion detector and lights) in Indigo, and then you create the trigger action.

Creating the devices

For this example, you create the motion detector and lights by following these steps:

1. **Click the Devices button at the upper left of Indigo's main window (refer to Figure 10-9).**

2. **Click the New button, at the top of the Devices pane.**

3. **In the Create New Device dialog that appears (shown in Figure 10-11), give the motion detector a name.**

Figure 10-11: Setting up Indigo for a motion detector.

4. **In the Type pop-up menu, choose Motion Detector.**

5. **Set the X10 address.**

   In this example, I set it to A5.

6. **Click the OK button.**

   You now see the motion detector in the device list. Now it's time for the next device.

7. **Click the New button to create a device for the light.**

8. **In the Create New Device dialog that appears, give the hallway light a name.**

9. **In the Type pop-up menu, choose the type of X10 control method.**

   The pop-up menu lists several types of plug-in lamp modules and the Socket Rocket screw-in module. Select Generic Light Switch to indicate an X10-controlled wall switch.

10. **Set the X10 address.**

11. **Click the OK button.**

Creating a trigger action

Creating a trigger action tells Indigo to turn on the light when motion is detected. You do three tasks to create a trigger action:

✔ **Specify the trigger:** In this example, it's a signal from the motion detector.

✔ **Set the condition:** The sun has set (it's dark outside).

✔ **Set the action:** Turn on the light.

The next three sections show you how to accomplish these three tasks.

Specifying the trigger

Follow these steps to specify the trigger:

1. **Click the Trigger Actions button at the left of Indigo's main window.**

2. **Click the New button at the top of the window.**

3. **In the Create New Trigger Action dialog that appears, give the trigger action a name, such as Motion in Hall is Detected.**

4. **In the Type pop-up menu, choose X10/RF Command Received.**

   This means that an X10 signal from the motion detector triggers the action you are creating.

5. **In the Received pop-up menu, choose On.**

   This refers to the On X10 command that is received from the motion detector.

6. **Click the Device option to select it. From the pop-up menu, select the name you gave to the motion detector.**

   The dialog looks like Figure 10-12.

The next task is to tell Indigo when to turn on the lights.

Setting the trigger condition

Unless there's a total solar eclipse, you don't need these lights to turn on in the daytime. You could schedule a time for the motion detector to start working, but sunset occurs at different times during the year. Indigo is smart enough to know that, so you can set the software to turn on the lights only after sunset. Just follow these steps:

1. **Click the Condition tab.**

2. **Select the If Dark, After Sunset option.**

   This prevents the light from coming on during the day.

The final task is to tell Indigo what it is you want it to do when the conditions are met.

Defining the trigger action

Now you can define the trigger action: to turn on the light. You usually don't need a hallway light to stay on all night, so you may want to set the light to go off 10 minutes after the last motion is detected. Follow these steps to do so:

1. **Click the Action tab in the Create New Trigger Action dialog to tell Indigo what to do when it hears from the motion detector.**

   The dialog shown in Figure 10-13 appears.

2. **From the Type pop-up menu, choose Send Device Action.**

3. **From the Action pop-up menu, choose Turn On.**

4. **From the Device pop-up menu, choose the name you gave to the light (Front Hall light, in this example).**

5. **Finally, tell Indigo to shut off the light after a certain amount of time. Select the Auto-off After check box and type 10 in the Minutes box.**

   To have your Mac mini say something at the time of the action, you can type a phrase in the Speak field.

6. **Click the OK button when you finish.**

Figure 10-13:
Define the trigger action, which is to turn on the light.

Chapter 11

Mac mini in the Kitchen

*T*he smell of fresh bread baking in the oven; the hiss of steam rising from pots on the stove; the friendly *boing* of Mac OS X booting up. What sensations better express the concept of home? The Mac mini, with its white and brushed-metal finish, fits perfectly in most modern kitchen decors. If you spend much of your life in the kitchen, you deserve to have a mini there.

If anything comes to mind for a kitchen mini, it's recipes. But there are other uses that a mini serves up as well. This chapter describes what you can do with a mini kitchen appliance and where to put it.

The New Kitchen Appliance

The kitchen is the nerve center of most homes. Family members start their day there with breakfast and end it by raiding the refrigerator for a midnight snack. The door of the fridge is where phone messages, shopping lists, reminder notes, the kids' art creations, and your niece-to-be's sonograms get posted. For less than the price of a high-end refrigerator, you can equip your kitchen with a Mac mini. The mini has several advantages over other computers for use as a kitchen appliance:

- ✔ **Size:** Space is always at a premium in the kitchen.

- ✔ **Cost:** The mini's low cost is a big advantage, particularly if it is your second (or third or fourth) Mac.

- ✔ **Flexibility:** You can choose peripherals that best match your kitchen needs.

Why you would want a computer in your kitchen might not be obvious, but a mini can play many roles. The next few pages describe a few of these. After that, I show you some things the Mac mini can do with recipes that you probably haven't thought about.

Entertain yourself while cooking

A mini can serve as an entertainment and communication center. You can listen to music on iTunes, play CDs and MP3s, or even watch a DVD movie while you cook. You can stay in touch with your friend using iChat instant messaging and videoconferencing and talk long distance to your mother in Florida using Voice over IP (VoIP). You can even keep up with the soaps if you buy a flat-panel TV for your display screen. The mini can also entertain your small kids in a place where you can keep an eye on them while you are working.

Tap the kitchen database

It's great having your address book, e-mail, and the proposal you need for work — and, of course, your favorite recipes — right in the kitchen where you spend so much time.

If you are interested in computers enough to have this book, there's a chance you already have some recipes in your existing computer, but more than likely, most are still in a 3 × 5–inch index card box. Keeping recipes on your Mac mini offers more than a box-load of advantages:

- ✔ The recipes don't become a soggy mess when food spills on the counter.
- ✔ It's easy to find recipes that use the foods you have on hand using Mac OS X's Spotlight search tool.
- ✔ You can easily e-mail recipes to friends, even changing them a little so that they are not as perfect as yours.
- ✔ It's easier to check for problem ingredients for friends or family who have food allergies, and to keep track of special diets for weight loss, diabetes, or other conditions.
- ✔ The recipes are preserved on the backups of your hard drive (you do back up, don't you?).

There is an old joke about the Windows user who couldn't double a recipe. The recipe called for an oven to be preheated to 375° F, and his oven only went up to 550° F. If you keep your recipes in a special recipe program, or just a spreadsheet program, changing the amount you make is a lot easier. The next section describes some recipe programs to run on your Mac mini.

You can find many recipe sites on the Internet, like the vast Epicurious (www.epicurious.com) or RecipeSource (www.recipesource.com). Google knows about most of them. It's best to search with a particular food or cuisine in mind. There is also a recipe Wiki, http://en.wikibooks.org/wiki/Cookbook, where you can add your own culinary creations and family dining treasures. Most online food-shopping sites did not survive the dot-com bust, but peapod.com still offers this service.

Organize your recipes

A good filing system for recipes makes them easier to find in a hurry. It can be as simple as a well-thought-out collection of folders, as shown in Figure 11-1. Like most cooks, you may have hundreds of recipes on slips of paper and in cookbooks. This is no problem. Just scan in your favorite recipes from *Cooking Basics For Dummies,* 3rd Edition, by Bryan Miller, Marie Rama, Eve Adamson, and Wolfgang Puck (Wiley). You can then drag the image files that the scanner creates into the Finder folders.

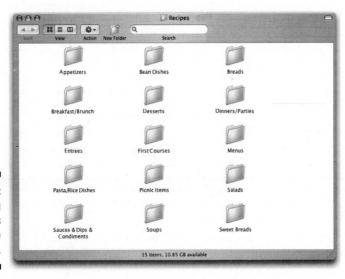

Figure 11-1:
Organizing your recipes in the Finder.

If you're willing to do some typing, you can use a word processor to store recipes, or type them in a specially designed recipe program.

Using a word processor for recipes

While several good recipe programs are available for Mac OS X, many cooks prefer to just use a word processor. It's a good idea to think about a standard format for your recipes. Here is an example, courtesy of Barbara Model Catering.

Peanut Butter Oatmeal

Great for people who don't eat oatmeal. If they like peanut butter, they like this. Serves one. Multiply proportions to the number of servings desired.

$^1/_2$ cup quick oats

1 cup water

1 tablespoon peanut butter

1 teaspoon maple syrup

$^1/_8$ teaspoon salt (optional)

*Put all ingredients into a saucepan over high heat.

*Bring to a boil and cook, stirring until thick for 1-2 minutes.

*Serve topped with cold milk or cream.

Variation: Try adding raisins and/or chopped fresh apples before cooking. To really tempt the skeptical, top the hot cereal with some vanilla ice cream and/or a sliced banana.

If you're using Microsoft Word to store recipes, type them in outline mode, with the titles as a heading. This way, you can collapse the document to display only headings, and view one recipe at a time by double-clicking the heading. (Close it up by double-clicking the heading again.) You can also use two or three levels of headings to list categories and sub-categories. Figure 11-2 shows a recipe file in outline view with the subheadings visible but with only one recipe showing.

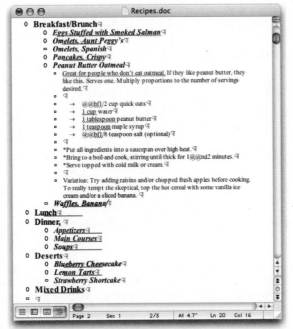

Figure 11-2:
Microsoft
Word's
outline view
is useful for
storing and
browsing
recipes.

A Word document can hold a lot of text — hundreds of pages worth — so you can store all of your recipes in a single file.

Connoisseur: iTunes-style recipe storage

iTunes has been so successful in managing music that Apple has replicated aspects of it in other software, including iPhoto, Address Book, and the Finder. One wonders why iLife doesn't include a recipe program.

There's no need to wait for Apple, however, because as you can see from Figure 11-3, Connoisseur is the iTunes of kitchen recipes. Connoisseur is a $20 application by The Little App Factory (www.thelittleappfactory.com) that is well worth the price. Think of each Connoisseur recipe as an iTunes song. Instead of playlists, there are recipe groups. Instead of smart playlists, smart groups automatically collect recipes based on your criteria. Sort and search for recipes just as you do for songs in iTunes.

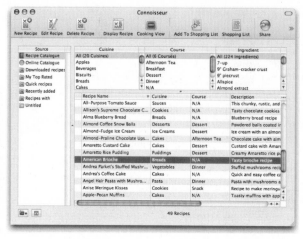

Figure 11-3: Connoisseur is one of the best ways to store, browse, and locate recipes.

If you already have your recipes typed up in a word processing file, Connoisseur can import them. It can also download recipes from the Internet. To get you started, Connoisseur comes with some recipes preinstalled.

Need to buy supplies for your big dinner party? Connoisseur can create a shopping list for your recipes to print or to copy to your iPod — just as iTunes copies songs to your iPod. When it's time to cook, you can switch to Cooking View (shown in Figure 11-4).

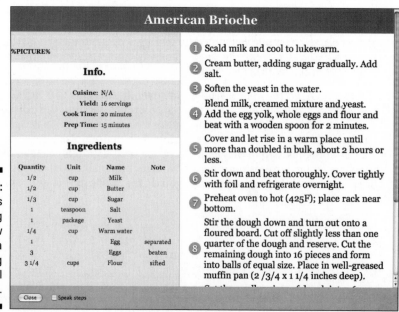

Figure 11-4: Connoisseur's Cooking View displays a recipe in big type, full screen.

The computerized kitchen of the future

Many futurists are predicting an electronic kitchen where the refrigerator and pantry will scan little radio frequency identification (RFID) tags on each food package. The tags will identify what came in the package and will store the expiration date. Smart shelves will weigh each package to determine how much is left. Electronic odor sensors will detect spoilage. All this will be attached to a kitchen computer that will check the Internet for the ingredients and nutritional value of each item, suggesting possible recipes and alerting you to possible food allergies for each family member. Dinner guests will presumably send you their dietary restrictions when they RSVP to an invitation. (People of the future will RSVP because they won't have anything else to do.)

The computer will learn your family's eating preferences and automatically order foods that they haven't had in a while, as well as all the staples you normally consume. Computerized recipes will automatically set times for the stove and microwave and preheat your oven. Will installing a Mac mini in your kitchen make all this possible? *NO,* thank heavens.

Other great features include unit conversion and recipe scaling — for example, taking a recipe for three people and increasing the quantities to serve seven people. All in all, Connoisseur is the best recipe manager for your Mac mini.

Enter the recipes you know by heart

Your favorite dish, simple things you make all the time, a salad, a casserole, a type of bread — you don't have to write them down. You know them so well that you can make these dishes in your sleep.

Then one day, you add a little rye with the flour or use beans instead of peas in the casserole. Maybe you were low on white flour or you forgot to buy peas. But you like it this way. And then you make other changes. Years go by and eventually you are making a completely different dish. Then one day you think "I used to make a simple whole wheat bread or a tuna casserole that would be perfect for this occasion; now what did I used to put in it?" Write it down now.

Finding a mini a Home in Your Kitchen

One fact of life about kitchens is that things get wet. Give careful thought about where you place your mini and what kind of peripherals to install. You could make a splash hood for your mini, perhaps out of a small baking sheet or out of some acrylic (Plexiglas).

Grease is another problem in most kitchens. Use the hood over your stove when frying or broiling. Keep its filters clean.

Locating the mini

You have a number of possible locations for a mini in the kitchen. Its small size lends itself to being installed under a kitchen cabinet, preferably not too close to the sink or stove.

Rather than having it sit on the countertop where you can spill orange juice on it, mount it directly to the bottom of a cabinet. You can build a simple bracket or modify an under-the-counter chrome wine glass rack from a home-decorator or kitchen store. For a tailor-made shelf, check out Newer Technology's Nu Clear mini (www.newertech.com). It's an under-the-desk acrylic shelf that you can easily install under a kitchen cabinet. You can buy it at Newer Technology's Web site or at other outlets for about $25-to-$35.

A table in the breakfast nook is another possible home for the mini, as long as it's a table that you don't use to prepare (or eat) food. Remember, your mini is not a toaster. Another place you could stash it is under the kitchen island. The mini could also be tucked between books on the recipe shelf, which is usually well away from drips and splashes, as long as the ventilation holes are clear. For a more adventurous approach, see the section "Computer on a Rope" in Chapter 22.

Displaying the display

You'll certainly want a flat-panel display in the kitchen. I recommend a smaller, 15-inch unit for a kitchen. You don't need a bigger display taking up room in a kitchen, and 15-inch flat-panels come at a good price. Smaller monitors are also easier to move around.

Another option is to plug into a flat-panel television that doubles as, well, a television. (See Chapter 9 for methods of connecting the Mac mini to TVs.) The Dutch electronics company Philips has a line of televisions with WiFi connectivity, called *Streamium.* These models allow you to view Internet content and computer-resident files through your TV sets without connecting cables.

Waterproof keyboard

A waterproof, flexible keyboard is available from www.clitheroelancs.co.uk. It is offered in red, blue, green, orange, purple, black, and hot pink. Be sure to order the USB version. A waterproof wireless Bluetooth keyboard is available from www.flexis.co.kr/web/fxcubebt.htm, but only in black.

You can find industrial-grade waterproof mice and trackballs, but they are pricey. Alternatively, you can try wrapping an optical mouse in a plastic bag or kitchen wrap.

Locating the Mac mini's power brick

It's a good idea to plug the mini's power supply and other electronic devices into an outlet that has ground fault interrupt (GFI) protection. Figure 11-5 shows a GFI outlet. Your house fuses only protect your home from fires caused by electrical overloads and short circuits. Only a GFI circuit protects against electrical shock. Newer buildings in the U.S. are required to have GFI outlets in the kitchen. If you have an older kitchen, consider having an electrician install some.

Figure 11-5: A North American– style GFI outlet.

A Day in the Life of the Kitchen mini

Here is a typical day that you might spend with a Mac mini in the kitchen:

Before breakfast: The mini checks your .Mac account and downloads a large file from that Kyrgyzstan outsourcing firm so that you can review it over your morning orange juice.

Breakfast: Read your e-mail, check the *New York Times* front page, and scan your favorite blog and other RSS feeds. Plug in your iPod to download a couple of podcasts and a new audio book for your spouse's long commute. Then tune in your favorite Internet radio station and enjoy your breakfast.

Mid-morning: Your cousin's daughter messages you to tell you that her date to tonight's party is lactose intolerant. You decide to whip up an additional side dish with the extra carrots you have on hand. Nothing looks good in your vegetable recipe folder, so you search some ethnic-food Web sites and find an interesting Laotian curry.

Check your stock portfolio and pay some bills online while tonight's stew is simmering.

Lunch: Join your weekly video lunch with your writers' support group on iChat. Write some notes for the book chapter you are working on.

After lunch: Exchange e-mails with your kid's Spanish teacher. Press F12 to bring up the Mac mini's weather widget. Looks like rain. Put together an iTunes playlist of late Beethoven chamber music for the dinner.

Mid-afternoon: The kids are home from school and hang out in the kitchen to work on their homework so that they can stay up past their bedtime for the party.

Dinner: Queue the chamber music playlist. Put the mini's display on the sideboard, and set the screen saver to show the photos of your recent trip to Copper Canyon.

During the party: Start a family video iChat call to your Aunt May, who couldn't make the party.

Late night: Check your watch list again. Add an entry about the party in your personal diary on a separate, FileVault-protected account.

Part V
Modding Your Car for the Mac mini

The 5th Wave   By Rich Tennant

"I swapped out gauges from my treadmill. Want to know how many calories we just burned in the last quarter mile?"

In this part. . .

*i*Pods in your car — yesterday's news. Why settle for
playing some songs, when you can store and play DVDs
and full-length movies, and not at the postage-sized resolution of the most recent iPods. The Mac mini can also
give you driving directions, access the Internet, and, oh
yes, hold a bigger music library than any iPod, particularly when you start adding FireWire hard drives. If it were
up to me, I'd have the Mac mini be a factory-installed
option.

These chapters are mostly Arnold's work. This stuff is
right up his alley. Let's face it, he's a geek. Well, I'm a geek,
too, but I'm a computer geek. Arnold is a rip-open-the-
dashboard-and-pull-out-the-seats type of hardware enthu-
siast. Here, he shows you how to hack your car to make it
mini-friendly.

Keep in mind that each car model is different. In fact, each
model year of each car model is different. So, we can't
show you where exactly you'll find everything you need to
get at in your particular car. Arnold does show you what
you can achieve, what you need to do to achieve it, what
you need to buy, and where to get information. Even if you
decide to have a professional do some or all of your auto-
mini installations, you'll want to read these chapters first.

Chapter 12

Planning a Mac mini Car Mod

The Mac mini somehow looks like it belongs in a car. It's compact, rugged, and complete, and shaped like many car-electronics components. And what could be cooler than driving a Mac-equipped automobile? While most of the neat things that a car mini can do can be done in other ways, the total cost can be several times what a mini installation will set you back — and your car will be filled with electronic gadgets. But before you start cutting holes in your dashboard, some planning is in order.

This chapter starts with some ideas of what you can do with a Mac mini in your car.

What's It Good For? Absolutely Everything!

In planning your Mac mini car installation, think about what you plan to use your auto-mini for. Your planned use dictates many of the design and peripheral components. You also need to think about where you'll put it, and who will do the installation, and how it will be done. Figure 12-1 shows a well-planned mini installation.

First, here are some of the uses for a car mini.

Figure 12-1:
A Mac mini
in your car:
Don't leave
home
without it.

Mini as a car stereo

Hooked up to a car audio system, the mini becomes a versatile car stereo, playing CDs, DVDs, MP3s, and cuts purchased from the Apple iTunes music store. Don't worry if you finished that audio book and still have 350 miles to drive. Find a wireless hot spot, and you can download a new one from www.audible.com. You can even load up your iPod from the mini for a walk break.

Playing movies for the kids

Mount a screen that's visible from the rear seat, and the kids (or grownups) can watch their favorite movies — no more "Are we there yet?" The mini can play any DVDs, of course, but you can also store the kids' all-time favorite titles on the hard drive so that they always have something to watch.

Driving directions

Okay, the Mac mini is one expensive car stereo, but it can be a money saver, too. For example, a car navigation system can cost more than a mini with a display. You can accomplish most of what car navigation systems do with a Global Positioning System (GPS) receiver and some software for the mini. Although most car-navigation software runs only on Windows, you can expect to see more coming to the Mac side soon. Right now, some good open source GPS software runs on the Mac.

Taking (or listening to) a memo

With voice recognition software, you can dictate memos and e-mails while you drive and edit what you wrote later. Mac OS X v.4, Tiger and later includes speech recognition. You turn on Speakable Items in the Speech pane of System Preferences. To see the commands you can speak, click the triangle at the bottom of the round window that appears when you turn on Speakable Items. You can also configure the various settings in the Speech pane.

For more powerful speech recognition software, try iListen from MacSpeech (www.macspeech.com). It also comes with a headset microphone.

Voice recognition requires a microphone to speak into. The catch is that the Mac mini doesn't have an audio-in port, so you have to use a USB-audio interface. The $40 iMic from Griffin Technology (www.griffintechnology.com) does the job. Then plug in Griffin's $15 Lapel Mic, clip it to your shirt, and tell your Mac mini what to do. A headset microphone is another option.

You can also use a text reader to read aloud your overnight load of e-mail as you drive to work. You configure the Mac OS X text reader (called text-to-speech) in the Speech pane of System Preferences. Click the Text-to-Speech tab. Here, you can set a key command to hit whenever you want to have the Mac read text to you. (It's good to use the Control key, because not many other commands make use of it.) To activate text-to-speech, you can select the text you want to hear (⌘+A selects all of the text in a document). Then hit your key command, and the Mac mini reads the document to you. Try doing *that* with a car stereo.

Wireless Internet access

Find a wireless hot spot, and you have the vast resources of the Internet at your disposal from your car. Many Starbucks cafés have signals that reach into their parking lots. Your mini-equipped car can also access your home WiFi network from the garage or driveway and download or upload work files, music, and movies. Use wireless to synchronize your calendar and other files with your home computer whenever your car is parked in your garage or driveway.

With a Bluetooth-equipped cell phone, your mini can dial in to the Internet from anywhere you have cell coverage. Not all cell service providers support this capability, so check with your provider. Switch providers, if you have to.

Office on the road

If your work keeps you on the road a lot, having a Mac mini in the car can make you more productive, serving as a focal point for your activities and data. The files you need are always there.

Home on wheels

The Mac mini is ideal for campers and caravans. It takes up little of the precious space that's available in a camper. With a flat-screen TV display, you can have a complete home entertainment center and an electronic office wherever your wanderlust takes you.

The mini versus iBook

You might wonder why you should go through all the trouble of modding your car to install a Mac mini. You can make a case for buying an Apple iBook or PowerBook and bringing it with you when you travel. You don't need to drill or wire anything, and aftermarket power supplies are available to power the iBook from the car's power outlet. And you can take the iBook with you to business meetings or to a coffeehouse.

On the other hand, a custom Mac mini installation has several advantages over using an iBook. A properly installed auto-mini is more kid friendly, especially for younger kids. A fixed Mac mini is also safer, because an iBook can fly about in a sudden stop or a crash. Or, the kids might spill their drinks (or worse) on the iBook keyboard — an expensive repair at best. You have to lock up the iBook or at least get it out of view every time you leave the car, and it's hard to use an iBook when you are driving without a copilot. And, anybody can bring along a laptop in the car, so it is far less cool than having an in-car Mac mini installed.

Of course, nothing is stopping you from doing both. Your laptop can sync to your auto-mini when it gets close enough to pick up a WiFi signal.

Installation Planning

Before you break out the tools, you need to thoroughly plan the installation. Most important is deciding where to put your mini, its display, and accessories. You have several issues to consider. Think through the following topics, and the location of the hardware should jump out at you.

The following is a list to get you thinking. The next few chapters go into more detail.

Safety

You don't want your mini to set your car on fire or become a missile in the event of a crash. You also don't want people scraping their knees on computer equipment every time they get into or out of the car.

User interface

User interface is a fancy name for all the ways you can communicate with your computer, such as reading from a screen, listening to the speakers, typing at the keyboard, or pointing with the mouse. Doing this in a car, particularly while driving, can be a problem.

Accessibility

You have several obvious candidates for where to put that mini and all its accessories — and there are perhaps a few not so obvious candidates, as well. The Mac mini's CD/DVD slot is in the front, and its electrical connections and On/Off button are located in the back. You need some way to get to both. The section "Mapping Out mini Locations," later in the chapter, discusses this.

Power

Your mini needs electricity to run: 100–240 volts AC and 50–60 Hz, with a maximum continuous power of 85 watts. Car electrical systems are 12 volts DC, and only a few high-end models come with 110-volt outlets. You have several ways to solve this problem. Chapter 13 describes these solutions.

Note that car batteries store 600 to 800 watt-hours of energy, enough for several hours of mini operation. Letting a car battery discharge fully can damage it, so it's not a good idea to run your computer for more than an hour without the engine running.

Heat

Your mini was designed to work in a home or office. Its operating temperature range is 50° to 95° F (10° to 35° C). It's not supposed to be stored outside a range of –40° to 116° F (–40° to 47° C). Relative humidity is supposed to be kept above 5 percent and below 95 percent and should be *noncondensing.* That means you should see no little drops of water, like those that form on that beer you take out of the cooler on a humid summer day.

A car parked in the sun with the windows rolled up can get much warmer than 116° F, so you shouldn't start up your mini until the car has cooled some. It's best to select a car with air conditioning for your mini project and to use a sunshade when you park your mini-mobile in the sun.

Vibration

Apple doesn't publish a vibration spec, but its equipment is generally pretty rugged. But it's not designed for car installation, and some additional protection from bumps and rattles is still a good idea, particularly if you plan to drive on dirt roads or off road or live in pothole territory.

Security

You don't want your mini stolen, so a good antitheft system is worth having for your car. You can also use the mini's security port in back, which allows you to physically secure the mini with third-party locking hardware. Computer Security (www.computersecurity.com) offers a lock made for the Mac mini; so does MeritLine (www.meritline.com). Kensington (www.kensington.com) has a line of locks for notebook computers that work on the Mac mini.

If you are concerned about someone breaking in and stealing your data, turn on the mini's excellent security features, like log-in prompting, FileVault, and WiFi Protected Access (WPA) for wireless networking.

Internet access

A mini that has built-in AirPort wireless can connect you to the many hot spots around the country. Some newer cell phones have Bluetooth wireless that can communicate with the mini, but not all cell phone service providers let you use this capability to connect to the Internet.

Estimating Costs

If you install the system yourself, your biggest expenses are the mini itself, the display, and a power converter. But accessories can also add up. The following sections describe some of the things you need.

The basics

Don't leave home without having these items installed in your car:

- **Mac mini:** Built in WiFi and Bluetooth can make a car mini much easier to use. A bigger hard drive makes sense if you plan to store lots of music or movies for the kids. $350 to $600
- **Flat-panel display:** The display should preferably have a touch screen. $275 to $600
- **Pointing device:** Use a mouse, or better yet, a trackball. Wireless Bluetooth devices are handy in a car. $20 to $70
- **Power supply:** This can be either a DC-to-DC power supply or an AC inverter (plus the mini's supply). $100
- **Wiring and mounting supplies:** $50

Optional stuff

Because you're already springing for the basics, consider these additional goodies:

- **Audio connection device,** such as an FM transmitter
- **USB extender or hub,** to bring connections to the front
- **DVI-to-VGA video adapter,** the one that comes with the mini does just fine

✔ **Remote on/off switch**

✔ **Wireless extender**

✔ **Additional hard drive,** for backup or a video library

✔ **TV receiver module**

✔ **Bluetooth cell phone**

✔ **Additional display for the rear**

A company in Japan called minidock.com (http://minidock.jp/) is sell-ing a docking assembly for the Mac mini that is designed for car mounting. It's a bit pricey, however, and it didn't have a U.S. distributor at publication time. The car dock costs about $1590, including an 8-inch touch-screen dis-play. You have to supply the Mac mini. Still, the pictures at the Web site are interesting to look at.

Tools

In addition to basic hand and power tools that the well equipped do-it-your-selfer might be expected to own, the following tools deserve special mention:

✔ **Soldering irons:** You need a small iron (25 to 40 watts) for fine work and a large one (100 watts or more) for heavy wire. A cordless or 12 VDC unit is handy for on-vehicle work. See Chapter 16 for more information on the fine art of soldering.

✔ **Battery-powered electric drill:** You should have at least a ⅜-inch drive. Battery power is convenient for working on cars, unless you like getting tangled up in power cords in small spaces. Just make sure that your drill's batteries are in good shape. They may need to be replaced if your drill has been sitting in its box since last Christmas.

✔ **Crimping tools:** Get good quality ones, especially for wire terminals. The more expensive crimping tools have a ratchet that prevents the tool from releasing until the crimp is fully made.

✔ **Metric socket set:** Almost all new cars use metric fasteners, even American cars. Trying to use English sockets on metric bolts is an exer-cise in masochism and can strip the bolt heads.

✔ **A set of locking pliers (Vise-Grips):** I'm not sure whether you need them, but Vise-Grips have gotten me out of more trouble than any other tool I own.

✔ **Hot-melt gun:** Also known as hot glue guns, these are handy for getting cables to stay put as you snake them around the car and for repairing dings in the car's linings that you accidentally made. Don't plan on hot-melting your mini to the dashboard, however.

Supplies

You should have the following supplies on hand before you start:

- ✔ **Hook up wire:** Number 10 AWG wire is a good size for power connections. Radio Shack sells spools of it in red and black. Get both so that you can color-code your work — red for +12 volts and black for ground.

- ✔ **Crimp-on wire terminals:** These wire terminals, as shown in Figure 12-2, make secure, professional-looking connections if you have a good-quality crimp tool and use it according to its directions.

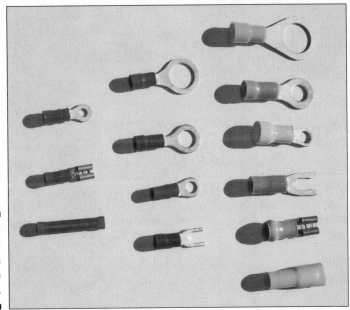

Figure 12-2:
Assorted
crimp-on
wire
terminals.

- ✔ **Wire nuts:** This is another way to make connections. A few are shown in Figure 12-3.

- ✔ **Wire ties:** These are handy little buggers for grouping wires into neat cables and securing them in place. But make sure that you know what you are tying to.

- ✔ **Solder:** The type that is traditionally best for electronics work is 60/40 tin-lead alloy with a noncorrosive rosin core. The new Restriction of Hazardous Substances Directive in the European Community severely restricts the sale of products containing lead, so newer lead-free solders are becoming available.

- ✔ **A small kitchen sponge and a dish to put it on:** Wet the sponge before you start soldering and use it frequently to clean your soldering iron's tip.

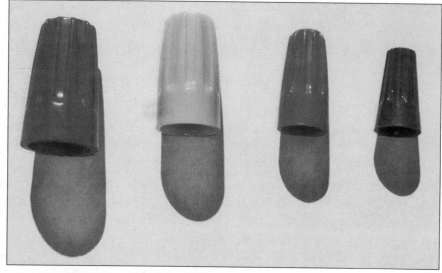

Figure 12-3:
Several
sizes of
wire nuts.

Hiring the pros

If you decide that this kind of installation is out of your league, many automobile electronics shops specialize in custom car electronics installations. You can find one in most major cities. Ideally, you can discover a shop that has done a Mac mini installation before — or at least a PC computer installation. If the shop gives you a hard time or tries to sell you another product, take your business elsewhere.

One company that offers professional Mac mini car installations is Classic Restorations in Sloatsburg, New York (www.classicresto.com).

Mapping Out mini Locations

Finding the best place in your car for your Mac mini can be tricky. There is no right answer. Every make of automobile presents different problems and opportunities. These locations are typical:

- ✔ **Under the dashboard:** Some cars have enough room for a mini slung under the dashboard; others don't.

- ✔ **In the dashboard:** Many cars have a radio compartment that's big enough to hold a mini. It should fit in what's called a double-DIN slot (DIN stands for Deutsches Institut für Normung, the German standards organization). Of course, you then have to figure out where to put the radio or head unit, if you still want one.

✓ **In the glove box or console between the front seats:** A mini in these locations can simply be placed there, with only the wires preinstalled. This lets you remove the mini from the car when you aren't using it. A between-seat console is also a possible location for a permanent location. Figure 12-1 shows a console installation that keeps the mini out of view while giving access to the CD/DVD slot while the console lid is closed. Whether these locations work depends on your make and model of car.

✓ **Under a seat:** This is my least favorite choice, because it's hard to get to and it's exposed to all the crud you track in when it's yucky out.

✓ **In the trunk:** This is often the easy way out, if your vehicle has one. You usually have plenty of room in the trunk, the mini can be reasonably well protected if you plan the installation carefully, and access is pretty easy. You do have to stop to change CDs and DVDs, however.

Video display locations

Possible locations for the video display are more constrained. Somebody has to be able to see it, so the trunk is out of the question. The top of the dashboard could block the driver's view. Mounting the display in the dashboard is great if you can find room. A roof mount makes sense for backseat Mac-ers.

Control options

Mounting the Mac mini in your car is one thing; figuring out how to control it in the car is another. Operating a keyboard and mouse while driving is a really bad idea. Some uses don't require you to have control while the car is in motion. You can pull over to start a video for the kids, for example.

You can set up the Mac mini to respond to voice commands, although this may be a little less reliable in the car due to road noises. (See the section "Talking or Listening to a Memo" earlier in this chapter.) For en-route GPS navigation, you need a video display with a touch screen that you can reach from the driver's seat. If you plan to write memos or compose e-mails while waiting for your next appointment, a Bluetooth keyboard and trackball come in handy. You can even buy software that lets you control your Mac mini using Morse code.

Hack Safely

Most automobile electrical systems run on 12-volt, direct current (DC) electricity. That voltage is much less than what is used in ordinary house wiring and is generally not considered a shock hazard. Amperage is another story, however. Automobile starters need a lot of power to crank a cold engine, so automobile batteries are designed to deliver very high current levels, up to several hundred amperes.

If a wire or terminal connected to the battery is short-circuited to any ground wire or metal connected to the car chassis, the short dissipates large amounts of energy and sparks fly. If the object that causes the short circuit is a watch band, bracelet, wedding band, or other piece of jewelry, it can quickly become very hot and cause a severe burn. In addition, a short-circuited battery can rupture or explode, spraying dangerous battery acid in the process.

Because I want you around to keep buying many more *For Dummies* books, here are some safety precautions you should follow before working on your car's or van's electrical system:

- Begin by reading your car's owner's manual, and follow the safety suggestions there.

- Don't run your car's engine inside a garage or other closed place without adequate ventilation. Carbon monoxide gas can build to lethal levels without you noticing anything is wrong.

- Remove all metal jewelry before you start work. (See the previous warning.) If you can't remove a wedding ring, get a copy of *Low-Calorie Dieting For Dummies,* by Susan McQuillan (Wiley), and wear rubber gloves in the meantime. If you have a body piercing you can't remove — I don't want to know the details — cover it with some tape.

- Wear eye protection, such as goggles, when working under the hood of a car or near a car or motorcycle battery.

- Disconnect the battery from the electrical system before doing any wiring work on the car.

- If you use an inverter, remember that its higher output voltage can cause a potentially fatal shock.

- If you are not sure what you are doing, have a professional do the wiring — or at least have a pro inspect it when it is done.

- Use good-quality tools and maintain them properly.

Installation Safety

I also don't want your finished auto-mini to be a hazard to yourself or your passengers, so follow these recommendations:

- Make sure that the computer is securely mounted so that it cannot come loose in a crash.

- Make sure that you have no sharp protruding corners or edges that can cause an injury in a crash.

✔ Do not block an air bag with the computer, video screen, or other accessory.

✔ Make sure that all connections to the car's electrical system are fused, but do not rely on the fuse for safety while working on the electrical system.

✔ Double-check every connection to make sure that it is properly made. A poor connection can get hot and potentially cause a fire.

✔ Tuck all wiring safely behind the dash or route it in a way that no one trips on it; ensure that people getting into or out of the car won't be able to step on the wiring.

✔ Follow applicable electrical codes when wiring the inverter output.

✔ When in doubt, have a professional check your work.

Legal Considerations

Many states in the United States (I've verified California, Illinois, Massachusetts, New York, North Carolina, Oregon, Pennsylvania, Texas, and Virginia — there are probably lots more) have laws prohibiting the installation of television screens where the driver can see them, with exceptions for GPS navigation systems and aids for backing up. Some states, including California and Illinois, have explicitly included computer displays in these restrictions.

Section 27602 of the California Vehicle Code, which went into effect on January 1, 2004, provides that "A person may not drive a motor vehicle if a television receiver, a video monitor, or a television or video screen, or any other, similar means of visually displaying a television broadcast or video signal that produces entertainment or business applications, is operating and is located in the motor vehicle at any point forward of the back of the driver's seat, or is operating and visible to the driver while driving the motor vehicle."

That's one heck of a long sentence, but it means that you can't drive if you're going to watch the TV jive. Here are several exceptions:

✔ A vehicle information display

✔ A global positioning or mapping display

✔ A back-up CCTV camera's monitor

✔ Equipment that is automatically disabled when the motor vehicle is driven

The code has additional exemptions for gas, telephone, or electric utility company trucks.

If you live outside of California, the U.S. National Committee on Uniform Traffic Laws and Ordinances rejected a proposal to prohibit television receiving equipment if the screen is visible from the driver's seat. The committee indicated that such a provision is inconsistent with current practice in luxury cars and that federal law may preempt it, at least for original equipment.

(If you're really into the legal mumbo jumbo, visit www.ncutlo.org/ RevisionstoUVC199.html.)

I'm not qualified to give legal advice. Check with a lawyer if you have concerns about what is permitted where you live. You might also want to check with your insurance company about vehicle modifications that you might make. Make sure that the computer and accessories are covered by your insurance policy.

Chapter 13

Getting Power to Your Car's mini

. . . .

. . . .

*P*roviding electrical power to your car's new mini is one of the first things you need to work out. The mini is actually two units, the computer and the power supply adapter. The latter, which is almost as big as the computer, converts the house-current AC voltage input to DC power that the computer uses.

You can provide power to your car's Mac mini in the following two ways:

✔ Find a way to get AC to Apple's power supply adapter. This requires a DC-to-AC converter, called an inverter.

✔ Replace the mini's power adapter with a power supply that runs directly off of your car's electric supply. This approach uses a DC-to-DC converter.

This chapter looks at both alternatives. It also provides the information you need to know about your car's electrical system for powering the display. For directions on how to install the display, see Chapter 14.

Facts about Your Car's Electrical System

Almost all cars on the road today use 12-volt power. The two major exceptions are antique vehicles, which often have 6-volt systems, and ex-military vehicles, including the military version of the Humvee, which use 24-volt systems. But the car that houses your Mac mini will most likely have a 12-volt system.

AC/DC isn't just a 1970s rock band

Two types of electric power exist. The simplest — the kind you get from ordinary batteries — has all those tiny electrons flowing the same way all the time; it's *direct current* or *DC*. A different kind has the electrons changing direction many times each second — 60 times a second in North America and 50 times a second in most other parts of the world. That's called *alternating current* or *AC*. AC makes it easier to step up the voltage for long-distance power transmission, so AC is what you get from your home's wall outlet. The integrated circuits in your computer want DC power, so the big white brick that comes with the mini and plugs into the wall converts the AC house current into the DC voltage that the mini wants.

By the way, the people who spend their lives worrying about such things have made up a fancy word, *hertz*, which means "times per second."

Here are some basics you should know about modern cars' electrical systems:

- ✔ Cars use a single-wire system, with a ground (or "earth," as the Brits call it) returned through the chassis.
- ✔ A car has two sources of power: the battery and the alternator.
- ✔ The battery's main purpose is to start the car. This takes a lot of current, so the wires in the starting circuit, including the battery connections, are very thick.
- ✔ The alternator powers the car when the engine is running and recharges the battery at the same time. The engine turns the alternator, usually through pulleys connected by the "fan belt."
- ✔ The power wire at the battery has positive polarity (+ or red), and the chassis is negative.
- ✔ Most modern cars use sealed, lead-acid batteries. Older batteries had vent caps for checking the water level, and the water could be tested using a hygrometer. Batteries contain sulfuric acid, which is very corrosive. The acid can be released if the battery ruptures from overheating, typically due to a short circuit.
- ✔ Battery voltage should be measured with a good-quality digital voltmeter. Analog meters are generally not accurate enough to give you a reliable indication of the state of a battery.

- ✔ The wiring in an automobile is color coded, but different car manufacturers use different color schemes. If possible, obtain a copy of your car's shop manual. Information is also available from www.12voltresource.com.
- ✔ The 12-volt supply can actually be in the range from 10 to 15 volts. A fully charged battery reads about 12.65 volts. A battery at 11.9 volts or less is considered to be discharged. Note that fully discharging a battery usually ruins it.

This information is useful to know when supplying power to the Mac mini and to a display.

Powering the mini with DC-to-AC Inverter

The easiest way to get power from a car is to use the cigarette lighter socket. Many new cars no longer come standard with cigarette lighters, but almost all cars still have the socket because so many accessories that need power are designed to plug into them. Some minivans have several of these outlets scattered around the interior. And many devices come with plugs that fit in auto power outlets (as shown in Figure 13-1).

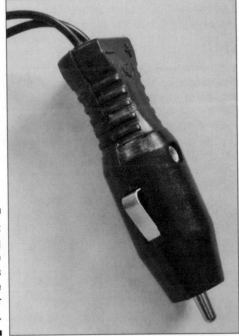

Figure 13-1: A plug designed to fit in a car's cigarette lighter receptacle.

Photo credit: Agr photo

If you travel with an iPod, you know that you can buy a device to charge the iPod from these auto power outlets. It should be no surprise that you can buy a device to power your Mac mini from an auto power outlet. The device you use for the mini is called an *inverter*. Inverters take DC power from your car and convert it into AC power. When you plug the Mac mini's power adapter into the inverter, the Mac mini's power adapter converts the DC back to AC. The whole conversion chain is thus DC-to-AC-to-DC.

This may seem like a lot of converting, but the reason that using an inverter is easy is that it typically has a standard wall outlet or two built in. These provide the same voltage and frequency that you find in your home (known as "house current"). In North America, that's 120 volts, 60 hertz. An inverter purchased in Europe is likely to supply 240 volts, 50 hertz. Your mini will work with either. The bottom line here is that the Mac mini thinks the DC-to-AC inverter is just another wall socket in your house. Great, isn't it?

The catch: power draw

Using an inverter box to power your Mac mini in your car sounds easy, but there's a catch. The units that come with a plug that's designed to fit into your car's cigarette lighter socket are lower-power units usually. Higher-power units will want to draw more power than the cigarette lighter outlet can provide. If the inverter needs more power than the cigarette lighter can supply, you must connect it directly to the car's electrical system. (See "Tapping in to the Electrical System" later in this chapter.)

If you're going to be using the inverter to power only the Mac mini, you might be able to get away with a low-power, plug-it-into-the-cigarette-lighter inverter. Your Mac mini's power adapter is rated at 85 watts, so you need an inverter that supplies more than that. An inverter that's rated at least a minimum of 100 watts of power will do the trick.

If you want to plug other accessories into the inverter — a display, a printer, or a hair drier — you may need an inverter with a higher power rating. Which means you might have to hard-wire it into the electrical system. Just how much of a power draw is too much for your car's cigarette lighter power outlet depends on the make and model of your car.

Some minivans and campers come with built-in inverters. If this is you, plug your Mac mini right into it. But if you have other things also plugged into your minivan's or camper's "AC outlet," check your owner's manual for the inverter's power rating.

Inverters and space

The reason you bought a Mac mini for your car was that it wouldn't take up much room. But using an inverter that plugs into your car's power outlet begins to eat up space, as you need a space for the following items:

  ✔ The inverter. It needs to be located somewhere you can get to it to plug things in. The trunk is not a likely option.

 ✔ The Mac mini power supply adapter.

 ✔ Power cables for the Mac mini and anything you want to plug into the inverter.

I'm not telling you to avoid a DC-to-AC inverter. It makes sense if you can plug it into the cigarette lighter adapter. But if you do have to hard-wire a DC-to-AC inverter, you might consider going with a DC-to-DC converter instead. This is described in the "Powering the mini with a DC-to-DC Converter" section, later in this chapter.

Whether you're hardwiring a DC-to-AC inverter or a DC-to-DC converter, you'll need to find power somewhere in the vehicle. The next section describes where to look.

Tapping in to the Electrical System

As I mentioned in the previous section, you may have to tie into your car's electrical system if your power needs are too great for an outlet. But hard-wiring a mini and display will give you a more custom look for your installation. The power inverter or converter will be out of sight and the mini will look like it was built into the car.

Tapping into the car's electrical system can be a bit tricky if you have no electrical experience. If you're unsure of your abilities, find some professional help, either to do a portion of all of the electrical work or to check your work.

Just how you connect to your car's electrical system depends on where you put the mini and power supply. Getting a copy of the car's service manual is a good first step.

Tapping into the fuse box

One of the better places to obtain power from a car is at the car's fuse box. Most cars have spare positions in the fuse box for optional accessories. If you didn't buy every possible option for your car, you probably have some fuse positions available. The fuse box in many car models is in the engine compartment. Other models have an under-dash fuse box.

Figure 13-2 shows the engine compartment of a 2006 Chevrolet Impala. The fuse box is the square black plastic item near the top of the image. Figure 13-3 shows the box after it has been opened.

Figure 13-2:
The fuse box is the black square box near the top in the Chevy Impala.

Photo credit: Agr photo. (Photo taken with kind permission of Porter Chevrolet, Cambridge, MA)

Figure 13-3:
A close-up of the battery and the fuse box with its cover removed.

Photo credit: Agr photo.

Radio Shack sells fuse taps (catalog number 270-1204). They provide an easy way to connect power leads to a vehicle's fuse panel. The tap fits over one end of the fuse and provides a blade connection that mates with crimp-on connectors.

Other car wiring approaches

In addition to connecting to the fuse box, as described above, there are a few other methods of connecting to your car's electrical system. These include hooking directly to the battery or tapping off some existing circuit in the passenger compartment, such as the car's radio circuit. In all cases, be sure to use an adequate wire size. Also check for adequate fuse protection. The supplies you need are available from Radio Shack and online dealers, such as www.sherco-auto.com/wiring.htm.

Monster sells cabling kits for high-power audio amplifiers that can be adapted for Mac mini cabling. They are also available from Radio Shack (catalog number 270-4135).

Powering the mini with a DC-to-DC Converter

If you've been paying attention, you might be jumping up and down saying, "Wait a minute; my car supplies DC power and the Mini uses DC power. Why can't I just use the car's DC power for the mini?" The answer is that you can, provided you overcome some problems first. The problems are caused by the fact that not all DC power is alike.

The mini uses a couple of DC voltages that don't exactly match what your car puts out. Also, your car's voltage varies quite a bit. While it is nominally 12 volts, it can range from 11 to 14 volts, depending on the state of charge of the battery, whether the engine is on or off, and if it's running, how fast it is revving. Even worse, you can get voltage spikes that go higher than this range, which can fry your mini. Fortunately, you can get around these issues by purchasing a DC-to-DC power converter (also called a DC-DC *regulator)* that produces the voltages your mini needs and regulates them to protect its delicate innards.

If you go this route, buy a power converter that is designed for use with the mini, such as the Carnetix P1900 (www.carnetix.com); these units typically come with detailed wiring instructions.

Using a DC-to-DC converter is the more elegant way to power your mini in the car than using an inverter, but it involves significant hacking of your car. Figure 13-4 is a wiring diagram of how a car's electrical system might be hacked for the Carnetix P1900. The next few sections describe the installation procedure for the Carnetix that will get you there.

Figure 13-4: Wiring diagram for a Mac mini car installation using a DC-to-DC power converter.

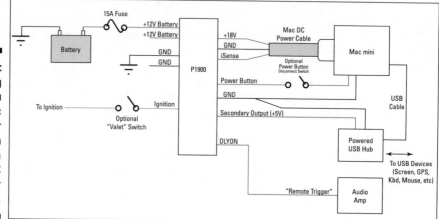

Diagram courtesy of carnetix.com.

Carnetix P1900 DC-to-DC supply

The Carnetix P1900 is a 140-watt power supply that's designed to operate off of an automobile electrical system; the power supply can survive engine cranking under full load over the entire temperature range. It can power both your Mac mini and your screen and USB devices. The P1900 measures 4.6 × 3.25 × 1.75 inches (117 × 83 × 45 mm) (L × W × H).

The P1900 comes standard with two outputs and an optional third output, which are described as follows:

✔ Jumper-selectable main output of +18, +19, or +20 volts at 6.3 amperes.

✔ Jumper-selectable secondary output of +12 or +13.5 volts at 3 amperes.

✔ Optional +5-volt, 3-ampere output using the CNX-P5V add-on (a recommended option). You can use this option to cut the power to USB devices when the ignition is turned off.

Mac mini sleep and the Carnetix

The P1900 includes a startup/shutdown controller that is compatible with the Mac mini, including sleep mode and "antithump" delayed remote control for audio amplifiers. It has a variable-speed fan, a user-replaceable fuse on the battery input, and a low-battery monitor that prevents draining of the battery, even while the Mac mini is in sleep mode.

The Mac mini will wake from sleep if it detects activity on any attached USB device, keyboard, touch screen, trackball, and so on. One way to prevent this is to attach all these devices through a powered USB hub that's connected to the secondary or tertiary output of the P1900.

Connecting the Carnetix to the car

The P1900 comes with two input return leads (black). Connect one of these to a car return wire with enough current capacity (10 gauge or bigger) or through a good connection to the car chassis. The same return connection should be used for all devices in your mini setup to prevent "ground loops" that can cause problems, particularly with audio and computer signals.

The second lead is not used. Cover it with electrical tape or shrink-wrap, and secure it with a tie wrap.

The unit also has two power input leads (red). Connect one lead to your car's 12-volt supply via a 15-ampere fuse. The other red lead is not used; insulate it with electrical tape or shrink-wrap, and secure it with a tie wrap.

Connecting the mini to the DC-to-DC converter

All that's left now is to plug the Mac mini into the DC-to-DC converter. Now, I don't mean to plug the Mac mini's AC power supply brick. You're bypassing AC here, so you need to connect the DC-to-DC converter directly to the Mac mini's power port on the back panel. This is easier said than done, however, as the mini's power input connector is an Apple-proprietary design and doesn't fit into any other mating plugs. This means that you have to cut the wire that leads from the mini to the power brick and do some fancy wiring. If you have no plans to use the mini outside of the car, you can just throw the mini's AC power supply brick away and connect the cut wire to the DC-to-DC converter.

Modding the power brick for plug-and-play

If you don't want to throw away the power brick, but want to preserve the option of running the mini on AC power in your house, you can add connectors to the wires you cut. This allows you to unplug the mini from the DC-to-DC converter in the car, and plug back into the AC power supply adapter when you need it in the house. This is the scenario that I describe for the remainder of this chapter.

To do this, you need to buy three sets of commercially available connectors, two female and one male. Radio Shack sells a four-pin Molex connector that's suitable for this purpose [catalog numbers 274-0234 (female) and 174-0224 (male)]. Alternatively, you can use disk drive power connectors scrounged from an old PC.

The flexible wire used in the mini's power cord can be difficult to work with. If this will be your first solder joint, you might want to practice on some spare wire, or you can hire an experienced electronics technician to do the work. There isn't a lot of risk in soldering wire, however. It's pretty tough to damage wire with a soldering iron. Just use the techniques described in Chapter 16.

The idea is to wire one female connector to the DC-to-DC converter and the other to the stub of wire left on the mini's power brick. The male connector gets wired to the cut end of the cable that plugs into the mini. After you do this, you can have your power cake and eat it too: The mini can run off the car's or the AC power supply.

Of course, all this wire cutting voids the warranty on the power supply adapter. If your mini needs service, you typically just send the mini, not the power supply, in for repair. Which means you can still send the mini in for repair without telling Apple that you've cut the power supply adapter wire.

Cutting and separating the power brick wires

Place your mini's power brick on a work surface. There are two cables coming out of the brick. One is the AC input cord, which has a connector that plugs into the wall outlet and another that plugs into the brick. Unplug this cable from the power brick and put it far away from where you are working. (If you can't see it, you can't cut it.) The second cable (shown in Figure 13-5) is attached to the brick and has a plug that goes into the mini itself. This is the one that you are about to cut.

Follow these steps to cut the cable and separate the internal wires:

1. **Cut this wire about 1 foot (30 cm) from the mini brick, as shown in Figure 13-5.**

   Leave enough cable on each side so that you can have a "do over" if you mess things up. *(Photos in this section are courtesy of carnetix.com.)*

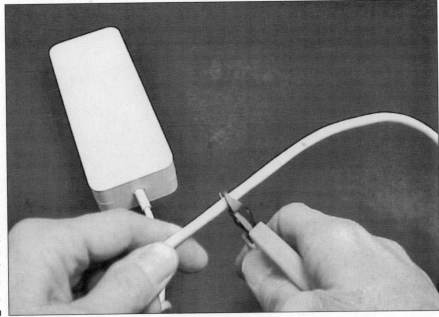

Figure 13-5:
Cut the cable that goes from the power brick to the wall.

2. **Carefully strip the outer insulation from both halves, as shown in Figure 13-6.**

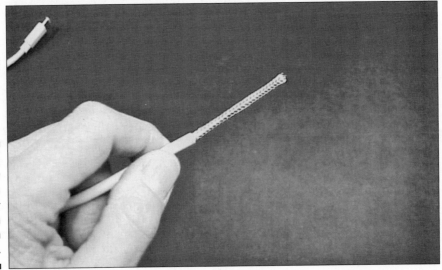

Figure 13-6:
Carefully strip the outer insulation from both halves.

3. **Push back the braided shielding, as shown in Figure 13-7.**

   You won't need to connect to the shield.

Figure 13-7:
The insides
of the mini's
power
cable. Note
the fluff.

4. **Separate the three wires: one red, one black, and a thinner gray one.**

5. **Cut off the cotton-like threads that are not wire, as shown in Figure 13-8.**

   Be sure that you don't cut any wires here.

6. **Strip the ends of each wire.**

   A good-quality stripper, like the one shown in Figure 13-9, is best for stripping the delicate gray wire.

   When all three wires are stripped, you should see what's shown in Figure 13-10.

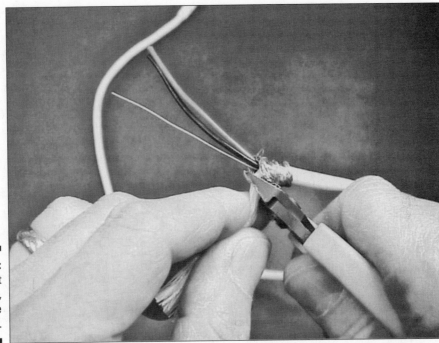

Figure 13-8:
Carefully cut
the fluff,
avoiding the
wires.

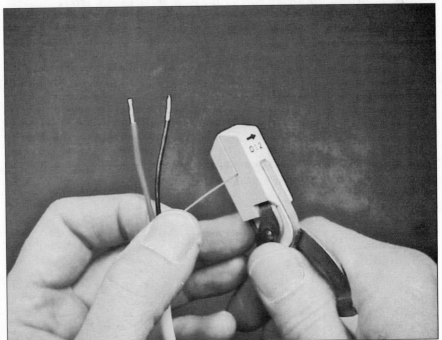

Figure 13-9:
Stripping
the wires.

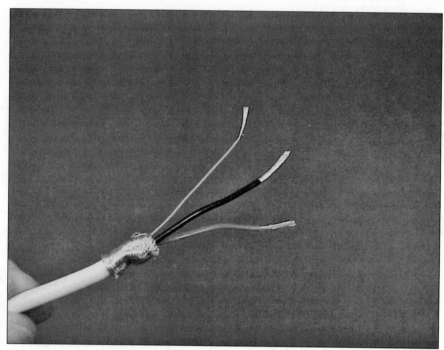

Figure 13-10:
The wires
are stripped.

Attaching Molex pins to the Mac mini supply wires

Now you need to attach pins to the wires that are coming out of the two ends of the Mac mini power cable that you just cut and stripped.

Open the Molex connector packages, keeping the male and female units separate so that you don't mix them up. (Connecters hate that.) Each connector comes with a strip of four crimp-on pins. The female pins have small holes at their working end; the males' do not.

Now attach the pins to the wires by following these steps:

1. **Attach one female pin (shown on the right side in Figure 13-11) to each wire on the cable that is still attached to the AC power brick.**

    Radio Shack sells a special crimping tool for this purpose.

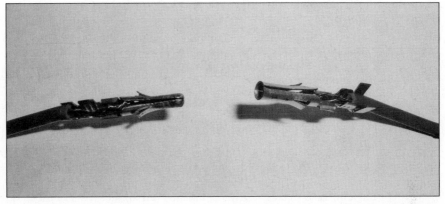

Photo credit: Agr photo.

Figure 13-11:
Male and
female pins
ready for
crimping.

2. **Attach one male pin (shown on the left side in Figure 13-11) to each wire on the section of cable that plugs into the back of the mini (the cable that is no longer attached to anything).**

Attaching Molex pins to DC-t0-DC converter wires and assembling

The P1900 has two black output wires and two red output wires. You also have a white "iSense" wire that connects with that little gray wire in the mini's cable. To add molex pins to these wires, do the following:

1. **Strip the white wire and one each of the red and black output wires coming from the P1900.**

2. **Attach female pins to each of these wires and crimp.**

   For extra credit, solder the crimped connections.

3. **Look at the connector bodies.**

   Each has a triangular feature at one side that ensures that the connectors can mate only one way.

4. **Insert the red wires of each assembly into the hole in the connector body that's closest to the triangular feature.**

   The pins click into place when they are pushed in far enough. (If you mess up, Radio Shack also sells a pin-extracting tool.)

5. **Insert the black wire's pin in the hole next to the red wire.**

6. **Insert the gray or white wire's pin in the hole on the other end of the connector body, leaving one middle hole unused.**

7. **Join the connectors, and check that the wire colors match.**

   Do this for both the P1900 and the mini's power brick.

8. **Plug the power cable into the mini. Attach each power supply (the P1900 and the AC brick) to its power source, and connect the new power cable.**

9. **Check that the mini is working properly on each supply.**

   Snap the cable from the Mac mini to the power supply brick and plug the brick into the wall. If the mini starts up, you did a good job. Now, shut down the mini and plug the power cable into the P1900 cable (assuming that it's installed in a car), and start the mini.

Carnetix also makes an adapter kit to control the On/Off button on your mini. See the company's installation manual (which is available online at www.carnetix.com) for details.

You can now power your mini either from your car or your AC power brick.

Chapter 14

Installing a Display and a mini in a Car

*P*robably the trickiest part of installing an in-car mini is mounting your display or displays; you can have more than one. Fortunately, a number of companies offer products to help. And you can tap the resources of the car PC market as well as the Mac specialists, so you have lots of choices.

This chapter describes your choices for displays and the guidelines to follow when locating and installing them. The chapter also presents ideas for mounting the mini in a car and describes how to connect it to the display.

For information on powering the display and the Mac mini, see Chapter 13.

Types of Displays

The market offers a bewildering variety of computer displays. Most take too much power, are too bulky, or are too fragile to use in your car, SUV, or mini-van. Even so, you still have a lot of models to choose from in several technology types.

Cathode ray tubes

Cathode ray tubes, or CRTs, are the television vacuum tubes from the 1940s. They are the Model T Fords of computer display technology, once ubiquitous but now obsolete. Bulky, fragile, and heavy, CRTs are difficult to mount and are potentially lethal in a crash. CRTs are a poor fit for cars.

Plasma flat-panel displays

Plasma displays are a type of flat-panel display that is popular for home viewing. They're very bright and can be seen well from a wide range of angles. (Other screens look dimmer when you are not looking straight at them.) Plasma displays also have a high contrast, which makes them great for watching movies. Their black is really black.

Plasma consists of two sheets of glass with a special gas in between. One side is coated with a phosphor that glows when excited by a high-voltage electrical discharge from the other side that ionizes the gas, cresting a plasma. And even though they are made of glass, they are fairly rugged.

Most are way too big for a car but could be spectacular in a mobile home or camper — part of a Mac mini-based mobile home theater, as described in Chapter 9. Plasma displays use a fair amount of power, though, which means you'd have to limit the time watching with the engine off to avoid draining the battery.

Liquid crystal displays

Liquid crystal displays (LCDs) are a popular type of display used in cars, as well as on everything from desktop and notebook computers to iPods. Displays used in cars are smaller than those used with desktop computers and are available at a reasonable cost. They also use relatively little power.

Slow LCDs and fast LCDs

There are two types of LCDs: passive-matrix and active-matrix. Both have hundreds of thousands of tiny, individual spots, or *pixels,* whose ability to transmit light is controlled electrically. A light source shines through the pixels from behind.

Passive-matrix LCDs are common in devices like personal digital assistants but are too slow for most computer uses. That's because the individual pixels are controlled one at a time.

Active-matrix technology is much faster because an entire column of pixels is updated at once; every spot on the screen is controlled by its own personal transistor. This gives rise to the nickname *TFTs,* which is short for thin-film transistor.

Head-up displays

One display type I'd like to see in a car are the head-up displays (HUDs) used by fighter pilots. A small, bright display is focused by special optics onto the inside of the windscreen or helmet. Airplane head-up displays are often designed to keep the display lined up with the pilot's line of sight so that the image overlays exactly what the pilot sees. This can be useful while flying in clouds or in the dark and trying to shoot down an enemy plane.

Manufacturers have toyed with using head-up displays in cars. They could give navigation clues — for example, a flashing arrow over that exit in the distance — as well as tell you your speed and the status of the car without your having to take your eyes off the road. Instant messages could float on the side of the highway like billboards. Critics claim head-up displays might distract the driver and could obscure some clue of upcoming danger, and they may be illegal in many jurisdictions. Still, an HUD would be the ultimate car computer experience.

TFT LCDs are the most popular display for in-car use, but they have some drawbacks. The viewing angle is limited. This means it is best if your display is mounted on some sort of swivel so that you can adjust it for head-on viewing. And LCDs tend to look washed out if direct sunlight shines on them.

LCD quality

TFTs come in several grades of quality. Less expensive models may have a small number of defective pixels, and their brightness may not be as uniform as the higher-priced models. TFTs are often marked with a letter code, with P for professional grade, S for standard grade, and V for value grade, the lowest quality. Smaller screens used in cars tend to have fewer problems because they have fewer pixels and are therefore easier to manufacture.

Projection displays

Projection displays, as their name suggests, work like a movie projector and shine an image on a reflective screen some distance away. They are reasonably compact but require a lot of power. Projection displays don't work too well for cars but would be cool to have at a campground.

Understanding resolution specs

While shopping for a monitor to use with a home mini, you don't spend much time on the technical details of display resolution. You can visit your local computer store (or, if you're lucky, an Apple Store) and see with your own eyes how different monitors look. Even if you order by mail, you can generally assume that all 17-inch flat-panels in a given price range will perform equally well, or at least you can read reviews of the displays.

But the small specialty monitors of the sort that work in cars are not generally available in retail channels, so it helps to know the gobbledygook. Table 14-1 lists the common screen resolutions currently on the market along with their *aspect ratio,* the ratio of the width to the height.

Table 14-1	Standard Display Resolutions and Aspect Ratios	
Code Name	*Resolution*	*Aspect Ratio*
VGA	640 × 480	4:3
SVGA	800 × 600	4:3
XGA	1024 × 768	4:3
WXGA	1280 × 768	15:9
SXGA	1280 × 1024	5:4
WXGA+	1440 × 900	8:5
SXGA+	1400 × 1050	4:3
WSXGA	1600 × 1024	25:16
WSXGA+	1680 × 1050	8:5
UXGA	1600 × 1200	4:3
WUXGA	1920 × 1200	8:5
PAL (Analog TV Europe)	576 lines (Analog TV Europe)	–
NTSC (Analog TV U.S.)	480 lines	4:3
HDTV	1920 × 1080	16:9

Note that while CRT monitors can support several display resolutions well, flat-panel displays generally have a "native resolution" that matches the number of built-in dots. Using something other than the native resolution generally gives less-than-adequate viewing results.

Choosing a video connector type

Your car's display needs a video connector that you can hook up to the Mac mini. It is always worth asking the display manufacturer whether a particular display will work with the Mac mini. If they tell you no — or more likely, we don't know — you probably can't count on much support.

The port on the back of the Mac mini, DVI (Digital Video Interface), isn't yet widely used in the small monitors that are suitable for cars. You can use a connector to plug in another type of connector. (See Chapter 2 and Chapter 9 for more on video connections to the Mac mini.)

VGA

The most common type of input connector for car computer displays is VGA, which stands for Video Graphics Array. You plug in VGA monitors using the Mac mini's VGA adapter.

Be aware that the adapter sticks out a couple of inches from the back of the mini. Plan for enough room for the adapter and the VGA plug that goes into it when you mount the mini in your car.

If you've really been paying close attention and have perused Table 14-1, you might be wondering, "If my monitor has a VGA connector, does that mean I only get 640 × 480 resolution?" No, fortunately, it doesn't. The original 640 × 480 VGA was hot stuff when it was introduced, but VGA now supports higher analog resolutions as well.

Analog and S-Video

You can also find car displays that use analog video, either through an RCA jack or S-Video. Some monitors have both analog video and VGA inputs. That's cool because it lets you plug a TV tuner or closed-circuit television camera into the analog input. You can then switch between the mini's display and the analog input.

If the display you are considering *only* has an analog input, forget it. Your mini can produce analog and S-Video output with Apple's $20 DVI to Video Adapter, but the quality will be so poor that it will be impossible to read text in menus. However, if you own a car that already has a built-in analog-only display — say, for a back-up camera — it might be worth experimenting with feeding it an analog signal from the mini.

See Chapter 9 for more on video connectors and adapters.

Touch screens in cars

If you've never tried to use a mouse while driving, you haven't been missing much. A touch-screen display is the easiest way to interact with your car's mini. Touch screens work like the computer's mouse, allowing you to move the cursor and indicate a mouse click.

Touch screens are transparent layers placed right on the display front that can tell the computer when and where they have been touched by a finger or a stylus. Several different technologies are available for sensing your touch, including resistive, capacitive, and ultrasonic surface wave. Resistive is the most common in automotive installations.

You need the following features in a touch screen so that it works with the Mac mini:

✔ **Built-in touch:** Adding touch-screen capability to an existing display doesn't work well.

✔ **USB interface:** The touch feature can plug into the Mac mini's USB port, just like a mouse or keyboard.

✔ **Software drivers for Mac OS X:** The driver package should come with a calibration utility.

When you calibrate a touch screen, you see a series of points appear one at a time. Your job is to touch them. You may have to hold your finger in place for a while until the mini acknowledges your touch with a friendly *beep*. If you own a Palm Pilot or similar personal digital assistant, you are probably familiar with this process.

If you install a touch-screen display, you can still use a keyboard and an alternate pointing device, such as a mouse or trackball. Just make sure that they are all USB devices. You can also hook up multiple touch-screen–equipped displays, and they all should work. Be sure to plan on installing a USB hub to support all these gadgets. See Chapter 15 for more on connecting peripherals to a car-based mini.

Mounting Your Display

Mounting your display is the trickiest part of installing the Mac mini in your car. You want it to be convenient to view, yet not obstruct the driver's line of sight, even while backing up the vehicle. You'll need some way to run wires to it. It must be sturdy enough to endure constant road vibration and not project in a way that would cause injury in an accident. Above all, it must not block an air bag, lest it launch as a missile in a crash.

First, you need display-mounting hardware. You could design and build this yourself. But if you buy a display that is built specifically for automobiles, mounting hardware and instructions should come with the display or be offered as an accessory. Ask before you buy.

Of course, a lot depends on whether you are installing the mini in an old jalopy or an expensive new car or SUV. In the former case, hack away. You can always patch any mistakes with body filler or duct tape. If duct tape doesn't match your sporty interior, do some planning or get some help.

Getting some help

If you're afraid of damaging a newer car and would rather have a pro install the display, you can use one of many local companies that install car electronics. The trick is to find them: You're not likely to find a listing under "Computer Display Installer" in the Yellow Pages.

The key is to look under "Automobile Alarm & Security Systems." Companies that install alarms generally do other car electronics installations, such as radios and high-end amplifiers. They are often listed under the automobile alarm heading because this heading comes early in the alphabetical listing.

Classic Restorations of Stony Point, New York (www.classicresto.com), is one firm that specializes in Mac mini car installations. Costs range from $2500 to $7000 or more for a complete installation, depending on the complexity of the installation and on how many additional components, such as dual screens, in-dash stereo, satellite radio, and subwoofers, the owner wants.

Figure 14-1 shows a deluxe installation by Classic Restorations with dual screens, a stereo, and a satellite radio. You can see the Mac mini under the armrest.

Figure 14-1:
A professional mini installation by Classic Restorations.

On-dashboard mounting

From a purely mechanical point of view, the dashboard is probably the easiest place to mount a monitor. Displays are available with swivel bases that are suitable for this use.

In-dashboard mounting

A number of companies sell monitors with a base that fits in standard DIN radio dashboard openings. You need to find another home for your car radio, or "head unit," unless your car has more than one slot. Figure 14-2 shows an in-dash display.

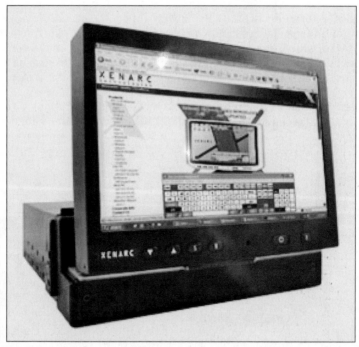

Figure 14-2:
A Xenarc
Model
700IDT for
in-dash DIN
mounting.

Photo courtesy of Xenarc.com

Roof mounting

Mounting the display on the roof of your vehicle has several advantages. The display can fold up when not in use, and it provides a central viewing location for backseat passengers. It is harder for kids to spill food and drink on a roof-mounted display, although yours may be up for the challenge.

Figure 14-3 shows a typical roof-mounted model. Note that the top plate has holes in it to bolt to the ceiling mounting hardware. The display pivots up to the top plate when not in use.

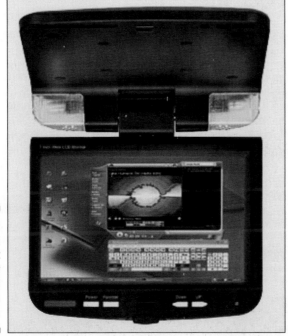

Figure 14-3:
A 7-inch roof-mount display (Xenarc Model 700TR).

Photo courtesy of Xenarc.com

Headrest mounting

You can also mount a display in the back of a headrest. This location is, of course, not viewable from the front seat. A proper headrest fitting requires some surgery. Before you go out and order such a display, press your fingers into the back of your headrest to see whether you find any obstructions.

The exact procedure for installing a headrest-mounted display depends on the mounting hardware. Xenarc has headrest installation instructions on its Web site at www.xenarc.com/download.html.

Xenarc also makes an adjustable aluminum bracket that's designed to bolt to the headrest supports and support a 7-inch monitor.

Mounting Your mini

The following sections give you a few ideas for places to tuck away the Mac mini itself.

The Mini Dock kit

One advantage to locating the mini in the dashboard is that you can easily insert CDs and DVDs while you're driving.

The Japanese company, Mini Dock (www.minidock.jp), is marketing a double-DIN kit that includes an in-dash dock for the mini and an 8-inch flat-panel, touch-screen display. Figure 14-4 shows the Mini Dock installed in a dashboard. At press time, Mini Dock's site is in Japanese only, but an English version is in the works. The price is about $1600, with the display, less the mini itself. The company also sells a do-it-yourself version without the display.

Figure 14-4:
A Mini Dock
installation.

Under the dashboard

If you have room to do so without banging your knees, hanging the mini under the dashboard is a relatively simple arrangement. You might look for brackets that are designed to mount mobile two-way radios that can fit your mini. If necessary, you can drill mounting holes in the side of the mini's outer casing, after you open the case as described in Chapter 4. Make sure that any mounting hardware you attach to the mini does not interfere with any of the mini's internal components when you reassemble the case.

Glove box

Your car's glove box or console storage compartment is another mounting candidate. No fancy mounting hardware is required, and you can easily pull out the mini and bring it into the house. Some glove compartments already have a built-in cigarette-lighter–style power adapter in the glove box; all you would need to do is route cables to the display.

As Figure 14-5 shows, it isn't pretty, and it forces you to find another place for your gloves.

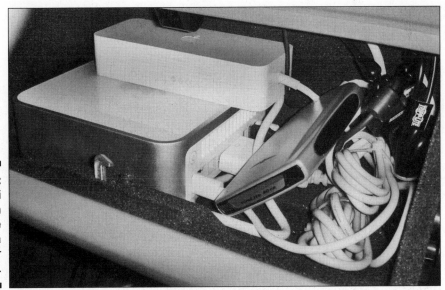

Figure 14-5:
A Mac mini installed in the glove box of a Land Rover Discovery II.

The trunk

No installation is easier than the trunk (or boot, for you Brits). The only problem here is long cable runs. Carefully scout out your car for possible avenues to route wires from the trunk compartment to the passenger interior. You may want to fabricate a sturdy cover for the mini to protect it from luggage being casually tossed into the trunk. Also, make sure that cooling air can get in.

Wiring the Display and mini

The final step is running wires between all of your car's computer components, both for power and signals. Exactly where and how you do this depends on where you located everything, what kind of vehicle you have, and how much you care about appearances. One advantage of keeping everything on and in the dashboard is a simplified wiring task. Everything can be tucked behind the dash.

If you mount the display or mini elsewhere, you will probably have to run cables through the passenger compartment. One possible route is under the carpet, perhaps near the doors or along the center console. Figure 14-6 shows a wiring job under the rear seat, which has been removed. A power supply is being located here, and you can see the Mac mini's power adapter brick at the top of the picture.

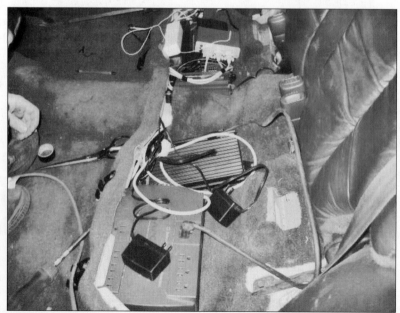

Figure 14-6:
A mini wiring job in progress.

Photo courtesy of Classic Restorations

If possible, run wires along paths where they will not be stepped on frequently. Repeated strain can cause wires to fail. The worst situation is when a wire breaks inside its insulation. This can cause you to pull your hair out trying to find intermittent problems, because the ends of the wires will sometimes make contact and sometimes won't.

Display power

Most displays sold for car use can run on the 12-volt DC power your car supplies. You can wire them directly to the car's electrical system or power them through a multi-output DC-to-DC converter, such as the Carnetix unit that I describe in Chapter 13. You should check with your display manufacturer to determine the current draw. Most LCDs have a modest power requirement, often less than 1 ampere. Installing a fuse in the line is still a good idea, however.

Connecting the display to the mini

If you use a touch-screen display, you need to connect several cables to your mini, such as the following:

- ✔ The VGA or DVI video cable
- ✔ A USB cable for the touch screen
- ✔ An audio cable that feeds sound from the mini to the display (optional)

You need the audio feed if you want to use the display's audio features. Some displays even support infrared headphones, which allow passengers to listen to the audio without disturbing the driver. (**Warning:** Don't even think of wearing headphones while you are driving. Not only is it dangerous, but it's also illegal in many states.)

Some car displays feature separate analog video inputs. You may also want to use these for a back-up camera or a TV tuner. That means more wire to run, coaxial cable in this case. You may want to use small-diameter coax cable rather than the bulky RG-6 type that's used for home cable TV installations.

A retro wiring tip

Wiring a car mini installation means managing multiple cables and wires running hither and yon. Your installation will be neater, and often more reliable, if you bundle wires going in the same direction. You can do that in several ways, but each has its drawbacks. Nylon cable ties are handy and cheap, but even if you carefully trim the excess portion, you always have a protruding bulge that is often quite sharp. These bumps can protrude through carpet and interior lining material. Another approach is to use spiral wrap or other wiring conduit solutions. These can be tedious to affix to the wires and add significantly to cable bulk. A different approach goes back to the early years of electronics, when wire bundles were formed into cables by stitching them with special cord, a process known as *cable lacing,* shown here. It is a relatively easy skill to master (you tie a series of overhand knots around the bundle and pull each one tight) and quickly turns a rat's nest of wiring into a professional-looking job without bulking up the cabling. Cable lacing cord can still be purchased from electronics supply companies, or you can simply use nylon packaging line.

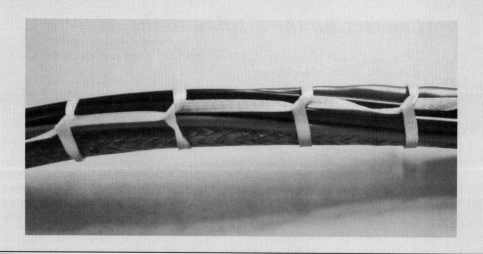

Chapter 15

Auto Audio and Peripherals

*I*nstalling a mini and a touch-screen display in a car, van, or motor home is one awesome upgrade. But you still have more to do. Your mini can play through the car's stereo speakers. The passengers can watch a DVD to the accompaniment of deep basses and high fidelity. It's the ultimate car theater.

Your mini can do even more for you: download your e-mail, tell you where you are, and so on. The possibilities are endless.

This chapter isn't endless, but it does cover some of your options. It describes the available choices for plugging into the car stereo and introduces some options for in-car Mac mini peripherals, including keyboards and TV tuners. No Mac mini is complete without an Internet connection, not even the mini in your car. And no automobile-based mini is complete without a global positioning unit to tell you where you are.

Wiring Your Car for mini Audio

Perhaps you just finished installing the Mac mini in your car in anticipation of a big road trip. You included a high-end audio system to help with the monotony of endless hours of driving. Now you need to connect the two. You're thinking, "All I have to do is plug one end of a cable into the mini's audio output jack and the other into the car stereo input jack," when — oops — the stereo doesn't have an input jack.

Don't give up. You can still plug in for full mini sound. The following sections describe the different ways you can do this, from the ridiculously cheap to the incredibly expensive.

On the cheap — FM transmitters and cassette adapters

If you're interested in quick, easy, and cheap sound, you may be tempted toward small FM radio transmitters that you can tune in on your car radio. Most are marketed to connect iPods to car stereos. Most connect to the iPod's headphone jack, which is the same as the Mac mini's. These transmitters get their power from the iPod and don't work with the Mac mini without modification. Radio Shack and Monster sell fairly inexpensive FM transmitters that can be powered by your car's electrical system.

This solution may be acceptable for an iPod that you carry with you, but most people who go to the trouble and expense of installing a Mac mini in a car will find FM transmitters unsatisfying. Heck, even iPod users hate them.

For one thing, the sound quality is limited by the narrow bandwidth of FM radio. Even worse, however, is the problem of reception and interference from FM radio stations. FM transmitters let you select one of several radio frequencies. The ones that work the best are those that don't have a strong radio station using your frequency or one near it. Before you drive off, you have to find the best frequency. As you drive around, however, you encounter new radio stations, and inevitably, the reception gets worse, and you have to change the station on both the FM transmitter device and your radio — a royal pain, especially when you're driving.

A far better on-the-cheap solution is for car audio systems that have a cassette player. For about $20, you can get an adapter from Sony and others that pops into the cassette slot. There's no hassle with changing stations, and the sound quality is superior to that of the FM transmitter.

If you want the best sound quality for your hot car stereo, however, find a way to plug the Mac mini directly into it.

Plugging into your car stereo

You can plug into the back of a car stereo unit — if you can get there. Pulling the stereo out of the dashboard can be a major headache. Some car manufacturers deliberately make it hard to do to deter car thieves. Others use a locking mechanism that is easier to use if you have the necessary key.

It's pretty much impossible to figure out how to get your car stereo out of the dashboard simply by looking at it. A little guidance goes a long way. A Web site called the Car Stereo Removal Guide (www.carstereoremoval.com) offers instructions on removing car stereos for less than $10. The site has instructions for a variety of makes, models, and years.

After you have the radio out of the car, either use one of the connections described on the next few pages, or find a way to modify the stereo's circuitry to accept line-level audio (the audio signal that comes out of the Mac mini's headphone port). A car audio repair shop might be able to do the latter for you, but you'll void the stereo's warranty for sure.

Regardless of how you connect to the car stereo system, you should use good-quality audio cable with a 3.5-mm plug at one end and the appropriate connector for your car stereo at the other end.

CD changer interface adapter

Some OEM car stereos (those sold by the auto manufacturer) have a jack in the back of the unit for connecting a car CD changer. A CD changer can hold a dozen CDs; the Mac mini can hold hundreds (electronically). If you're lucky enough to have a car stereo with this jack, just tap into it and you're good to go. Well, it's not that simple. These jacks aren't standard audio input ports, and they vary with the car make and model. Some of these jacks have 8 pins, some have 12 pins, and others have 13, 16, 20, or some other number of pins.

The way to tap into this port is to buy a CD changer interface adapter that connects to the CD changer port. These adapters cost about $50, and you can buy them at Blitzsafe (www.blitzsafe.com) and Logjam Electronics (www.logjamelectronics.com).

CD changer interface adapters usually provide stereo RCA jacks. A mini headphone-to-RCA converter cable can plug your Mac mini into the interface adapter. (See Chapter 9 for more on audio cables.)

Because you need to get at the back of the radio, getting to the jack inside the dashboard can be tricky. Not only that, but the jacks aren't in the same location in all cars. In some cars, the jack is located behind the radio; in others, it's behind the tuner.

To get an idea of what you're in for, Logjam Electronics has instructions posted for various models of cars (http://store.yahoo.com/logjam/wiringx.html). These instructions don't reveal anything about getting into your dashboard, though.

Aftermarket head unit

Many mid- to high-end aftermarket car stereos (known as *head units*) provide an auxiliary input jack that you can plug the mini's audio port into. Yeah, I should have told you that before you ordered your new car. If you are about to buy a car and are thinking of adding a mini, talk to the dealer or an aftermarket car-audio vendor first.

If you are adding the mini to that old wreck you are driving, include an aftermarket head unit in your budget.

Extreme makeover, car audio edition

While you have the interior of your vehicle torn apart to install the mini and its accessories, why not go whole hog and put in that killer audio system you've always dreamed of? I'm talking a satellite radio, multi-hundred-watt amps, top-of-the-line speakers, a TV tuner — the works. Just make sure that one of the boxes has a line-in jack for the Mac mini's audio.

The one thing you don't need is a CD changer or DVD player. Plenty of car audio installation shops might consider the mini one more component that they can install.

If you install a custom audio system, you may be annoyed by a loud popping sound every time you turn the unit on. To eliminate this problem, many amplifiers have a remote trigger. If you use a DC-to-DC power supply, like the Carnetix unit described in Chapter 13, you can connect its delayed output, "DLYON," to the amplifier. (See Figure 13-4.)

Among the hottest products in car audio these days are vacuum-tube amplifiers and preamps. A basic Mac mini has enough digital signal processing horsepower to make any conceivable sound. Tube enthusiasts say that no transistor amplifier sounds as smooth as a pair of 6L6 beam-power tetrodes running Class B, a design classic first marketed back in 1936 and still manufactured in Russia and Eastern Europe. The tubeheads have graphs and charts to prove it, and I'm not going to argue. A Milbert BaM-235 ten-tube amplifier (www.milbert.com) only sets you back $2500. That's the unit shown in Figure 15-1. It can accept output directly from the mini, using nothing more than an inexpensive 3.5-mm–to–RCA stereo cable, although you might prefer the gold-plated cable from Monster if you've gone this far.

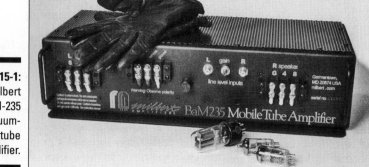

Figure 15-1:
The Milbert
BaM-235
vacuum-
tube
amplifier.

Gizmos and Gadgets

You might want or need to install a variety of other devices in your car to go along with the Mac mini. Just remember that they all need power and cabling. Installing your multiheaded Mac mini in a Cooper Mini may present some resource issues.

Hub of the universe

If you've been keeping a list of all the things you will need, you've probably noticed that a lot of them require a USB jack. What could be more cozy? Regrettably, your mini only comes with two USB (Universal Serial Bus) ports, both in back, where they can be hard to get to in some mini mounting schemes. If you need more USB ports — and you will — plan on adding a *USB hub,* a multitap extension cord in USB-land. Having USB ports accessible from the passenger compartment makes it easy to connect portable devices such as digital cameras and VCRs when you want to download their files to the mini. A USB hub fitted into a car's center console is shown in Figure 15-2.

Figure 15-2:
A USB hub custom-fitted into a car console.

Photo courtesy of Classic Restorations

Before you pick a USB hub off the shelf at your local supermarket, check to see whether it is powered or unpowered. The USB standard requires the mini to allocate about 5 volts to each plugged-in device. But if all the devices you are using exceed this allocation, your mini will complain and shut off power to the device. An unpowered hub splits this available power among all the devices plugged into it. You'll be happier with a powered hub that supplies its own 5 volts to the devices that are plugged into it. You still need to get that power from someplace. The Carnetix power supply that I describe in Chapter 13 has an optional third output that can be used for this purpose.

Voice control

Typing on a keyboard is difficult to do while driving. A better alternative is to control your car mini with the voice-command feature that's built into Mac OS X. You can also use voice control to dictate memos or to make Voice over IP (VoIP) phone calls when you are near a wireless hot spot. That's a great idea, except for one problem: the lack of an audio input jack on the mini. You don't have a place to plug in a microphone.

Adding a place to plug in a microphone

Another gadget can come to your rescue. The iMic, from Griffin Technology (www.griffintechnology.com), is a small, inexpensive (about $40) plastic disk that plugs into a USB port and has a 3.5-mm sound input jack that can accept a microphone. (It also provides another line-level output if you need it.)

You may still encounter a problem with road noise. The sound level may be too high for reliable voice recognition. A well-placed, directional microphone could help here. Training Mac OS X to recognize your voice is also important.

Turning on speech recognition

You turn on speech recognition in the Speech pane in System Preferences, as shown in Figure 15-3. With a microphone connected, follow these steps:

1. **Click the On radio button (next to Speakable Items).**

2. **Click the Listen Continuously with Keyword radio button (next to Listening Method).**

   You need to do this because you don't want to have to press a key while you're driving.

3. **Change the default keyword and how often you need to say it in the Keyword Is pop-up menu.**

4. **Click the Calibrate button, and speak the listed phrases into the microphone.**

   You also have to adjust a slider, as directed by the dialog.

5. **Click the Done button when you're finished calibrating.**

6. **Speak the keyword you selected in Step 3.**

7. **In the small, round Speech Feedback window that appears, click the triangle at the bottom and choose the Open Speech Commands window.**

   A list of commands appears.

8. **Say a command in a normal voice.**

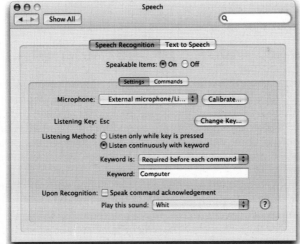

Figure 15-3:
Turn on and calibrate speech recognition in the Speech dialog.

Television tuner

Why miss your favorite TV shows on long trips? If the displays you installed have an analog video input, you can buy a standard car TV tuner from an outfit like Quality Mobile Video (www.qualitymobilevideo.com). The company also sells TV antennas for cars. But for about the same amount of money, you can buy a tuner that connects to your mini. Tuners are available for USB 2.0 and FireWire. Most FireWire units work with Macs, but not all USB tuners have Mac drivers. Most tuners also let your Mac serve as a digital video recorder (DVR), allowing you to record programs and watch them later. Most work with both U.S. and European broadcast standards and are available from Mac-oriented online computer retailers.

For more about using your Mac mini as a DVR, see Chapter 9.

A broadcast TV tuner works only within range of a TV station and can be frustrating to watch on long trips (unless you pull over to watch TV). At least one company, KVH Industries (www.kvh.com), sells a satellite TV tuner for car installation in the United States with the DIRECTV system. These devices are pricey, about $2300, and require a 31-inch-diameter, pancake-shaped antenna to be mounted on your car's roof. Satellite TV makes more sense on mobile homes.

Connecting to the Internet

Just because you're driving around doesn't mean that you can't stay connected to the Internet. You would need an awfully long cable to stay connected to your cable modem or DSL service. Wireless is the only way to go.

Long range: Mobile phones and satellite

For broad Internet coverage while you're on a road, you can use a mobile phone to connect the Mac mini to the Internet. The Mac mini needs built-in or add-on (USB) Bluetooth. The mobile phone needs to have built-in Bluetooth, and your wireless phone provider needs to support it. Your service provider can tell you whether your plan supports Bluetooth, and should be able to tell you which phone can do the job.

To set up Mac OS X, you have to pair the mobile phone with the Mac mini using the Set Up Bluetooth Device command in the Bluetooth status menu on the menu bar. You must also go to Network Preferences in System Preferences and set up a Bluetooth port. Here, you type in your access phone number and username, and other information from your wireless service provider. Next, go to the Modem pop-up menu in the Bluetooth Modem area of Network Preferences.

You make the network connect as you would dial-up a modem, using the Internet Connect application. Here you select Bluetooth as the configuration.

For really long-range connectivity, install a satellite phone from Iridium Satellite (www.iridium.com). Its phones are expensive and per-minute charges even more so, and the connection speed is painfully slow. But the coverage is truly global.

Short-range Internet access via WiFi

WiFi wireless was first popularized by Apple under its AirPort trademark, and has taken over the world of Internet connectivity in short ranges of less than 300 feet. The WiFi card in your mini sends radio messages in the 2.4-GHz frequency band to an AirPort Base Station or other WiFi access point, which connects to a wired network.

If you have a wireless access point in your house, you can probably connect your mini to your home wireless network from your garage or driveway. If not, you can add a wireless range extender, such as Apple's AirPort Extreme or the Linksys WRE54G at some point closer to where you park the car. Connections from the parking lots of stores equipped with a WiFi hot spot are also possible.

Several cities have set up "Freenets" in their downtown area, giving you free access to the Internet as you drive around. WiFi services are also available for a fee.

If your mini is mounted in the trunk or somewhere else where its WiFi antenna is shielded from picking up outside signals, you can install a WiFi range extender in the car, perhaps with an antenna in the roof.

For more information on WiFi, check out *Wireless All-In-One Desk Reference For Dummies*, by Todd W. Carter (Wiley).

WiFi security

Out of the box, WiFi networks have no security. Anyone nearby can listen in to what you are sending and receiving. Directional antennas are available that allow signals to be intercepted from more than a mile away. The mini and most newer wireless access points support three security modes: WEP, WPA, and WPA2. WEP, or Wireless Equivalent Privacy, is the oldest and most commonly used security mode. Its encryption protocol is easily broken, however. WPA, or Wireless Protected Access, and WPA2 are both much stronger and provide good protection with one proviso: You must choose a password for your access point that is much more complex than what you typically use for other computer accounts. I suggest at least 20 random characters.

Apple's OS X Tiger and later operating systems have a Password Assistant that helps you pick strong passwords. To use it, you have to start setting up a new user account. You don't actually have to save the new account, though. Select Accounts in Systems Preferences and click the plus sign (+). Then click the key icon next to the password field in the New Account screen. Don't fill in anything else. In fact, you can click the Cancel button at this point. The Password Assistant still works. I suggest that you select the Letters and Numbers option and set the length to 14 or more. Write down the password suggested and enter it into your access point as the WPA *personal shared key,* or PSK. See your access point's manual for instructions. For other ways to choose a password and for additional AirPort security suggestions, visit `www.diceware.com`.

War driving

Many people feel that a wireless access point with no security enabled is a friendly invitation to share the connection, although this interpretation is legally questionable in many jurisdictions. The practice of hunting for and logging in to such open access points is known as *war driving,* and a Google search on the term produces many Internet sites devoted to the activity.

Navigating with GPS

The Global Positioning System (GPS) is a system that uses a network of satellites in Earth orbit to help you figure out exactly where you are anywhere on the planet. To use it, you buy a GPS receiver. Some receivers are specifically designed for car navigation and include a map display and a street database with software that can tell you how to get to any address that you enter from where you are at the moment. Such systems give very precise directions in a friendly, but authoritative, human voice, such as, "Turn left at the next street, 300 feet ahead." These systems typically cost over $1000.

You don't have to lay out that kind of money with a Mac mini in the car. You can connect the mini to a less expensive, hand-held GPS receiver. Garmin (www.garmin.com) is a popular manufacturer of hand-held GPS receivers. Mid- to high-end versions can be plugged into a computer using an NMEA-0183 interface. Bluetooth models that avoid the need for a special cable are also available. Deluo Electronics (www.deluoelectronics.com) sells a GPS receiver with USB cable and navigation software that runs on Mac OS X for about a hundred dollars.

Most of the major GPS manufacturers have been reluctant to support Macs, so third-party software solutions are often necessary. Here are a few of them:

- **GarminUSBTool** (www.chrigel.ch/software/) reads and writes GPS data in GPX format between a Mac and a Garmin GPS device connected via USB.

- **GPS Connect** (www.chimoosoft.com) is a free Mac OS X utility that works with Garmin GPS receivers.

- **GPSy** ($50, www.gpsy.com) is a shareware program that supports a wide array of popular GPS receivers. The developers also have recommendations on receivers to buy. Unfortunately, GPSy is not Mac OS X native, and it runs under the Classic environment.

Mount your GPS receiver where it will have a clear view of the satellites orbiting in the sky. A spot on the dashboard is a common choice. Higher-cost roof-mount units are also available.

Part VI
Maxi mini Mods

The 5th Wave   By Rich Tennant

"Wow, I didn't know OSX could redirect an email message like that."

In this part . . .

*I*f you want to know how far you can go in hacking and modding a Mac mini, this part is for you. Turn the Mac mini into something unrecognizable, or upgrade the un-upgradeable. Many of the mods in this section have no practical purpose whatsoever. But, hey, there are plenty of practical mods described in the first five parts of this book. This part is about fun.

I start by describing the techniques you'll need to take on these and other projects: soldering, painting, cutting, and gluing. Not for the faint of heart. Potentially destructive, absolutely. Time consuming, sometimes. And yet, not incredibly difficult. But I do encourage you to practice these techniques before you try them out on your mini.

I've also included a chapter here on software hacks and mods. With a few text commands and some free or cheap software, you can radically alter the look and feel of Mac OS X in a way Apple never intended.

The last two chapters actually do have a tiny bit of practicality in them. I'll show you how to hack the Mac mini to accept a hard drive that is almost the size of the mini itself. You get a faster and higher-capacity drive, with a faster hardware interface than you could otherwise get. I end up showing you how to take a soldering iron to the motherboard itself to make your Mac mini a little faster. In many ways, it's the ultimate hack.

Chapter 16

Maxi mini Mod Techniques

• •

In This Chapter

▶ Soldering techniques

▶ Cutting techniques

▶ Gluing techniques

▶ Painting techniques

• •

Don't get me wrong; the screwdriver is a great tool. It was a great technological innovation of the 15th century, when it was used to screw together parts of a knight's armor. But it's time to move beyond the screwdriver, because maxi mods often require some skills with other tools.

This chapter presents techniques to use on the projects described in Part VI and on projects you may come up with on your own.

I start the chapter by describing how to solder electronic parts and wires. Next, you discover how to cut materials you are likely to run into or use for a Mac mini mod, such as metal, plastic, and acrylic. There's also a section on painting these materials to get professional-looking results. For each of these techniques, I describe the best tools to use.

Soldering Electronics

Soldering is the original electronic hardware hacker's tool. It's how Steve Wozniak created the first Apple motherboard. While modifying the Mac mini, you may solder a few electronic parts (as Chapter 20 describes), but you may also be soldering wires to boards or wires to other wires.

The basic concept is simple. You heat the two items you are joining to above the melting temperature of the solder. You then touch solder to the hot components, and the solder melts on the components and solidifies. You may also need to *desolder,* that is, to melt and remove the solder on an existing solder joint.

About solder

Solder is any metal alloy with a low melting point that's used to join other metals. Tin-lead solder, the type used for electronics, has a melting temperature of about 360° to 370° Fahrenheit (F), depending on the exact composition. The interesting thing is that this melting point is lower than that of either tin or lead, which are 450°F and 621°F, respectively. This is true for other metal alloys, and it's even true for solutions as well. Salt water has a lower melting point (freezing point) than pure water.

To the novice, the hot iron of soldering sounds dangerous and difficult, but it actually isn't. With a little care, soldering is safer than using many power tools, and the soldering tools are a lot cheaper. Learning to solder takes a little practice but doesn't take long. You should use extreme care, however, if you are putting a soldering iron to the Mac mini's motherboard.

Soldering tools

Soldering tools don't cost a lot, probably because they have no moving parts.

Soldering iron

For electronics soldering, you need a pencil soldering iron, shown in Figure 16-1, which you hold like a pencil, not like a gun. These irons can cost from $5 to $40 or more; somewhere in the midrange should be fine.

Figure 16-1:
Use a pencil-style soldering iron for electronics.

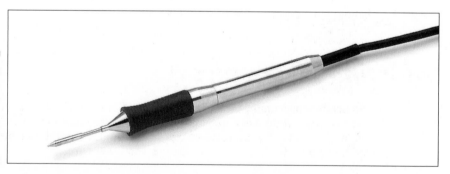

The ability to replace tips gives you versatility. You use a very fine tip for small parts (like the jumper resistors in Chapter 20) and bigger tips for wiring pins. Soldering tips also wear out due to repeated heating and reaction with oxygen and molten solder.

An iron in the power range of 25 to 45 watts is sufficient for electronics and circuit boards. For bigger hunks of metal, such as thick wire, you might need a second soldering iron that runs at 150 watts.

A more expensive setup is a soldering station ($70 or more), which includes a stand for the soldering iron, a holder for a sponge, and a temperature control and regulator that keeps the soldering tip at a constant temperature. The temperature control and regulation features are more of a luxury than a necessity for hobbyists. It allows you to crank up the heat for bigger solder joints, something you can easily and more inexpensively achieve with a second, bigger soldering iron.

Solder

You use different types of solder, with different mixtures of metals, for different purposes. For electronics, use 60/40 tin-lead, rosin flux-core solder wire. Solder usually comes in a spool of wire, and, solder pastes with mixed-in flux are also available.

Flux-core means that the center of the solder wire contains soldering flux made out of rosin, which removes oxides that hinder the creation of good solder joints. The flux removes the metal oxides from the surface of the metal to give you a pure metal-to-metal contact. Rosin is an organic material that's created from pine sap.

Damp sponge

You use a sponge to wipe the tip of the iron clean while you're using it. It's important to keep a soldering iron tip clean, so give it a wipe every few minutes. A clean soldering tip gives you better conduction of heat to the items you are joining. It also slows the deterioration of the soldering tip.

Soldering stand

For a few dollars, you can buy a soldering iron stand, as shown in Figure 16-2, to hold the hot iron and the sponge.

De-soldering braid

This braid of thin copper wire, also known as *solder wick*, is named after Soder-Wick, a brand-name copper braid from Chemtronics. A desoldering braid uses capillary action to soak up melted solder. Desoldering braid comes in a spool.

How to solder

As you can see from the steps in the following sections, soldering is not difficult. It is important to follow all the steps, however. Skipping a step can make it impossible to create a good solder joint.

Figure 16-2:
A soldering
stand
provides a
holder for
the sponge
and the
soldering
iron.

Preparing

Before you solder, you must prepare your materials:

1. **Prepare the surfaces by wiping, cleaning with alcohol, or in the case of heavily oxidized metal, gently abrading.**

   Surfaces must be free of grease, fingerprints, or heavy oxidation. Solder can't bind to a dirty service but instead beads up into globules.

   A rubber eraser works well for removing a layer of oxidation on metal.

   Dirty surfaces are not just annoying, but can do harm. In your frustrating attempts to get the solder to adhere, you'll be tempted to apply more heat, which only damages the circuit board or the part you're soldering.

2. **Heat the soldering iron by turning it on and letting it sit for a few minutes.**

Creating a solder joint

After you make the necessary preparations, you're ready to create a solder joint; just follow these steps:

1. **Clean the soldering iron tip by wiping it on the damp sponge.**

   Again, all parts to be soldered must be clean and free from dirt and grease.

2. **Tin the iron tip by touching the solder wire to the hot tip, letting the molten solder coat the tip.**

   Tinning the tip helps with heat transfer from the iron to the parts. You'll also replace the tip less often if you always keep some solder on it; this prevents the air from reacting with the hot tip.

3. **Heat both of the surfaces you want to solder by touching the iron to both of them at the same time, as shown in Figure 16-3. For a circuit board, heating should take from 1 to 3 seconds.**

   For a small surface-mounted part, you can press down on the part with the soldering iron. (See Figure 16-4.)

Figure 16-3:
Heat both
surfaces
with the
iron, and
apply solder
to the
surfaces.

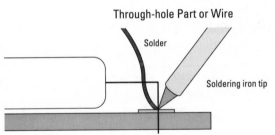

Through-hole Part or Wire

Solder

Soldering iron tip

4. **Touch the solder to the heated parts, *not to the soldering iron*.**

   The solder should melt around both parts. Apply solder sparingly to a circuit board.

   Don't push the solder around with the iron. This is not going to help the solder adhere, and applies too much heat.

TIP

Figure 16-4:
You can
hold down
a small
surface-
mounted
part with
the iron.

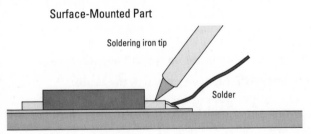

Surface-Mounted Part

Soldering iron tip

Solder

5. **Stop adding solder when both parts are covered. Keep the soldering iron on the part for another second.**

6. **Remove the soldering iron.**

   In Steps 3 through 6, the soldering iron should only be touching the circuit board for a few seconds.

   Don't move the parts until the solder has cooled and solidified. Don't blow on the solder joint to cool it.

7. **Clean the tip of the soldering iron by rubbing it on the damp sponge.**

8. **Tin the iron tip with a small amount of solder before putting it down.**

9. **Repeat these steps for each solder joint, including wiping the iron tip.**

10. **Tin the tip of the soldering iron before you turn off the power.**

Trim any extra material or wire lengths after soldering. You can clean off flux residue with a Q-Tip and some alcohol.

Evaluating the solder joint

A good solder joint looks shiny, smooth, and tapered. A joint that looks balled up or grainy and dull is known as a *cold* solder joint. A cold joint is mechanically weak and can have poor electrical connectivity. The following factors can cause cold solder joints:

- ✔ Surfaces that were dirty prior to soldering
- ✔ Parts that weren't hot enough before the solder was applied
- ✔ Components that were moved before the solder cooled

You can fix a cold solder joint by removing the solder, as the next section describes, and reapplying the solder.

Desoldering with a braid

To remove the solder from a joint, use a soldering iron to heat the solder joint and use a desoldering braid to soak up the molten solder. Follow these steps:

1. **Place the desoldering braid on top of the solder joint.**

2. **Press the hot soldering iron on top of the braid.**

   The solder melts and the braid wicks it up. This should only take a few seconds.

3. **Remove the iron and the braid** *at the same time.*

   If you let the solder cool in the braid, the braid may adhere to the circuit board.

4. **If necessary, repeat the desoldering in another location of the solder joint using a clean section of braid.**

   Wipe the soldering iron tip on the damp sponge between applications.

Practicing

Before you turn your iron to your Mac mini, practice soldering and desoldering on an old circuit board. You can find old circuit boards in old radios, stereos, or other discarded appliances. You can also buy circuit boards to practice on at an electronics supply store such as Radio Shack. You can use the latter to practice soldering pins and wires onto the board.

Cutting

Experienced computer modders employ a stable of cutting techniques for cutting windows in equipment, for cutting slots and holes for wires or cables, and for cutting new material to build new cases. Although you could probably build a wood case for your Mac mini, this section focuses on techniques for cutting metal and several different types of plastic.

What to wear when cutting

Cutting plastic with a power tool heats the plastic, which releases toxic fumes. It can also release toxic particles into the air. When cutting metal, the particles are heavier, but sharp and nasty. You don't want any of this material in your lungs or eyes. So, when cutting material with power tools, protect your eyes and lungs with safety glasses or goggles and a respirator mask.

When cutting metal, you may also want to wear thick gloves to protect your hands from the shards of metal on the cut edges and from those flying into the air.

Cutting tools

The premier cutting tool for modding is a hand-held rotary tool casually known as a Dremel, as shown in Figure 16-5. Officially, the name refers to the Dremel Company (www.dremel.com), which makes the tool, but other companies offer similar hand-held rotary tools. Dremels are easy to handle and are great for cutting on curves. Cordless Dremels are common. They're also versatile in that you can use them for cutting, grinding, and polishing rough metal edges, depending on the type of bit you're using. Figure 16-5 shows a Dremel with a grinding bit. Figure 16-6 shows a cutting bit. Dremels sell for $50 to $100. You can buy kits that include sets of bits for different tasks.

If you're cutting a lot of metal, a hand-held jigsaw is helpful. Jigsaws are good for cutting precision curves in sheet metal. You can use a Dremel to make the initial cut and then insert the jigsaw.

You can also use a Dremel to cut plastic. In this case, you would first need to drill a pilot hole to get started. When cutting sheet plastic, acrylic, and laminate, you can also use scoring tools and a ruler. To smooth out the cut edge, use a file and sandpaper.

Clamps are useful to hold down your parts during various types of cutting.

Figure 16-5:
A hand-held rotary tool known as a Dremel, shown here with a grinding bit.

Figure 16-6:
A cutting
blade on a
hand-held
Dremel.

Cutting plastics

Plastic is a common material in modding projects. You find it in the cases of computers and peripherals, in raw material you buy at a hardware store, and in found material you might be using for your mod, such as a piece of a CD jewel case or a reused bit from an old toy. For the purposes of cutting, you can lump plastics into thick-and-bumpy and flat-and-thin pieces.

Cutting thick, uneven plastics

You usually need to use a power tool such as a Dremel when cutting plastics found in cases for computers and computer peripherals. You can use a cutting disk bit, as shown in Figure 16-6, but you get better results using a special spiral bit that's designed to cut plastic.

Using a rotary tool can cause the plastic to melt from the friction, creating toxic fumes. This makes ventilation a good idea.

Here is the procedure for cutting thick plastic pieces with a spiral bit:

1. Draw your cut lines on the surface with a pencil.

Don't try to eyeball it with your cutting tool.

2. **Using a drill bit, drill a pilot hole in which to insert the spiral cutting bit.**

   The hole should be on the inside of your drawn line.

3. **Place the spiral bit into the pilot hole.**

4. **Using a slow rotational speed, move the tool slowly along the inside of the pencil line to make the cut.**

   A fast rotational speed can melt too much plastic.

5. **After you finish cutting, use a file to remove bumps and to smooth gashes at the cut edges.**

6. **Use 220-grit sandpaper to smooth the edge, and then use a finer-grain sandpaper to finish it off.**

7. **If you're working with clear plastic, you may want to continue sanding the edge with an even finer sandpaper, up to 1800 grit.**

   Sandpaper with this fine a grain is often wet sandpaper, which you can use under running water to remove the fine dust.

Another option for clear plastic is to continue finishing with polishing compounds after sanding.

Cutting thin, flat plastics

For thin sheets of plastic, you may be able to score the material with a knife and then snap the material along the score line to break it. Use a straight edge to guide the knife several times along the same line, cutting a groove in the material. Then snap the plastic along the groove, bending away from the cut. It helps to place the line at the edge of a table.

Plastic laminate, also known by the brand name Formica, is a tougher material than ordinary plastic, so you can't use a knife to score it. Hardware stores sell a special diamond-tipped scoring tool for cutting laminate.

Not all types of flat plastic break evenly when scored, so it's a good idea to run a test on a spare piece.

Cutting acrylic

Acrylic, also known by the brand names Plexiglas and Lucite, is a good material for building clear cases and for turning old iMacs into aquariums. Acrylic is a kind of miracle material. It doesn't yellow or crack with age, even when exposed to strong sunlight. It's also very strong. Acrylic that is an inch thick or more resists bullets, which is why the Pope-mobile has an acrylic shell.

The strength of acrylic also makes it more difficult to cut than plastic. For instance, if you are using a power tool to make curve cuts, it's best to use a carbide bit at a high speed.

The best way to make straight cuts in acrylic is to use a scribing tool to score a line. You can do this with acrylic sheets of up to ³⁄₁₆ inch thick. You can use a scoring tool made of metal or a diamond-tipped scoring tool that's made to cut plastic laminate (Formica). You can also use a matte knife with a sharp (new) blade.

Clamp or firmly hold a straight edge along the line you want to cut, and score the material about seven times. To complete the cut, break the sheet by pressing down while holding the sheet over an edge, with the score line at the edge.

To dull the edges of the cut, scrape them with a knife edge. You may not want to do this if you're planning to apply glue to the edge, however.

You can also sand the edges of acrylic for a smoother finish by using sand-paper wrapped around a block. Start with 120-grit sandpaper, and then use 220-grit. You can finish with some wet 400-grit sandpaper. Be careful not to scratch the main surfaces of the sheet.

Cutting metal

When cutting metal with a rotary tool, use a high rotational speed and move the tool slowly. Use a disk bit on the Dremel. To get the best results, follow these steps:

1. **Use a pencil to mark your cut lines.**

   Alternatively, you can add masking tape where the cut lines go and mark the lines on top of the tape. This prevents scratching the surface. Apply masking tape to protect the metal-case surface from scratches. Then draw or trace on the tape the lines you plan to cut.

2. **Place the Dremel blade on the inside of your line and press down to cut.**

   Don't cut right on the line, but cut slightly inside the line, leaving some space to make a mistake.

It's also a good idea to clamp the part while cutting it.

3. **Repeat this downward motion along the line that you've drawn.**

   Make sure that you stay inside your marked line.

4. **You can use a grinding bit on the Dremel to grind down parts that protrude or are misshaped.**

5. **Smooth the edges with a file, and then use sandpaper for the final finish.**

For a finished look, cover a cut metal edge with plastic or rubber tubing that you've slit lengthwise.

Cutting thin metal

For cutting thinner metal, such as the EMI shielding inside of a Mac mini or other computer, you can use tin snips, which are shown in Figure 16-7. Remember, though, tin snips are designed to cut sheet metal. You'll ruin them if you try to cut thicker metal.

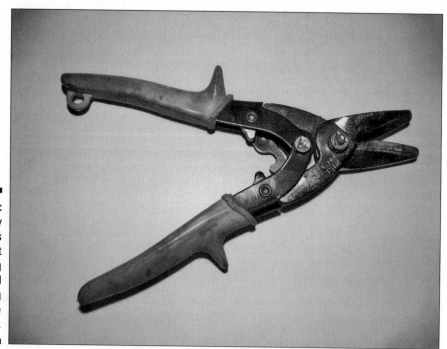

Figure 16-7:
My trusty old tin snips are great for cutting the metal shielding inside computers.

Gluing

The following sections provide suggestions regarding which glues work best with various materials. Others may work as well, so you might benefit from poking around your local hardware store and reading the fine print on the labels.

Surfaces should be clean and free of grease before applying adhesives, and some surfaces benefit from a little sanding to improve adhesion.

Precautions

Many types of glue give off toxic fumes. Use glue with a respirator in a well-ventilated area. Goggles are good for some glues, because the fumes can damage your eyes.

Some adhesives are also harmful to the skin. Read the label and wear gloves if recommended by the manufacturer.

Gluing plastic to metal and other mixed materials

If you're gluing plastic or acrylic to metal, try using a hot-glue gun. These guns are great for gluing together dissimilar materials, even if they are uneven and not flush with each other.

Hot-glue guns are inexpensive (the gun shown in Figure 16-8 is particularly cheap). The glue comes in the form of sticks that you insert. Squeezing the trigger forces the glue into the gun, where it melts. The activated adhesive comes out the tip at the front. Glue guns are fun to use, and don't require clean up.

Different types of glue sticks are available for different purposes, so read the labels before you buy. One type of glue stick is good for gluing cloth-like material, for making your Mac mini look like half a pair of pink fuzzy dice, or for covering the mini with red leatherette.

The strength of the bond varies with the type of glue stick, but an adhesive may not hold up if mechanical stress is being applied to the joint.

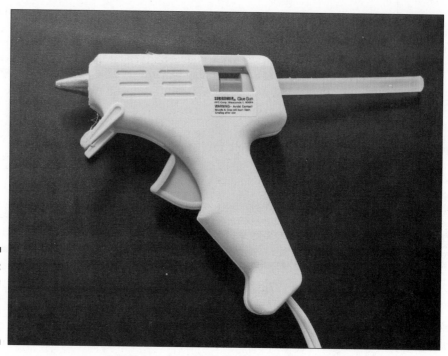

Figure 16-8:
A hot-glue
gun with a
glue stick in
the back.

A two-part epoxy can give you a stronger plastic-to-metal bond than hot glue. Epoxy's high strength is a bit overkill for most computer modding projects, though. Epoxy is also a pain to use, because you have to mix a resin with a catalyst. After you mix the two parts, you have about 10 minutes to glue everything together before the epoxy turns rock hard.

Gluing plastics

Gluing plastic to plastic is fairly easy, and you have a wide choice of adhesives. Here are your best choices, in no particular order:

- **Hot glue:** This is a forgiving adhesive that you can move around for a while after you press the parts together. If you think that you might want to take the pieces apart in the future, you can always reapply the adhesive with a hot-glue gun.

- **Tensol cement:** This adhesive creates a strong bond between certain types of plastics. You brush it onto both parts and clamp for 24 hours. If you can't clamp the parts, however, tensol cement is not as effective.

✔ **Cyanoacrylate (also known by the Krazy Glue brand name):** This is very easy to use, especially on small parts. Just apply a few drops to each piece and hold them together for 20 seconds or so. Cyanoacrylate only works on flush joints; it doesn't fill gaps. Be careful: You can easily glue your fingers together. Using rubber gloves can help prevent this.

✔ **Contact cement:** This adhesive is good for gluing a sheet of plastic to a surface. If you want to cover your Mac mini in Formica, contact cement is for you. You apply it with a brush to both surfaces and let it sit for a half-hour. After that, you roll the plastic onto the surface. After a few hours of drying, the adhesive creates a permanent, tough bond.

✔ **Two-part epoxy:** This is a good choice if the parts being joined are not flush (that is, you need to fill gaps) and you need a strong bond. After you mix a resin and the catalyst, you have about 10 minutes to glue everything together before the epoxy hardens. Clamping the two parts together helps ensure a good bond.

Acrylic (Plexiglas)

You may have chosen acrylic because of its transparency, so you want a clear adhesive to join acrylic pieces. For tight-fitting, flush joints, a watery adhesive works well. Weld-on number 3 or number 4 from IPS Corp. (www. ipscorp.com) is made for this purpose. Cyanoacrylate also works.

Before you glue acrylics, roughen the edges a bit with 220-grit sandpaper. Be careful not to scratch the sides of the acrylic.

Isopropyl alcohol works for cleanup afterwards.

Painting

Painting can be the finishing touch for your mod. Or, maybe you just want to paint the Mac mini a cool new color. Whatever your motive, plan on spending some time on the paint job. Crummy-looking painting is quick and easy. Good-looking painting takes time. A good paint job requires preparing the surface and then applying multiple coats of primer and paint, sometimes with sanding in between coats.

Aerosol spray paint can get you good results, and is what I describe in the following sections. You can get even better, more consistent results with airbrushes and spray applicators, but they take some skill and funds and aren't the place to begin. How professional you get with your results is up to you. Here I describe moderately ambitious procedures that can give you great results. You can ramp it up from there if you want to, or pick and choose between the techniques I describe.

Removing paint from plastic

A lot of plastic is colored throughout rather than painted. Sometimes, however, you may run into painted plastic or acrylic. (The iBook has an acrylic shell that's painted on the inside, for instance.) If you want to paint such a surface, try removing the existing paint with isopropyl alcohol. Let the alcohol soak for 5 to 10 minutes before scrubbing off the paint with a brush.

Don't use paint thinner on plastic; you may end up melting or otherwise disfiguring it.

Sanding

Sanding both smoothes and roughens surfaces. Sanding before you paint roughens a surface to help the paint adhere. Sanding in between coats smoothes out irregularities and wrinkles in the paint. Your results won't be nearly as good if you don't sand.

Hand-sanding mini-sized painting projects works better than power sanding. Hand-sanding small parts gives you control and prevents burning of the material. You can still wear your surface down too much with hand sanding, but you're more likely to do so with a power sander.

When hand-sanding flat surfaces, wrap the sandpaper around a block. Use a circular motion on the surface to get the best results.

Prep sanding

Metal should be sanded before painting to create a good surface for paint adhesion. In addition to roughing the surface, sanding removes residual layers of invisible goop that may have accumulated on the surface.

With plastic, you may not want to sand before painting. For instance, you may want to keep a texture in the plastic. You can also create textures in the plastic that you wish you hadn't. Still, sanding does help paint adhere to the surface. If you do a prep sand, go lightly and briefly.

For metal, you can start with an 80- or 100-grit sandpaper and work your way up to 320-grit, with 150- and 220-grit steps in between. For plastic, use a 220-grit sandpaper to prepare the surface for painting.

Sanding between coats

A coat of paint can leave a number of nonsmooth artifacts, such as wrinkles and bumps that look like the surface of an orange. A light sanding between coats can give you a smooth finish.

The first coat you lay down on the surface should be a primer or sealer. After this dries, sand it with 220-grit sandpaper, the same as you used on the bare surface.

If you're going for a glossy finish, consider giving the primer coat another sanding with 600-grit wet sandpaper. You use wet sandpaper (usually black) under running water, which keeps the surface clean from the ultrafine dust being created. Then, give the primer a wet sanding at 800 or 1000 grit. Do the same in between the color coats.

Finally, if you are applying a clear top coat, finish the last color coat with an 1800-grit wet sand to give the clear coat an ever-so-slightly rough surface to adhere to.

If you're not going for a slick finish, you don't need to go to these lengths; just use light 600-grit sandpaper in between coats.

When sanding paint coats, use a light touch and watch what you're doing. You want to remove as little of the paint as possible while still smoothing out the bumps and wrinkles.

Masking

If you aren't painting an entire part, remember to mask off the areas of your part that you don't want to be painted. Masking gives you clean lines and good results.

Look for blue masking tape for your modding project. Don't use the regular beige masking tape that you would use to bind cardboard boxes. It can leave a nasty glue residue behind, particularly if it's exposed to sunlight for a few days, in which case the residue becomes rock hard. The blue masking tape is designed to not leave a glue residue and is not affected by the ultraviolet light in sunlight. The official name of 3M's blue tape is 3M Safe Release Blue Painters Masking Tape.

Where to paint

I recommend painting outdoors. When you use aerosol spray paints, the fumes can be unbearable and are certainly unhealthy. Go into the backyard, throw a tarp on a table or on the ground, and get to work. Or paint in the garage with the garage door open.

If you must paint indoors, spend $25 on a respirator mask. That little dust mask that you might wear when sanding doesn't stop you from inhaling the toxic fumes.

Types of paint

For the types of surfaces that you're painting in computer modding projects, spray paint gives you far superior results than brush-on paint. A variety of sprayers are available, including automobile sprayers and artist's airbrushes. You can also get great results with aerosol spray paints. They are easy to use, require no mixing or thinning, and are readily available.

Different sources, different paints

You have two main sources for aerosol spray paints: a hardware store and an auto parts store. Each sells paint that has been designed differently. In hardware stores, Krylon is a major brand. In auto parts stores, Valspar is a big name.

The auto spray paints are intended for touching up cars, and therefore try to approximate the high-gloss look of an automobile finish, at least when used under a clear coat. If that's the kind of look you're after, it's off to the auto parts store you go. You may find a bigger selection of colors at a hardware store, however.

Different layers, different paints

You may be using different types of aerosol spray paint in multiple layers. Here's a list of them in the order that they would be applied. Don't worry; you don't need all of these paints. The ones you use depend on what you're doing.

- ✔ **Conditioner:** Glossy plastic can use a conditioner before the primer coat is applied to help the primer coat adhere. Otherwise, all your paint layers can peel off like a pancake from a Teflon pan. A conditioner isn't needed for nonglossy plastics or any metal surface.

- ✔ **Primer/sealer:** This forms a bond between the surface and the paint, and gives you better results than if you don't use it. Primer is often available in gray, brown, or white.

- **Krylon Fusion Plastic Paint:** This is a special paint from Krylon that doesn't require a primer on plastic. It's designed to bind right to plastic. If you are painting plastic, Krylon Fusion could be the only paint you need.

- **Color paint:** By this I mean ordinary paint, the color that you want the item to be.

- **Clear coat:** This is a transparent paint that you spray on as the last coat to give you a hard finish. Clear coats are available in high gloss as well as satin. Krylon offers an acrylic clear coat, as does Valspar, which is sold in auto parts stores. You can also apply multiple coats of clear coat to build up a durable finish.

Applying paint with aerosol cans

The previous few sections refer to multiple coats of paint. There are two reasons for applying multiple coats: coverage and durability.

- **Coverage:** When covering another color or surface, you get better results with multiple thin coats than with fewer thick coats. Thick coats of sprayed-on paint have a greater chance of bunching, wrinkling, and running.

- **Durability:** Multiple coats resist chipping and wear better than a single coat.

The procedure for applying each coat of primer, color paint, and top coat is the same. Follow these steps:

1. **Position the part horizontally on blocks or on a stand.**

   Placing the part directly on the work surface can cause it to stick to the surface.

2. **Shake the aerosol can for a minute, or for the duration noted on the directions on the can.**

3. **Shake the can frequently during painting, every 30 seconds or so.**

4. **Hold the can 8 to 12 inches from the part while spraying.**

   The paint will be too concentrated in one area if you hold the can too close, causing runs.

5. **Apply the paint with a side-to-side motion, followed by an up-and-down motion.**

   This gives you an even coverage of paint, without missing spots and without accumulating too much paint in one spot.

   Don't keep the can in a stationary position while spraying, and don't spray in circular patterns, or you deposit too much paint in one spot.

   Don't keep spraying over the same spot. Remember, multiple thin coats give you better results than fewer thick coats.

6. **Allow primer to dry completely between coats. For the finish color, wait an hour between coats.**

For a high-quality finish, be willing to allow time for multiple coats and for the drying time between coats. For a top-notch job, it's not out of the question to do two or three primer coats and half a dozen or more color coats, followed by two or three clear coats. Considering the drying time, this could take a week or more.

Of course, you can use fewer coats. I've spray-painted metal with three or four coats of Krylon paint and have been satisfied with the result. It all depends on what you are trying to cover, how well your thin coats cover it, and how much of a stickler you are for a quality paint job.

Chapter 17

Fun mini Case Mods

• •

In This Chapter

▶ Things to be careful of

▶ Wrapping your mini

▶ Gluing stuff to your mini

▶ Painting your mini

▶ Ripping apart the cover and replacing the white plastic with another material

• •

*W*ith some of the mods in this book, you have to weigh whether the mod is really worth the trouble, or whether you would get as much functionality by going out and buying some peripheral.

With the Mac mini makeovers in this chapter, you don't have to go through this process. There is no practical reason to do any of these mods. You do them because you need a change, because it's art, or because you want a weekend project — because they're there.

This chapter explores changing the look of the Mac mini by making alterations to the top casing. I start with the easy stuff, wrapping the mini in designer vinyl and gluing found objects to the case. I move up to the more drastic measure of painting your mini. The chapter ends with a maxi mini mod: ripping apart the top casing to replace the plastic top with something else — say, oak, acrylic, or maybe polished granite. How about a mini in a soccer ball? It's up to you.

Precautions

Other than obvious prohibitions like drilling a hole in the hard drive or cutting through the motherboard, there are only a couple of things to avoid with a Mac mini case mod. One is overheating, and the other is blocking wireless reception.

Preventing overheating

The most important thing to avoid with a case mod is interfering with the Mac mini's ability to keep cool.

The Mac mini draws in cool air through vents in the bottom. After the air blows past the motherboard and other internal parts, the air flows through a channel in the internal frame and out the vents in the back of the unit. The fan helps move air, but convection is a big factor in the design. As cooler air is heated, it rises up through the mini and exits, thus drawing in more cool air from the bottom.

Here are some precautions to take when positioning the mini on its bottom and side, and a note about the rear:

- **Bottom:** The sides of the Mac mini don't extend all the way down to the base. They stop ⅛" from the bottom, where air vents (shown in Figure 17-1) suck in cooling air. If you're wrapping the mini in some decorative material, keep these vents clear.

  If you're replacing the mini's outer casing with your own invention, the new sides must not go down all the way to the base. If you're placing the mini inside of another box, leave some room around the base of the mini to allow for airflow. And make sure that air can enter your box at the bottom and leave near the top.

  Don't run the Mac mini while it's sitting on a soft surface. A Mac mini mounted on a velvet pillow or shag rug may be an expression of your inner artist, but doing so can block the air vents. The mini should always sit on a flat surface or be mounted in the air via a bracket.

- **Side orientation:** You can safely turn the Mac mini on its side to operate it. Doing so doesn't block the bottom vents. It throws off the convection design, though, so the fan may run more often when the mini is operated on its side.

- **Rear:** The vents above the ports at the back allow warm air and heat to leave the mini. If you're building a new enclosure, put some ventilation holes near where the back of the Mac mini will be.

Interference with wireless and optical

Apple warns users not to place anything on top of the Mac mini because an item on the top of the mini could hinder reception for internal AirPort and Bluetooth. This makes sense when you consider that the antennas for both sit on top of the optical drive just under the cover.

Figure 17-1:
Don't block
the air vents
that ring the
bottom of
the mini.

Apple also warns that putting something on top of the Mac mini could interfere with the optical drive. If the object you are placing on top is another electronic device, it could create electronic interference that can hinder the DVD
drive's ability to read or write discs.

Wrapping and Sticking Stuff to the mini

The first assault on the stock look of the Mac mini is to cover it up. Gray and
white — how boring. Try using colors, patterns, fur, or plastic army men.

Adding prefab skins

One way to mod the mini case is to cover it with a vinyl decal, known as a *skin*.
Figure 17-2 shows you one example. This is the easy, cheap, and nonpermanent
method of case mods. Sure, you *could* cover it with shelf paper, cutting a hole
in the paper for the DVD slot. For a better look, get a skin that is tailor-made
for the mini. Use solid colors, interesting patterns, and pictures — even *your*
photos.

Figure 17-2:
A vinyl skin
can turn
your mini
into a Power
Mac G5 —
at least, on
the outside.

There's more than one way to skin a mini. Here are three companies that take different approaches:

- **Decal Girl** (`www.decalgirl.com`) sells about five dozen stick-on vinyl decals that cover the top of the Mac mini for $10 each. The Apple Mac Mini Skins only cover the white portion on the top, leaving all the aluminum exposed. You can remove the skins and reuse them without leaving glue goo behind on the mini.

- **SkinIt** (`www.skinit.com`) offers four-piece vinyl skins that cover the Mac mini's top, front, left, and right sides. For $20, you can choose from hundreds of designs — one of the biggest selections available. For $25, the selection becomes infinite, because SkinIt can make a mini skin from your own image file. Like Decal Girl, SkinIt uses nonpermanent adhesive so that the decals are easily removable.

- **We Love Macs** (`www.welovemacs.com`) offers skins called Mac Mini Skin Tattoo Protectors, for $20; the skins cover the top, sides, and even the back of the mini (without blocking the air vents and ports). These skins come in more Apple-related themes, such as giving the Mac mini the look of other Macs or of various iPods. The skins are also more sensitive to the Apple design; they don't cover the Apple icon in the center of the mini's top, and they leave exposed the quarter-inch rim of aluminum that bands the top. Classy. We Love Macs also gives you a free Mac OS X desktop background image that matches the skin. Doubly classy.

Gluing things to the mini's case

As long as you don't block the ventilation holes along the bottom and at the rear, there's no reason you can't cover your mini with your own materials. Make your own skins, or glue found objects to the mini.

A hot-glue gun works well for attaching your own skins to the mini's case. Don't fold the skin under the bottom of the case, or it won't fit on the mini properly. A hot-glue gun also works for fixing larger objects to the mini's case. A nice thing about a hot-glue gun is that with a soft glue stick, you can change your mind. Within a period of a day, you can pull off an object and scrape off the soft glue. Some of the other adhesives that I describe in Chapter 16 can also do the job for large and small objects.

First, you have to decide what kind of mod this is going to be. A lot of the PC mod Web sites go for the slick look of highly polished paint. You, too, can achieve this look with paint. PC users go for this look because most of their PCs are bland beige. But because the Mac mini already has a polished look, a real change would be a retro look, a carnival look, a Goth look, something kitschy, or something comfy.

Here are some ideas for your own skins:

- **Use textiles.** A fabric store is a great resource. Cloth gives you an interesting look, although you may want to Scotchgard it first. You can choose from solids, paisley, herringbone, and flowers, among others. Burlap is interesting. Vinyl leatherette can be cool.

- **Use real leather.** Make your mini match your Italian leather sofa. Or, go butch or punk and add some metal studs.

- **Cover your mini in fuzzy pink fake fur.** Very '60s.

- **Use mixed media.** Try applying leather on the sides and cloth on the top.

- **Glue LED strips to the perimeter.** This is another popular item among PC modders. SciLux (www.scilux.com) has some very sci-fi-looking choices. Some change color. You need to plug them into a wall socket for power.

For found objects, almost anything works if it's done right. I find toy stores to be an unbounded source of glue-able mini art. Try the following add-ons:

- **Glow-in-the-dark stars.**

- **Green plastic army men.** This is a classic way to get in touch with your inner child. Also along those lines are Barbie shoes.

- ✔ **Baubles, bangles, and beads** for the carnival mini.
- ✔ **Pennies.** Try laying down a layer of flat black fabric or plastic as a base.
- ✔ **Strips of bamboo.**

As Yul Brenner once said, "Et cetera, et cetera, et cetera."

Painting the mini

When it comes to a new paint job, the comparison to a car may be the reason why many PC modders go for the shiny polished look. The prefab skins can get you partway there, but a new paint job is the real deal.

Leaving it to the experts

If you're not interested in the process of painting your mini, you may find the procedure that I describe in Chapter 16 a chore. You do have an option, which is to get someone else to do it. Find a professional.

Color-Ware (www.colorwarepc.com), of Winona, Minnesota, specializes in paint jobs for computers and, in particular, for Apple computers and iPods. The company offers 22 colors. Color-Ware paints the entire Mac mini cover, including the white top. Color-Ware does, however, retain the big white Apple logo at the top center.

Color-Ware charges $99 (plus shipping) to paint the cover of the Mac mini. For an extra $49, Color-Ware paints your keyboard and mouse the matching color. You ship your hardware to Minnesota; Color-Ware paints it and ships it back to you.

When you go to the Color-Ware Web site, look under Apple Services to find the mini modding proposal.

The average person trusts his mini to the shippers. As a modder and hacker, you have other skills. Remove the mini's outer casing and ship that to Color-Ware. Keep the mini's electronics at home — and out of the hands of the delivery companies. And remember, you can keep on using the mini while Color-Ware paints the outer casing.

Painting it yourself

Chapter 16 describes the prepping and spray-painting techniques that you need to use to get a decent paint job — or a fabulous paint job, depending on how much time (and layers of paint) you're willing to put into it. Here are some ideas about what to do with the paint and your Mac mini, and how to keep from damaging the mini.

To do the job right, use an aerosol spray paint, such as a Krylon, for primer coats and the basic color coats. You can detail the paint job using an artist's paintbrush or stencils. Or, for an abstract impressionist look, squirt on different colors of paint with plastic squeeze bottles.

 Instead of painting the entire mini, remove the mini's outer casing and apply the paint to the outer casing only. Otherwise, paint may find its way through the air vents and on to the interior electronics or connectors, where it could do some damage. You can also get a cleaner look by painting the outer casing separately.

Spraying paint

When painting with an aerosol can, the goal is to get even and complete coverage without bunching up the paint. This goes for the primer as well.

 For $5 or $10, you can buy a spray can holder that makes it much easier to paint evenly with an aerosol can. The holder snaps onto the rim of the can, turning the can into a spray gun. You squeeze the trigger to release the spray. It also keeps your hands clean. Krylon makes the Snap & Spray, which is carried by Ace Hardware (www.acehardwareoutlet.com) and other hardware paint supply stores. You can find other brands as well.

You can paint the entire outer casing one color, but with some extra effort, you can paint the plastic top surface a different color. A combination of flat paint on the sides and glossy paint on the top reflects the stock Apple look. To accomplish this, mask off the plastic center while painting the aluminum and then mask off the aluminum when spraying the plastic center.

 Another way to create a two-toned mini is to remove the plastic center from the aluminum ring, as I describe in the next section. Then you can spray each part separately. The benefit is that you get a cleaner break between the two colors than you can with masking. The drawback is that the plastic center is tough to remove without bending the metal tabs that hold it in place, and it's not easy to get the plastic center back in place.

Detailing the paint job

If you're artistically gifted (or at least have a steady hand), you can use an artist's brush to add a trim design, racing stripes, or a hand-painted figure. Enamel works well here. Hobby shops and auto-supply stores may also carry suitable paints. You can also find paint pens in gold and silver and other colors. Stencils can also add interesting patterns or images to a paint job. Art supply stores and hobby shops carry stencils and paint pens.

Mac in a box

A Mac mini makeover doesn't have to be limited to changing colors or textures. You can also change the mini's shape and material by building a new case. Use wood, metal, or plastic, or adopt a found object as the new home.

It's difficult to build a new top casing that snaps into place like the old one. You would have to re-create the inside grooves to accept the plastic tabs. But you probably want a new shape anyway. For instance, you can use half of a soccer ball to create a hemisphere mini like the white-and-chrome table-lamp iMac.

You could put the entire mini inside a new case. Be sure to remove the top casing first for better cooling. Because you can use screws or a hinged door, your new mini enclosure can be easier to get into than the factory mini. You need holes for the ports and holes or slots for air cooling.

It's really annoying to spend a lot of time building a case only to find that the mini doesn't completely fit or that the portholes are in the wrong place. Building a full-scale model out of foam core can prevent this. When you perfect the model, use the walls of the model to create a paper template that you can use to cut your building material. This approach won't work with a soccer-ball mini, however. In that case, make sure that you have several soccer balls to use as prototypes.

Maxi Modding the Outer Case

A decal with the look of real wood still looks like a decal. In the following sections, I show you how to remove the shiny white plastic top from the aluminum casing. After you remove it, replace it with real wood, metal, or acrylic. Or, don't replace it at all.

The white plastic top is attached to a metal electromagnetic interference (EMI) shield, as shown in Figure 17-3. Small plastic rivets fix the plastic sheet to the EMI shield. The EMI shield is held in place by metal tabs that fit into slots in the aluminum case. To remove the plastic top of the outer casing, you basically push on the metal outer shielding until it pops out. You are likely to bend the shielding and break some of the plastic rivets in the process.

If you're adding a solid top, such as metal or another type of plastic, you should plan on replacing the EMI shielding under the new covering.

Removing and replacing the plastic top

Apple did not design the white center plastic sheet at the top of the outer casing to be removed. This doesn't mean that you can't remove it, but doing so is more difficult than opening the mini. You don't need to cut anything to remove the white top, but you do have to bend some things.

Figure 17-3:
The white plastic top is attached to the EMI shield with small plastic rivets.

If you change your mind after you remove the top or are just removing it to paint it, you can reassemble it, with difficulty. Reassembly isn't an issue, of course, if you're replacing the top with something new.

Removing the top of the outer casing

If you're ready, here's how to hack the outer casing:

1. **Place the outer casing upside down.**

2. **Remove the metal tape, as shown in Figure 17-4, that is in each corner of the inside of the casing.**

   If you are planning to replace the metal EMI shield, take care not to rip or mangle the metal tape. This is not easy, because it is easily ripped. If you want to keep it, try scraping it with a knife blade to lift a bit of the end and then pull it up with a pair of tweezers. Another method that works well is to push down on the EMI shield with your thumbs to loosen the tape and then slip the tweezers behind the tape.

3. **Pick up the outer casing and place your thumbs in the two corners near the rear of the outer casing.**

   The rear is the side with the big notch, as shown in Figure 17-4.

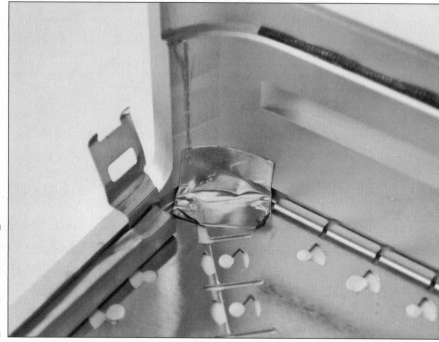

Figure 17-4:
Pull up the
metal tape
in the
corners of
the casing.

4. **Push down with your thumbs, slowly and steadily, until the edge of the top pops out of the aluminum frame, as shown in Figure 17-5.**

   If you plan on reinstalling the plastic top, try to break as few plastic rivets as possible. (These are the rivets that hold the plastic top to the EMI shield.) In Figure 17-5, you can see that because some of the rivets have broken, the corner of the top has separated from the EMI shield. You *will* break some of these — it's unavoidable.

5. **Turn the outer casing right side up, as shown in Figure 17-5.**

6. **Lift the open end of the top and tilt it back until the top is clear of the aluminum frame.**

Separating the plastic from the EMI shield

If you're not going to use the plastic top, but want to reuse the metal EMI shield, you can separate the two. Slip a screwdriver in between the two and carefully pop the plastic rivets as you pull the two apart. You may mangle the shield a bit, but it's stiff enough to resist major crimps.

You can't go back after this step. After the rivets are popped, you can't get them back in.

Figure 17-5:
When you push with your thumbs, the top pops out.

Replacing the plastic top or the EMI shield

If you need to replace the plastic top/EMI shield assembly because you painted it, or if you're replacing the metal EMI shield by itself under a new top, the following sections are for you.

Replacing the top is more difficult than removing it. You must pop the tabs in the slots on all four sides of the interior of the outer casing. Refer to Figure 17-5 to see the tabs. They are very stiff and not easily bent.

The replacement procedure is a little different for the plastic top/EMI shield assembly and for the EMI shield alone.

Plastic top/EMI shield assembly

The best way to get the top assembly back in place is to reverse the removal procedure. With the outer casing upside down, place the tab in the groove under the optical disc slot. Be careful of the rubber flange that surrounds the optical disc slot. It's easy to pinch this rubber under the tabs.

With the tabs in the groove under the optical disc slot, pivot the assembly down to try to get all the tabs in the grooves. I found that I was not able to force in the two tabs closest to the optical disc slot on either side. I ended up using a pair of pliers to bend these tabs up and out of the way.

It takes some manipulation to get the tabs on opposites sides into their grooves. Pressing down on the center of the metal side to bend it enables you to succeed. This action also pops some more of the rivets, unfortunately.

If you've popped too many of the plastic rivets and the plastic top won't stay down, use some double-sided tape in between the top and the EMI shield.

Shield alone

With the absence of the plastic top, the metal EMI shield is more flexible and can bend more, which makes it easier to get the tabs in the grooves. You also don't have to worry about popping the plastic rivets, which means you can bend it farther without fear of damage.

Start the process by placing the metal tabs in the groove under the optical disc slot. Pivot the assembly down to try to get all the tabs in the grooves. You should be able to manipulate the shield into place without resorting to bending any of the tabs with pliers.

Adding a new top to the outer casing

The following sections consider using wood, metal, and acrylic for the new top, as well as using no top on the outer casing.

The woody mini

There's nothing like the look of real wood, especially on a computer.

To create the wood top for the aluminum frame, use the plastic top that you previously removed as a pattern to draw on your wood. I'm sure that Norm Abram (www.newyankee.com) would have the best idea about how to cut the wood with rounded corners. A jigsaw would work if you have one. After the top is cut to the right size and the edges are sanded, stain it and apply varnish or another top coat.

If you want the wood top to fit flush with the aluminum rim the way that the old plastic top did, install the old EMI shield first. Use ⅛"-thick wood, which can rest on the EMI shield. To keep the wood from falling out, place some double-sided tape on the EMI shield on the edges, in the corner, and in the center. You can also use epoxy to cement the wood top to the metal shield. Use the epoxy sparingly at the corners and the center. Again, you should have the EMI shield fitted into the outer casing before gluing the wood to it.

Metal

Use metal on the top for an industrial look. Poke around your local hardware store for something you can use. A metal grate or wire mesh might work as well. Because the EMI shield helps to hold the top piece in place, you should use it even with a metal top.

The visible mini

You've ditched the plastic top and you're proud of it; you don't have to add a replacement. The visible mini (see Figure 17-6) is an interesting mod in itself, acting as a window into the mini. Just replace the aluminum casing. Another variation to this mod is to cut out the Apple icon from the plastic top and glue it to the DVD drive.

One benefit to this mod is that it makes it easier to remove the outer casing. Instead of inserting a putty knife into the tight crack on the bottom, you can move the plastic tabs from the top, where they are now visible. Use a plastic tool, though. You shouldn't stick metal into the guts of your mini.

One trick you can do with a topless outer casing is to replace the RAM module without removing the casing. Just stick the flat end of a pencil into the space on either side of the RAM module and press down on the tabs to release the module.

With this mod, and with the next, you won't be replacing the EMI shielding. The metal shield is designed to keep stray EM signals from interfering with other electronic devices, and to keep EMI out of the mini to prevent problems. In practice, however, I've operated many a computer, including the mini, with the top off for weeks at a time without a problem.

The acrylic mini

This mod is a lot like the previous one in that it is also a visible mini. Here, though, you add a cover — this time, a transparent one. The difficulty is cutting the round corners. You can use a router. If you don't have one, you can simply cut the corners off.

An interesting variant on this is to add a thick acrylic layer to the top. Newer Technology's NuClear Mini ($25, www.newertech.com/macmini) is a 1.5-inch-thick solid acrylic base that's meant to sit under the Mac mini. You can scrape the feet off and place it on top of the visible mini. Another model, the NuBlue Mini ($30), includes an LED embedded in the acrylic.

Plastic Smith (www.plasticsmith.com) offers similar products. The Mini Skirt ($20) is half as thick as the NuClear Mini, at ¾". You can also buy a version with embedded LEDs called the Mini Skirt Glow ($35).

These are all fairly hefty, so when placing one on top of the topless Mac mini casing, you may not have to attach it to the outer casing.

Chapter 18

Mac OS X Hacks and Mods

● ●

In This Chapter

▶ Using Terminal to type commands

▶ Hacking the Finder and the Dock

▶ Improving iTunes

▶ Getting more utilities for modding

● ●

Hardware isn't the only thing you can mod on your Mac mini. You can also mod your Mac mini's operating system software, Mac OS X.

I'm not talking about setting preferences or changing icon sizes. I'm talking about hacking the way Mac OS X works, adding new options and removing others, abandoning the way Apple tells you to do things, and even changing the look of Mac OS X.

This chapter describes some of the hacks and mods that you can create using the Mac OS X command line and third-party utilities. As with some of the other mods in this part, there is danger lurking in these methods. Even if you do everything right, there's a chance your particular system may experience some flaky behavior.

None of these hacks are permanent. For command-line hacks, I show you how to undo them to get back to what came with your mini. Before you install a utility, check to see whether you can uninstall it. An installer program may have an uninstall option, or you may have some other method of getting rid of it.

Now that I've warned you properly, let me say that I'm confident that none of these hacks will blow up your system, and that they should work in Mac OS X v.4, Tiger.

Hacking in Terminal

One of the semi-secrets of the Mac that Apple doesn't trumpet is the command line in Mac OS X, the operating system that runs the Mac mini. Yes, the company that brought the graphical user interface to the masses has a command line in its operating system. As it turns out, the command line is very handy for hacking Mac OS X.

You access the command line in the Terminal application, which resides in the Utilities folder in the Applications folder. Terminal provides a complete Unix command-line environment, as shown in Figure 18-1.

Figure 18-1:
The Terminal application gives you access to your mini's command line.

Be sure to type the commands in this chapter exactly as they are printed here. To successfully execute the commands, here are some things to remember:

✔ Unix commands are case sensitive. If you ignore a capital letter or capitalize something that is supposed to be lowercase, the command won't work.

✔ Remember to type spaces in between the terms. Spaces separate the different "ingredients" of a command.

✔ Press Return after each line that you type. This sends the command to the operating system, which then executes the command.

Terminal lets you have multiple command-line windows open at the same time. This is useful if you have a lot of data displayed in a window but need to run some more commands.

To find out more about the commands that you can use in Terminal, check out *The Mac OS X Command Line: Unix Under the Hood,* by Kirk McElhearn (Sybex).

Hacking the Finder and Dock

If you're new to Mac OS X, the Finder is the environment that includes the Desktop and the windows that display your files and folders. Apple gives you some settings that you can change, but you can do much more with text commands.

 If typing commands isn't your thing, the free TinkerTool (www.bresink.de/ osx/TinkerTool.html) does several of the mods described in the following sections, including adding a Quit command to the Finder menu and hiding the Dock.

Adding a Quit command to the Finder menu

Just like iTunes, Word, or Nanosaur, the Finder is an application that runs in Mac OS X, with one big difference: The Finder doesn't quit. If you use the Force Quit command on the Finder, it temporarily quits and then automatically relaunches.

Most of the Finder hacks that you write in the Terminal application require you to restart the Finder. By default, Mac OS X gives you one way to restart the Finder: Open the Force Quit dialog from the Apple menu (or press Option+⌘+Esc), select the Finder, and then click the Force Quit button.

If you were already in Terminal hacking Mac OS X, it would be convenient to be able to relaunch the Finder with a command without bringing up this dialog. You can do exactly that with this simple command, followed by pressing Return:

```
killall Finder
```

The Finder briefly quits, with Finder windows disappearing only to reappear seconds later. Other open applications (including Terminal) are unaffected.

That's not bad, but if you're not already in Terminal, it's kind of a pain. With another simple command, you can add a Quit command to the Finder's application menu, just as you find in every other application. Type this in Terminal:

```
defaults write com.apple.finder QuitMenuItem yes
killall Finder
```

Of course, the second line merely restarts the Finder, as required for the hack to take effect. When you go to the Finder, click the Finder menu. A Quit Finder command appears at the bottom, as shown in Figure 18-2. The Finder also gains the standard keyboard Quit command, ⌘+Q.

Figure 18-2:
Add a Quit
command to
the Finder
menu.

To revert to the standard Finder menu, type the same command, but use `no` instead of `yes`.

Right and left justification of the Dock

Mac OS X puts the Dock smack-dab in the middle of the bottom of your screen. The Dock setting in the Apple menu lets you move it to the left or right sides of the screen, but it's still center-justified.

Here's a hack that changes the Dock's center justification to a right/left justification (or to an up/down justification if the Dock is positioned vertically on one side of the screen).

To position the Dock at the right side of the bottom of the screen (or to give a bottom-justification if the Dock is vertical), follow these steps:

1. **Type the following line in Terminal:**

   ```
   defaults write com.apple.Dock pinning end
   ```

2. **Launch Activity Monitor in the Utilities folder.**

   You need to use the Activity Monitor to do the equivalent of force-quitting the Dock.

3. **Locate Dock in the Process Name column, and click the Quit Process button.**

   This will quit and relaunch the Dock. The Dock briefly disappears and reappears in the new position.

To position the Dock with left justification (or top justification if the Dock is vertical), type the following line in Terminal:

```
defaults write com.apple.Dock pinning start
```

Then relaunch the Dock.

To restore the Dock's original center justification, type this line in Terminal:

```
defaults write com.apple.Dock pinning middle
```

Then relaunch the Dock.

Top Dock, disappearing Dock

Not everyone is a fan of the Dock. It can get in the way, and you have alternatives, including the ⌘+Tab keyboard command for switching between open applications, the sidebar for launching items, and third-party utilities such as DragThing ($29, www.dragthing.com) and TinkerTool (free, www.bresink.de/osx/TinkerTool.html).

The Hiding feature doesn't really get the Dock out of the way. It makes the Dock temporarily disappear, but then up it pops just as you're reaching for an item in an application or on the desktop.

Here are two ways to get rid of the Dock. The first is complete removal. The second keeps the Dock in case you want to get it back, but makes it more difficult to unhide a hidden dock.

Removing the Dock

To completely remove the Dock, follow these steps:

1. **Type the following two lines in Terminal:**

   ```
   cd /System/Library/CoreServices
   sudo mv Dock.app ~/Documents/
   ```

2. **Log out from the Apple menu, and then log back in.**

When the Finder comes back up, the Dock will be gone.

Should you want to bring the Dock back, follow these steps:

1. **Type the following two lines in Terminal:**

   ```
   cd /System/Library/CoreServices
   sudo mv ~/Documents/Dock.app
   ```

2. **Log out from the Apple menu, and then log back in.**

If you do remove the Dock, you may want to create a Trash icon on the desktop, as I describe in the section "Creating a desktop and sidebar Trash icon," later in this chapter.

The next hack makes a hidden Dock much harder to bring back.

Moving the Dock to the top, making the unhiding area smaller

You can hack the Dock to dramatically shrink the activation area that causes a hidden Dock to reappear. In fact, you can shrink this activation area to a line that is a single pixel in width. This means that the Dock won't appear unless the tip of the cursor falls exactly on that one-pixel-wide line, making it less likely you'll unhide the Dock accidentally.

To do this, you need to use a Unix command to move the Dock to the top of the screen, where you normally don't have the option of putting it. Here's what you do:

1. **Launch Terminal, type the following line, and press Return:**

   ```
   defaults write com.apple.Dock orientation -string top
   ```

2. **Launch Activity Monitor in the Utilities folder.**

   You need to use the Activity Monitor to do the equivalent of force-quitting the Dock.

3. **Locate Dock in the Process Name column, and click the Quit Process button.**

   The Dock moves to the top of the screen, just under the menu bar, as shown in Figure 18-3.

Figure 18-3:
When you hack the Dock to the top, it takes on unique hiding properties.

4. **Switch to the Finder, click the Apple menu, select Dock, and then select Turn Hiding On.**

The Dock hides. To bring it up, you have to move the cursor over the correct pixel. This is tough to do accidentally, so the Dock is as good as gone.

To bring back the Dock, just go to the Apple menu and select a position (left, right, or bottom).

Creating a desktop and sidebar Trash icon

If you've used Windows or the old Mac OS 9, you may have fond memories of a Trash can (or Recycling Bin) on the desktop. In Mac OS X, when you hide (or get rid of) the Dock, it takes the Trash with it. Yes, you can still delete files by selecting them and pressing ⌘+Delete. But you can also do better.

You can hack Mac OS X to create a Trashcan of sorts, one that can live on the desktop, in the sidebar of Finder windows, or in the toolbar of Finder windows. To do this, you create a folder, assign it a folder action (an AppleScript), and then give it a Trash-like icon.

Creating the folder action

First, create an AppleScript folder action to enable a folder to move items to the Trash:

1. **Open Script Editor, which is located in the** `/Applications/Apple Script/` **folder.**

2. **Type the following in the Script Editor window:**

```
on adding folder items to this_folder after receiving
        these_items
tell application "Finder"
repeat with i in these_items
move i to trash
end repeat
end tell
end adding folder items to
```

3. **Save the script with the name Trash to the** `/Library/Scripts/ Folder Action Scripts` **folder.**

Creating the folder with icon

Next, create the folder that will act as the surrogate Trash and give it a Trash icon:

1. **Create a new folder on the desktop by switching to the Finder and choosing File⇨New Folder.**

2. **Name the new folder** `Trash`.

3. **Click the Trash icon in the Dock to open it and press ⌘+I to bring up the Trash Info window, as shown in Figure 18-4.**

Figure 18-4:
Copy the
Trash icon
from the
upper-left
corner of
the Trash
Info
window.

4. **Click the Trash icon and copy it.**

5. **Click the new** `Trash` **folder on the Desktop and press ⌘+I to bring up its info window.**

6. **Click the generic folder icon and paste the Trash icon.**

The folder will have a Trash icon. The icon doesn't change when you empty the Trash, however. The new `Trash` folder will always have an empty icon or a full icon, depending on which one you chose. If you copied the Trash icon when the Trash was empty, you get the empty icon. If you copied the icon when the Trash had items in it, you get the full icon.

Attaching the AppleScript to the folder

Finally, attach the AppleScript to the folder as a folder action:

1. **Control+click the new** `Trash` **folder on the desktop and select Enable Folder Actions.**

2. **Control+click the new** `Trash` **folder a second time and choose Attach a Folder Action.**

3. **Browse to the** `/Library/Scripts/Folder Action Scripts` **folder and choose Trash.**

Using the new Trash folder

You can now drop items into your desktop Trash to delete them.

To add the `Trash` folder to the Finder Sidebar (as shown in Figure 18-5), just drag it there. To add it to the Finder toolbar, Control+click the toolbar and drag the `Trash` folder to it.

You can buy a utility that gives you a desktop Trash icon that changes when it's emptied. I wouldn't buy a utility just for this purpose, but these utilities provide other functions as well. Check out iCan (`www.kanzu.com/`) and DragThing (`www.dragthing.com`).

Figure 18-5:
A Trash in a
Finder
window.

Making hidden apps look different in the Dock

Open applications in the Dock look the same whether they are hidden (with the Hide command in the Application menu) or not. The following hack makes hidden applications transparent in the Dock so that you can differentiate them from visible open applications. Here's how to do it:

1. **Launch Terminal, type the following line, and press Return:**

   ```
   defaults write com.apple.dock showhidden -bool yes
   ```

2. **Launch the Activity Monitor in the Utilities folder.**

   You need to use the Activity Monitor to do the equivalent of force-quitting the Dock.

3. **Locate Dock in the Process Name column, and click the Quit Process button.**

   The Dock quits and automatically relaunches.

Figure 18-6 shows several open applications. The transparent icons, iTunes and Address Book, are hidden. Safari and iCal are solid, and therefore are not hidden. As always, clicking the icon of a hidden application brings it to the front, in which case its Dock icon becomes solid.

Figure 18-6:
With this
hack, you
can tell that
iTunes and
Address
Book are
hidden.

Showing invisible folders

The Finder hides a lot of files and folders, including Unix folders and the music files on mounted iPods. You can show the Finder who is boss: Force it to show invisible files and folders by following these steps:

1. **Type the following line in Terminal:**

```
defaults write com.apple.finder AppleShowAllFiles
    -bool yes
```

2. **Relaunch (force-quit) the Finder.**

When the Finder returns, it displays all the Unix directories, such as /bin and /usr. This can be useful for getting access to a file you want to edit in TextEdit instead of Terminal, or just for browsing folders to see where a file is located.

The modified Finder also shows music files on an iPod. They're in a set of numbered folders beginning with *F*, which are in a Music folder, which is in the iPod_Control folder.

There is a danger to showing all the invisible files. If you accidentally delete or change the wrong file or folder, or even change the name of a file or folder, you could prevent the Mac mini from working properly or even prevent it from booting.

Should you want to hide all the previously invisible files, use the same command as before, but use no for yes, like this:

```
defaults write com.apple.finder AppleShowAllFiles -bool no
```

Then relaunch (force-quit) the Finder.

An iTunes Mod

iTunes has a great marketing scheme for the iTunes Music Store: those little arrows next to the names of songs, artists, and albums. Click an artist's name, and iTunes takes you to a page that contains nothing but songs by that artist. If you hold down Option while you click an arrow, iTunes does something useful — it brings up all the artists (or songs or albums) that are in your Library.

I don't know about you, but I need to go to my own Library far more often than I need to go to the iTunes Music Store. That's why I mod all my Macs to switch the behavior of these arrows. Follow these steps:

1. **Quit iTunes if it's already open.**

2. **Type the following line in Terminal (and then press Return):**

```
defaults write com.apple.iTunes invertStoreLinks -bool
    YES
```

When you launch iTunes, clicking any of the arrows displays a list of songs from your own Library. If you want the arrows to take you to the Music Store, hold down Option while you click.

If for some reason you want to revert to the default behavior, type the line shown in the previous list, but use NO instead of YES.

Utilities That Change the Look and Feel

Mac OS X is nice enough, but you may want to customize it in ways that aren't offered by Apple. For instance, you can add features or looks that are similar to Windows, or do things a different way. In earlier sections in this chapter, I mention a few utilities that can make this happen, including TinkerTool (www. bresink.de/osx/TinkerTool.html), iCan (www.kanzu.com/), and Drag-Thing (www.dragthing.com). In the following sections, I show you a few more. Most of these utilities let you try them out for free for a period of time.

Utilities that mod Mac OS X often break or cause flaky behavior of the operating system when you install an upgrade to Mac OS X. Be prepared to uninstall the utility when you upgrade the OS, and wait for the developer to upgrade the utility.

Adding files and folders to the Apple menu

The only applications and files that you can open from the Mac OS X Apple menu are recently opened apps and files. Install Unsanity's Fruit Menu ($10, www.unsanity.com), and you can customize the Apple menu, adding folders and removing standard items. In this way, the Apple menu functions similarly to the Windows Start menu, except that the Apple menu is on top of the screen instead of at the bottom.

Fruit Menu lets you put any folder or drive on the Apple menu. You can then open folders inside these folders with hierarchical menus. A useful setup is to add your home folder and your Application folder to the Apple menu, which lets you open most of the files you need from one place.

Fruit Menu also lets you add System Preferences to the Apple menu. When you click the Apple menu, a hierarchical menu appears, listing all the System Preferences items.

Getting rid of brushed metal

I've never understood Apple's reasoning for using the brushed-metal look on Finder windows and in other places throughout Mac OS X. If you like it, that's great. If you don't, you're stuck with it — unless, that is, you use Unsanity's ShapeShifter ($20, www.unsanity.com). In place of the brushed-metal look, you can assign one of many themes, such as iT5. Its look is similar to that of iTunes 5 and 6. You download themes from within ShapeShifter and make the assignments from System Preferences.

ShapeShifter doesn't stop at windows, however. It modifies just about every aspect of Mac OS X, including buttons, menus, and dialogs.

Macintosh Explorer

If you come from the Windows world, you may rue the fact that Mac OS X doesn't include an equivalent to Windows Explorer on PCs. Rage Software's Macintosh Explorer ($16, www.ragesw.com/) gives you the file-browsing and -management features of Windows Explorer, but with a Mac feel. Mac users who have never clicked a Windows Start menu may also like the structured view of your files that Macintosh Explorer gives you. It supports tabbed browsing to go to different views of subsets of files.

Macintosh Explorer comes with an arsenal of file-management tools, such as the ability to change the names of batches of files, and you can preview thumbnails of batches of graphics files all at once.

Chapter 19

Modding for Bigger Form Factor Hard Drives

*T*hroughout this book are descriptions of using the Mac mini for purposes other than what Apple had in mind. One of these is as a server: an audio server, a movie server, or a server of whopping-big files. The main drawback to the Mac mini as a server is the relatively slow speed and small storage capacity of the internal hard drive.

Chapter 7 describes replacing the Mac mini's 2.5-inch drive with a faster, slightly bigger 2.5-inch drive. This chapter describes replacing the Mac mini's 2.5-inch drive with a way-faster, way-bigger 3.5-inch drive.

Practical? Well, upgrading the 2.5-inch drive is easier, and adding an external FireWire drive is a lot easier. But this hack is about speed; it's a maxi-mod. Sometimes we must mod because we can. I hack, therefore I am.

Like some of the other extreme mods in Part VI, this is a potentially dangerous mod. If you get the pins wrong, you could burn out both the hard drive and the Mac mini's motherboard. So please, don't ignore the warnings in this chapter, read everything, and proceed with caution. Or, just read for the fun of it.

What's Involved

The Mac mini is designed to contain a notebook computer hard drive, known as a 2.5-inch drive. The name refers to the size of the platters spinning inside the drive. The advantage of this type of drive is its small size, but the drawbacks are small capacity and slow speed. This chapter describes how to hack the mini to accept a bigger, faster 3.5-inch drive. There are several reasons why this is superior to upgrading the internal drive or adding an external FireWire drive:

- ✔ **Spin rate:** The 2.5-inch drives that Apple installs in Mac minis spin at 4,800 rpm or 5,600 rpm. The 3.5-inch drives spin at 7,200 rpm. But so do other 2.5-inch drives and FireWire drives, so this by itself isn't reason enough for this mod.

- ✔ **The IDE interface:** This mod uses the internal ATA/IDE interface, which is faster than the 400-megabits-per-second (Mbps) FireWire interface. Not only are you going to install files on this drive, but you are also going to boot the Mac mini from it. A Mac mini booted from a FireWire drive runs slower than one booted from an ATA/IDE drive.

- ✔ **Capacity:** The 3.5-inch drives are available in capacities that are hundreds of gigabytes larger than 2.5-inch drives.

- ✔ **Big capacity, small bucks:** With 2.5-inch drives, you're paying for the small size. Not so with 3.5-inchers, where you can get 400GB for just over $200.

That's the motivation.

To accomplish this, you remove the old 2.5-inch hard drive and connect new cables and connectors for the 3.5-inch drive. The following sections describe what's involved in doing this.

Size

You can see from Figure 19-1 that the 3.5-inch drive, shown on the left, is significantly larger than the native 2.5-inch drive. There is just no way on this green planet that the replacement drive is going to fit inside the Mac mini. But while the new drive is going to be physically located outside the mini, it is still technically an "internal" drive because it uses the internal IDE interface. This also means that you have to get a cable from the connector inside the mini to the drive outside of it.

Power

The Mac mini has no provisions to power a 3.5-inch drive. You could try to steal power by hacking the mini's motherboard with a soldering iron. But I just didn't have the guts to ask you to do that when an easy, cheap solution exists: Buy an external drive housing and power the drive from that. It's not a lot to ask for when you're already keeping the drive outside the Mac. There's no gee-whiz factor, but it works.

Figure 19-1:
A 3.5-inch hard drive is a lot bigger than a 2.5-inch unit, more so than the names imply.

Converting between IDE connectors

The Mac mini has an ATA100 bus that supports the DVD drive and internal hard drive. It's a bus that can support a 3.5-inch drive using an IDE cable. But here's the rub: 2.5-inch and 3.5-inch drives use different IDE connectors. Figure 19-2 shows the pins of the 3.5-inch hard drive and the female receptacle like the one in the Mac mini.

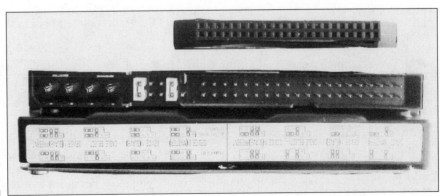

Figure 19-2:
The challenge is converting between different IDE connectors.

The task here is to use some combination of adapters and cables that keeps the right signals on the right pins. For example, the signal that appears on pin

1 of the connector in the Mac mini has to get to pin 1 on the hard drive. If that signal gets to pin 2 instead, you can damage both the hard drive and the motherboard.

Gathering Parts

Here is the parts list for this project:

- **2.5-to-3.5-inch (44-to-40-pin) IDE adapter:** This is the "something" that converts from the smaller 44-pin female IDE connector in the Mac mini to the larger 40-pin male connector on the 3.5-inch hard drive. This can be one of the following:

    - A special connector or cable that you build yourself.

    - A rare connector that someone else builds for you. This is *not* a stock item.

- **3.5-inch hard drive:** It should be set as a "master" IDE drive, which is the default.

- **IDE ribbon cable:** If you have a converter connector in the Mac mini, you would use a standard 40-pin cable, as shown in Figure 19-3. You could also use a special converter cable here. This is described in the next section.

- **External 3.5-inch drive enclosure:** The main purpose of this is to power the big drive. Because you are using an IDE interface to the Mac mini, it doesn't matter if the enclosure is USB or FireWire; buy whatever is cheaper or looks cooler. Just make sure that it comes with a power supply, either built-in or external, one that plugs into a wall. (These are sometimes called *kits.*) Good sources include Tom's Hardware Guide (www.tomshardware.com) and PC Pitstop (www.pc-pitstop.com/external_enclosures/).

Chapter 7 describes putting your old internal hard drive into an external FireWire case. You may still want to do that, but remember, you need a 2.5-inch FireWire hard drive enclosure. For the purpose of powering a big enclosure, be sure to order a *3.5-inch* enclosure.

For the best-looking, space-saving enclosure, look at the NewerTech miniStack (www.newertech.com), an enclosure that fits right under your Mac mini and has the same aluminum finish. It costs $100 but has built-in USB and FireWire hubs, and it's quiet. Remember, though, you must cut a slot in it to get the IDE cable into it from the Mac mini.

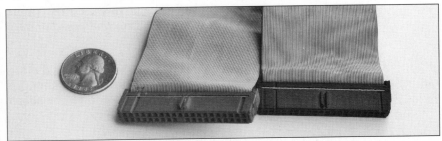

Obtaining a 44-to-40-pin converter

In order to connect the 3.5-inch drive to the mini, you need a cable or connector with a male 44-pin IDE connector to plug into the Mac mini and a female 40-pin IDE connector to plug into the 3.5-inch drive. The job of converting between the two different-sized IDE connectors is not just to enable you plug everything in. You also need to keep the path of the pins straight. This is not as easy as it sounds.

The connector for 2.5-inch drives has 44 pins; the connector for 3.5-inch drives is bigger, but has 40 pins. Both have the same 40 data and control pins in the same locations. The 2.5-inch-drive IDE connector has 4 extra pins for power. That's because 2.5-inch drives are powered through the IDE connector. The 3.5-inch drives don't have these 4 pins because they are powered through a separate connector. This means you can ignore the 4 extra pins on the 2.5-inch drive connector.

The 40 pins that both types have in common are in the same place relative to each other. Your job is to keep it that way when you connect the two together.

What doesn't work

The 2.5-inch internal drive used in the Mac mini is the standard size used in notebook computers. It is not uncommon for people to want to use a notebook hard drive in a desktop PC. Because of this, you can find ample availability of converter connectors and cables that let you plug a 2.5-inch drive into a PC motherboard's 3.5-inch IDE connector.

Unfortunately, this solution does not work for the reverse situation, putting a 3.5-inch drive in a notebook computer, which, in this case, is your Mac mini. Figure 19-4 shows one of these connectors. You can tell right away that it's the wrong cable because of the power cable hanging off of it. (The power connector is meant to direct power from a PC's motherboard to the connector to power the 2.5-inch drive.)

You can also see that the gender is wrong. The small end, the 44-pin end, is female, but so is the connector in the Mac mini. The temptation is to add a male/male gender changer, shown in Figure 19-4, to get the adapter to plug into the mini. Avoid this temptation.

The problem is that a gender changer mirrors the pins, which has the effect of switching the placement of the two rows so that pin 1 is where pin 2 is expected. Plugging in a 3.5-inch drive with this connector setup and powering up the Mac mini can cause permanent damage to both the mini and the hard drive. Do not try the setup in Figure 19-4 at home.

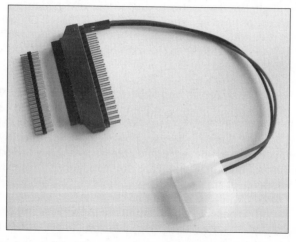

Figure 19-4:
Beware:
This
converter
adapter and
a gender
changer
don't work.

This is tough to visualize, but you can think of it as taking a cable and connector and rotating one of them 180 degrees. You'd discover that pin 1 on one connector meets pin 2 on the other. This can fry your motherboard.

Buying a converter that does work

If you Google around, you'll find plenty of adapters that don't work, like the one in Figure 19-4. What you need is a cable or connector with the small 44-pins (male) on one end and the bigger 40-pins (female) on the other end, but which does not switch the two rows. This kind of converter is very hard to find; it is not a standard part.

In fact, it's so difficult to locate that in my research for this book, I was able to find only two sources of converters that work, both in Australia. One source is an Australian company called Unitech Electronics Pty. Ltd. (www.unitechelectronics.com). It sells an IDE cable with a male 44-pin IDE connector on one side and a female 40-pin IDE connector on the other. The cable is designed to let you connect a 3.5-inch drive to a notebook computer, which is what you really are doing here, with the mini playing the role of the notebook. The part number for the cable is C01220, and it costs $45 Australian, or about $35 US.

Even if you're going to build your own cable, it's worth taking a look at the diagram of the C01220 cable at Unitech's Web site. It shows you why its cable works for this chapter's mod.

You could have a similar cable built to order at many computer cable companies. Just tell them you want to connect a 3.5-inch drive to a notebook computer. It won't be cheap, however, especially if you need only one.

The second source I found is not a company, but an Australian Mac mini modder named Adam Eberbach. He built an IDE adapter connector for plugging in a 3.5-inch drive into the Mac mini. It has male pins on both sides, and plugs into the Mac mini on one side and a standard 40-pin IDE ribbon cable on the other side. The connector is more than just a straight gender changer; it crosses the pin signals that the signals go through to the right pin.

Adam originally built one converter for his own use, but now offers to sell you one for $23. Adam isn't selling these on a Web site, but he did give me permission to print his e-mail address. If you'd like one of Adam's adapters, you can e-mail him at aeberbach@hotmail.com.

Growing your own converter connector

To wire your own IDE connector, you need to avoid the mirror-image trap that I describe in the previous section, and make sure that the correct pins route through. With some connector and circuit board stock, you can build a converter connector like the one from Adam Eberbach described in the previous section. It would plug into the Mac mini and a standard 40-pin IDE ribbon cable. It would have to be more than just a straight gender changer; you need to cross the pin signals.

You can think of this converter as connecting the two IDE connectors in Figures 19-5 and 19-6. The one in Figure 19-5 is a standard 40-pin IDE cable leading to the 3.5-inch hard drive. The connector in Figure 19-6 is the connector in the Mac mini.

Pin 1   Cable key   Pin 39

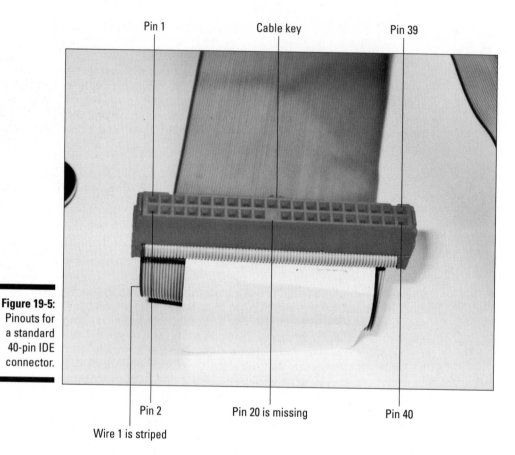

Figure 19-5:
Pinouts for
a standard
40-pin IDE
connector.

Pin 2   Pin 20 is missing   Pin 40

Wire 1 is striped

Figure 19-6 shows a 44-pin IDE connector on the interconnect board in the internal frame. This is a view with the hard drive removed; the DVD drive is at the bottom. Pin 1 is the pin in the lower right in this view. It's marked "J1" on the interconnect board. Pin 2 is in the upper right, pin 43 is in the lower left, and pin 44 is in the upper left.

Table 19-1 lists what is on each pin. This is purely for reference, just in case you need it. What's really important in making your connector converter is making sure that pin 1 goes to pin 1, pin 2 goes to pin 2, and so forth.

It's a good idea to test your creation with a voltmeter to make sure that pin 1 on one side reaches pin 1 on the other side.

Pin 44   Pin 2

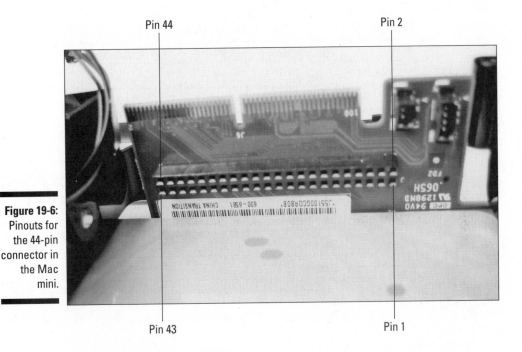

Figure 19-6:
Pinouts for
the 44-pin
connector in
the Mac
mini.

Pin 43   Pin 1

Assembling the Mod

After you get the issue of the cable converters out of the way, the procedure of replacing the internal drive with a 3.5-inch IDE drive is a lot like
the straight replacement of the internal drive with another 2.5-inch drive,
which is described in Chapter 7. The difference is that the 3.5-incher
doesn't fit inside the Mac mini.

Transferring data and settings

When you install the new 3.5-inch drive, it's going to be blank. You can install
Mac OS X and the Apple software from the Restore discs that came with the
Mac mini. You can also move data directly from your old 2.5-inch drive by
installing it in an external 2.5-inch FireWire enclosure.

Chapter 7 describes some of the different strategies that you can use to move
data and settings to the new drive. If you want to back up anything on your
drive, you need to do so before you take apart the Mac mini.

Table 19-1		**IDE Pinouts**	
Pin	*Description*	*Pin*	*Description*
1	Reset	23	-IOW
2	Ground	24	Ground
3	Data bit 7	25	-IOR
4	Data bit 8	26	Ground
5	Data bit 6	27	I/O channel ready
6	Data bit 9	28	SPSYNC: Cable select
7	Data bit 5	29	-DACK 3
8	Data bit 10	30	Ground
9	Data bit 4	31	RQ 14
10	Data bit 11	32	-IOCS 16
11	Data bit 3	33	Address bit 1
12	Data bit 12	34	-PDIAG
13	Data bit 2	35	Address bit 0
14	Data bit 13	36	Address bit 2
15	Data bit 1	37	-CS1FX
16	Data bit 14	38	-CS3FX
17	Data bit 0	39	-DA/SP
18	Data bit 15	40	Ground
19	Ground	41	+5 volts (Logic) (Optional)
20	Cable key (pin missing)	42	+5 volts (Motor) (Optional)
21	DRQ 3	43	Ground (Optional)
22	Ground	44	-Type (Optional)

Installing the cable and connectors in the Mac mini

After you have a 44-to-40-pin conversion scheme worked out, you can install the cables.

If you haven't read the earlier section "Obtaining a 44-to-40-pin converter" on creating this conversion, go back and read it before proceeding. It's for your own good. Then follow these steps to install the cable and connectors:

1. **Remove the Mac mini's outer casing, as I describe in Chapter 4.**

2. **Remove the internal frame, as Chapter 5 describes.**

3. **Remove the hard drive from the interconnect board, as I describe in Chapter 7.**

4. **Plug your 44-to-40-pin converter or cable into the 44-pin connector on the Mac mini's interconnect board.**

   This is located on the internal frame (refer to Figure 19-6).

5. **Fold the ribbon cable so that it makes the turns required to route from the interconnect board, up through the space between the DVD drive and the RAM module, and out.**

   Figure 19-7 shows that this required one diagonal fold and two right-angle bends.

6. **Carefully replace the internal frame on the Mac mini, taking care to route the folded ribbon cable over the RAM module, as shown in Figure 19-8.**

   Note that power has not yet been supplied to the drive.

Figure 19-7:
Fold and bend the ribbon cable to create 90-degree turns.

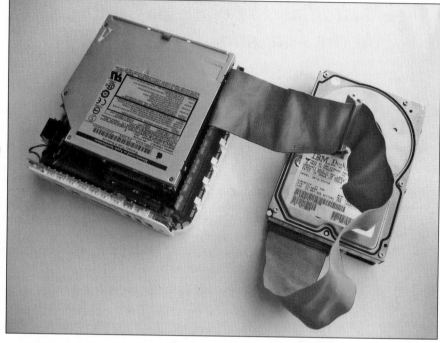

Figure 19-8:
The
installed
cable
comes
out of the
Mac mini
between
the RAM
and the
DVD drive.

7. **Replace the three screws that secure the internal frame to the bottom chassis, as Chapter 5 describes.**

As you can see from Figure 19-8, the Mac mini's cover doesn't have a design feature for the new drive. You have to either leave the cover off or lightly place the cover on top and carefully press down. Don't force it, or you'll damage the ribbon cable.

Modding the hard drive enclosure

The final step is to get power to the 3.5-inch drive. You can do that by installing it in a powered external 3.5-inch drive enclosure. Plug the enclosure's internal 4-pin power connector into the drive.

Of course, you're not using the USB or FireWire interface of the enclosure, so you have to cut a hole or slot in the enclosure to allow for the IDE ribbon cable. Where you do this depends on the enclosure, but you can fold the ribbon cable inside the enclosure to direct it to a place in the enclosure that's easy to cut. After you do this, you can screw the enclosure shut.

Chapter 20

Overclocking for a Faster Mac mini

In This Chapter

▶ Deciding to overclock your Mac mini

▶ Tools for overclocking

▶ Overclocking your Mac mini

▶ Reassembling and testing the Mac mini

*T*he need for speed is a demanding force. This book has descriptions of how to install a faster hard drive and how to increase performance with a bigger RAM module. In this chapter, I turn my attention to speeding up the processor. You can't replace the Mac mini's processor because it's soldered to the motherboard. But you can use a soldering iron to *overclock* the processor, that is, to make it run faster than normal. This means that you can take a lower-end 1.25-GHz Mac mini and turn it into a higher-end 1.42-GHz Mac mini — or faster.

Overclocking is not, however, like replacing your hard drive or RAM. I want to be clear that I am *not* urging you to overclock your Mac mini. This is one of the most extreme mods in this book. You face a great risk for a moderate performance gain — about 30 percent at most. But you gain a very high coolness factor. If you overclock correctly, it does work, and it gives you bragging rights as a techno wiz.

You should do this only if you've handled a soldering iron before. If you haven't, read Chapter 16 for information about soldering techniques and then practice on an old circuit board. Even if you have soldered before, a little warm-up practice beforehand couldn't hurt.

Processors and Clocking

The term *overclocking* comes from the measure of a processor's speed. The *clock rate,* or frequency, is the number of instructions that the processor can execute per second. For example, a processor with a clock speed of 1.25 GHz (gigahertz) can execute approximately one and a quarter billion instructions per second — mind-boggling, when you think about it.

Overclocking is a hardware setting that makes the processor run at a faster clock rate. It's a matter of resetting a set of jumper resistors from one position to another. With some processors in some computers, this is a simple matter of pulling out jumpers, each of which bridges two pins, and moving each jumper to another pair of pins.

It's not such a simple matter with the Mac mini. Here, overclocking requires you to use a soldering iron to remove tiny surface-mounted jumper resistors on the motherboard and then resolder them in a different position.

Why it works

Overclocking is possible because processors are manufactured with the ability to run at different clock rates, that is, the 1.25-GHz Mac mini uses the *same* processor as the 1.42-GHz Mac mini. The only difference is the setting of the jumpers on the motherboard.

Processors are manufactured with the ability to run at different clock rates. The manufacturer tests a sample of processors from a given batch to see at what clock rate most of them can run the most consistently. The manufacturer then labels the whole batch as running at that clock rate. Sometimes, a manufacturer labels a batch of faster-clock-rated processors at a lower clock rate because of the demand for the lower-speed processors.

Issues to consider

You take some risks when overclocking a processor. This risk is greater if you overclock to the maximum possible setting, so most experts don't recommend this.

The following sections discuss some problems that can occur with overclocking the Mac mini.

Instability

Overclocking can cause the processor to create errors in the instructions it executes. The result is instability or crashing of the computer. At below maximum clock rates, these types of problems don't usually occur. This is why I don't recommend overclocking to the highest setting.

Heat concerns

Overheating of the processor is another consideration. Executing more instructions per second creates more heat, and too much heat can cause the computer to malfunction and crash.

Overclocking the Mac mini won't require you to immerse it in liquid nitrogen or even add extra heat sinks or fans. But you must follow some precautions, which I list here:

 ✔ **When reassembling the Mac mini, make sure the motherboard is properly replaced.** The section "Reassembling the Mac mini," later in this chapter, describes this procedure.

 ✔ **Be careful where you place the Mac mini after you overclock it.** Don't block any of the air vents at the bottom. Because the mini dissipates heat partly through its outer casing, don't place anything on top of the Mac mini or directly adjacent to the sides.

Bungled soldering

You can cause hardware havoc if you solder the jumpers in the wrong place or if you bungle the soldering by applying excessive amounts of heat to the motherboard or by making incomplete soldered joints.

Tools You'll Need

The overclocking mod requires basic soldering tools, tools for taking the mini apart, and tools to deal with the small size of the jumpers. Here's a list of these tools:

 ✔ **Magnifying glass mounted on a stand:** The jumper resistors are small — *really* small. Unless your friends call you "Eagle Eye," a magnifying glass is clearly a requirement.

 ✔ **Small-tipped soldering iron, with a 1.5-mm tip or smaller:** Some irons have removable tips. (See Chapter 16 for more about soldering irons.)

   ✔ **Braided solder wick:** Also called a *desoldering braid,* this consists of braided wire and is used for removing solder. You need a narrow solder wick.

   ✔ **Flux solder wire:** This is the solder.

   ✔ **Precession tweezers:** Use these to pick up and replace the jumper resistors.

   ✔ **Small glass jar:** This is a good container in which you can place the jumpers when you remove them. A baby-food jar works well. Having a lid is a good idea.

   ✔ **Screwdrivers for disassembling the Mac mini:** You need a jeweler's Phillips #0 and a standard Phillips #1 screwdriver.

Performing the Mod

Although the heat sink is on the top side of the motherboard, the processor and the jumpers are on the bottom side. This means that you need to remove the motherboard to get at the processor and jumpers. The next step is to locate the jumper resistors and to remove some of them. Then, if necessary, you solder any needed jumpers back in a new configuration and reassemble the Mac mini.

Removing the motherboard

Overclocking is one of the few mods that require removing the Mac mini's motherboard.

Take all static-discharge precautions before handling the motherboard. After removing the outer casing, touch the DVD drive with the mini's power cable plugged in. Wear an antistatic wrist strap if you have one.

When you're sure that you're static-free, follow these steps to remove the motherboard:

1. **Remove the outer casing, as I describe in Chapter 4.**

2. **Remove the inner frame, as described in Chapter 5.**

3. **Remove the RAM module by pressing down on the tabs on either side of it, then lifting the module out.**

4. **Remove the screw that secures the motherboard.**

   This is visible in the upper-left corner of Figure 20-1.

Figure 20-1:
The screw that holds down the motherboard is in the upper left.

5. **Disconnect the power-on cable from the connector on the motherboard in the corner nearest to the heat sink.**

   This is visible in the lower-right corner of Figure 20-1.

6. **Disconnect the LED cable from the motherboard.**

   Pull up from the connector, not the cable.

   You can see the LED cable in the lower-left corner of Figure 20-1 and to the left of the battery in Figure 20-2.

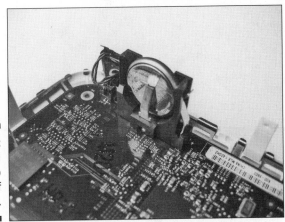

Figure 20-2:
The LED cable is to the left of the battery.

7. **Carefully push and hold the plastic LED panel a small distance away from the motherboard.**

   The LED panel is the vertical plastic rectangle to the left of the battery in Figure 20-2.

Don't put the LED panel out too far or it could break off.

8. **Carefully lift the motherboard from the side that the battery is on (the left side, as pictured in Figure 20-1).**

This pulls the port connects out of their holes in the back panel.

Locating the jumpers

Searching for the jumper resistors on the bottom of the motherboard gives meaning to the term *microelectronics*. These things make the screws used inside the Mac mini look like lag screws by comparison. I'm talking grains-of-sand, specks-of-dust small. Trying to find them by looking around the motherboard is like trying to find your house in a satellite photo of your county.

Although you may need a magnifying glass, you don't have to look at every square millimeter of the motherboard. In this section, I guide you to the jumpers by zooming in on that satellite photo — not of your county but of the Mac mini motherboard.

The first place to look is on the bottom side of the motherboard, as shown in Figure 20-3. (The graphics chip is also on the bottom side.) The jumpers reside in the upper-right quarter, as the board in Figure 20-3 is oriented.

Figure 20-3:
The bottom
side of the
motherboard.

The jumpers sit on the bottom side of the motherboard, opposite the processor and heat sink that are situated on the top side. Zooming in a bit, you can identify the jumper location on the bottom side by the four black plastic posts, which hold the top-side heat sink in place. With the port connectors facing to the right, this is the upper-right quadrant of the bottom side of the motherboard, as shown in Figure 20-4.

Figure 20-4: Zooming in on the neighborhood between the four posts.

Zooming in some more on the four posts, in Figure 20-5, you can see the resistors and their labels. Finally, in Figure 20-6, the four jumper resistors come into view. They are labeled R362, R358, R355, and R351. These labels are rotated 90 degrees in this view.

Figure 20-5: Zooming in on the four posts, you can see the tiny resistors and labels.

Figure 20-6:
The four
jumper
locations
have ID
numbers
written
vertically
above them.

Determining the jumper configuration

Before you take soldering iron to motherboard, check what jumper configuration you have and what configuration you want to create.

Each of the jumper locations — R362, R358, R355, and R351 — can either have a jumper resistor or can be left empty. Table 20-1 shows the combinations of empty and filled jumper locations that set the possible processor clock rates. An *X* indicates that jumper exists.

In Figure 20-6, the left jumper location (R362) is empty. The next location to the right has a jumper. The one to the right of that is empty, and the last location on the right has a jumper resistor in it. From Table 20-1, you can see that the processor in Figure 20-6 is set to 1.42 GHz.

Table 20-1	Placement of Jumpers and Clock-Rate Settings			
Clock Rate, GHz	*R362*	*R358*	*R355*	*R351*
1.25	X	X	X	Open
1.42	Open	X	Open	X
1.50	Open	Open	Open	Open
1.58	Open	X	Open	Open

The table shows that the easiest clock rate to configure is 1.50 GHz. To set this rate, you remove all the jumpers and don't replace any. This means that you don't have to solder any jumpers to the board.

To increase from 1.42 GHz to 1.58 GHz is also easy. Simply remove the jumper at R351, and you're done.

Desoldering a jumper

Check which jumpers you need to remove. You may not need to remove all of them. Each jumper is held in place by two solder joints, one on each side. To remove the jumper, you remove the solder at each joint.

It's a good idea to use a magnifying glass while removing jumpers. You don't want to remove the wrong resistors. You need two hands for desoldering, so you need to mount it to a stand of some sort, or even a desk lamp.

After taking precautions to free yourself of static, follow these steps to remove a jumper:

1. **Plug in the soldering iron and let it heat up.**
2. **Place the motherboard upside down.**
3. **Heat the solder wick with the soldering iron for about a half-second.**
4. **Place the solder wick on top of the solder joint on one side of the resistor.**

   Don't put the soldering-iron tip directly on the motherboard or the resistor when desoldering a joint. The direct heat from the iron could damage them.

5. **Place the tip of the hot soldering iron on top of the wire braid for about a second.**

   The solder will liquefy and the braid will soak up the solder through capillary action.

6. **Repeat Steps 3 through 5 for the other side of the resistor.**
7. **Remove the resistor with tweezers and place in a glass jar.**

   Don't discard the jumper resistors. You may need them to reclock, as I describe in the next section.

Soldering the jumpers in a new place

As I mention in the earlier section "Determining the jumper configuration," some clock speeds don't require you to solder jumpers back on the board.

If you want to avoid soldering, see whether one of those settings works for you.

It's helpful to have a magnifying glass mounted on a stand for this procedure, because you need one hand to hold the soldering iron and the other to hold the jumper in place.

If you do need to replace a jumper resistor in a new location, follow these steps:

1. **Coat the tip of the hot soldering iron with solder by touching the solder wire to the tip of the iron.**

   The solder melts on the solder tip. Give it an ample coat of solder.

2. **Use tweezers to position and hold the jumper resistor on the board so that it bridges two solder pads.**

   You may find it easier to hold the jumper resistor in place by pressing down with the tweezers.

3. **Briefly touch the tip of the soldering iron to one end of the resistor.**

4. **Apply more solder to the tip of the soldering iron.**

5. **Briefly touch the tip of the soldering iron to the other end of the resistor.**

   That's it. Now you can reassemble your mini.

Reassembling the Mac mini

Putting the mini back together is easier than disassembling it. Follow these steps to reassemble the mini:

1. **Make sure that the square thermal pad is in place on the surface of the bottom housing.**

   The thermal pad is the square item at the front of the bottom housing, as shown in Figure 20-7. It comes into contact with the graphics processor to conduct heat away from it.

2. **Reinsert the RAM module by pressing it into the slot until both tabs come up and lock it into place.**

   It's easier to insert the RAM module when the motherboard is out of the bottom case.

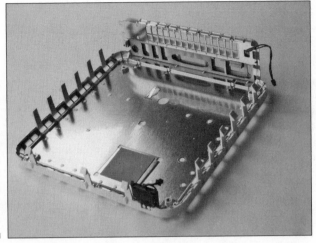

Figure 20-7:
The bottom housing, with port holes in the back panel and the thermal pad at the front.

3. **Insert the port connectors on the motherboard into the openings in the bottom housing (see Figure 20-7).**

   To do this, tilt the motherboard, as shown in Figure 20-8.

Figure 20-8:
Pull the black LED panel back slightly while you lower the mother-board.

4. **Gently hold the black LED panel away from the motherboard as you lower the board into the bottom housing, as shown in Figure 20-8.**

   Don't pull the LED panel out too far or it could break off.

5. **Press the motherboard down into place, and then release the LED panel.**

6. Plug the LED cable (next to the battery) into the motherboard.

7. Plug the LED power-on cable (shown in Figure 20-9) into the motherboard.

Figure 20-9:
The power-on cable is located in the corner near the power switch.

8. Replace the motherboard screw in the corner near the RAM module.

You can see the location in Figure 20-10.

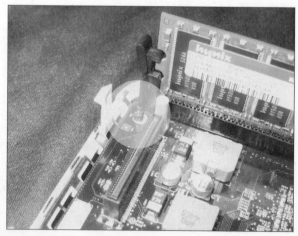

Figure 20-10:
The motherboard screw.

9. Replace the internal frame, as I describe in Chapter 5.

Before you replace the outer casing, you should test your Mac mini for stability, as I describe in the next section. If everything checks out okay, replace the outer casing, as I describe in Chapter 4.

Testing Your Pumped-Up Mac mini

After you complete your overclocking mod, you should test your Mac mini to see whether it is running in a stable manner. If the mini fails one or more tests, consider going back and setting the jumpers to a lower clock rate. Here are some of the things you can do to test your pumped-up mini:

- **Choose Apple⇨About This Mac.** The dialog that appears should list the new clock rate that you set. If it displays a weird result (such as a number well below the original clock rate), you should reclock at a lower speed.

- **Run a variety of applications to see whether they function properly.**

  If applications are unstable or otherwise don't work properly, go back and lower your clock rate. Unstable behavior could include suddenly quitting and freezing.

- **Run a benchmark testing application such as Xbench** (www.xbench. com). Xbench is a free utility from Spiny Software. (The Web site asks you for a voluntary donation, but it isn't required for the download.) Your overclocking is a success if Xbench can complete its tests without giving error messages.

  The numbers that Xbench gives you as the results don't matter, unless you want to compare the speed of your original clock setting to that of your overclocked processor. In this case, you need to run Xbench before you start your overclocking project.

  Xbench also displays the frequency of your processor in GHz. If it gives you a wrong number, consider going back and setting the jumpers to a lower clock rate. The same is true if Xbench returns a lot of error messages.

Part VII
The Part of Tens

The 5th Wave   By Rich Tennant

"Ironically, he went out there looking for
a 'hot spot'."

In this part . . .

Don't tell the publisher I said this, but this book is not the last word on mini mods. One place to turn to for more words is the Internet. The problem is, the Internet is such a huge virtual place. In Chapter 21, I describe the top ten Web sites to visit for information and ideas on Macs, Mac mods, and mods in general.

In Chapter 22, Arnold describes the top ten other things you could do with a Mac mini that we couldn't fit in this book. The tough part here was limiting the list to ten.

Chapter 21

Ten Web Sites to Go to for Ideas and Help

● ●

*T*he Web knows all, including Mac mini hacks and mods. The Web holds secrets of how-to information, ideas for new projects, the latest news, software to download, products to discover, answers to problems, and places to shop for hardware and tools. The ever-changing Web can keep you up to date on new developments and cool new mods that other people dream up.

The problem is mining the Internet to get at all this information — the Web is just too big. It's not always helpful when Google returns 1,364,598 results for your search. Neither is spending 10 minutes clicking through a site only to discover that it doesn't have what you want. This is why this chapter is here.

This chapter presents ten very different Web sites that can help you find what you need, whether it's information or products. I list the best Web sites in each category, the sites that offer the best (and most) content, and the sites that are the easiest to navigate. Some of these Web sites even have their own Dashboard widgets (which, like your other widgets, appear when you press F12) for getting directly to content with a single click. (I suspect this is a trend that will grow.)

Some of these Web sites are about the Mac mini; some are about Macs in general. Some are about Mac mini mods or just mods in general. And some of these Web sites aren't specific to the Mac or the mini, but are helpful nonetheless.

MacInTouch

www.macintouch.com

Long before Webcasts and pop-up ads, there was MacInTouch. Not only was MacInTouch one of the first (if not *the* first) Macintosh Web site, but it's also one of the longest-running Web sites of any kind. Ric Ford started MacInTouch in 1994, only two years after the release of MacWWW, the first Web browser for the Macintosh, and three years after the Web became publicly available.

These days, I never install a new update to Mac OS X or application software without first consulting MacInTouch. That's because new software often breaks old software. MacInTouch can tell me what is likely to break if I install an upgrade. As soon as a new version of software becomes available, MacInTouch posts notes from readers reporting on the bugs and quirks that they've discovered. This list of reports grows every day until you get a good idea of the risk you'll take by installing the update. If none of the reports has anything to do with the software you are running, go ahead and install the upgrade. If you do find a report that scares you, hold off on the upgrade until a fix becomes available.

MacInTouch also has the latest Mac news, updated daily. Occasionally, this site posts reviews of major Mac-related software and hardware such as the Mac mini. The reviews aren't a regular feature, but they are in-depth and full of useful information.

Apple's Macintosh Product Guide

http://guide.apple.com

If someone tells you that something isn't available for Macs, don't take his word for it until you consult the Macintosh Product Guide, a database of hardware and software for Macs. When this book was published, the Macintosh Product Guide listed no less than 23,000 entries. Here, you're likely to find items that you never thought existed, from utilities that hack the way Mac OS X looks to USB credit card swipers. You can click a software or hardware category, then click subcategories, and you can search at any of the levels. When you get a list of items, click one to get a short description and a link to the product's Web site.

Version Tracker

www.versiontracker.com

Version Tracker is similar in concept to the Macintosh Product Guide but differs in several significant ways. Unlike the Guide, Version Tracker lists only software. It's the first place I go to look for freeware and shareware applications and utilities, but commercial software is also listed. Version Tracker also updates its entries for new versions of software and describes what is new in the latest release, including beta (prerelease) versions. It even describes updates to Dashboard widgets.

Each entry includes reader reviews and an average grade. Be careful about relying too much on the user reviews, however, because some readers will assign the lowest grade for irrelevant reasons, such as a problem downloading.

The best way to use Version Tracker is to use the search field at the top of the home page. Type a keyword or a word that you think might be in the name of the software.

Version Tracker has its own Dashboard widget, but it's not all that useful because you can't search from it. To get a searching widget, you have to pay $50 a year for a Version Tracker Pro subscription. The free version asks you to select a category. The widget then displays only the top five or ten returns for the most recent updates in that category. Hopefully, future versions of the free Version Track widget will include searching. For now, you'll have better luck finding software in your Web browser at the Version Tracker home page.

Apple Discussion Forum

http://discussions.info.apple.com/

The Apple Discussion Forum is the largest Mac-related discussion board. When you have a question or a problem that you need to solve, post an item at the Apple Discussion Forum. To find an instant answer, browse through the postings or use the search field to find entries that concern your topic.

Check out the Mac mini section for several subsections of mini-related threads. Don't miss the sections on Mac OS X, Bluetooth, AirPort, and some of the software categories.

Apple employees don't usually post, but plenty of other Mac-savvy readers are ready to share their experience. I once saw a post called "My Son Spilled Milk on My Mac Mini" that received 20 responses with advice on how to handle the problem.

MacMod

www.macmod.com

"Your Mac Mod Headquarters" focuses on mods and hacks, but for all Macs, not just minis. This means that you have to look for mini-specific material, or just be inspired to create your own mods based on what people are doing to other Mac models. But you can find a few Mac mini modifications and links to mini mods at other Web sites, including a Mac mini Robot and a Mac mini Millennium Falcon model mod.

Also, check out the Modding Techniques section. It describes some of the modding procedures that you can use for the Mac mini. The users' forum is a great place to share tips and ask questions of other modders.

123Macmini

www.123macmini.com

123Macmini, the most complete Mac mini Web site, provides news and information about Mac mini–related products, reviews, books, and links to Mac mini mods around the Internet. The news isn't just announcements of new products. For instance, you can see a Mac mini installed in an antique Lotus Roadster. The site also offers a generous helping of photos of various mini mods on its home page and adorning various news sections.

The Gallery section has more photos, which displays photos of mini-specific peripherals and of users' Mac mini setups. Click a photo, and you get a large photo with a discussion board below it. It also has an active discussion forum section, with thousands of posts on various mini-related topics.

The Accessories section describes hardware that's specifically designed for the Mac mini and includes reviews with lots of photos. 123Macmini does its own reviews and also provides links to other mini-related reviews and news.

123Macmini also has its own Dashboard widget, as shown in Figure 21-1. It displays the latest articles at the site. Click a title, and the widget launches your Web browser and takes you to the article. You can also click to get the forums and news sections. You can download the widget at Apple's widget site (www.apple.com/downloads/dashboard/).

Figure 21-1:
The 123
Macmini
widget.

MacVroom

www.macvroom.com

This is one of the most topic-specific Web sites in this chapter. Not only is it a Mac Web site, not only is it a Mac mod Web site, not only is it a Mac *mini* mod Web site — but it's also a Mac mini *car* mod Web site.

The biggest section is Mac'd Rides, which is a kind of clearinghouse for car mods. It summarizes Mac mini installations in different types of cars for different purposes, and it provides photos. My favorite is a Volkswagen Touareg that has three Mac minis installed in it. Here, the Mac minis actually *drive* the car. Most of these car mods are from other Web sites across the Internet. MacVroom provides links to the modders' Web sites, where you can get more information.

MacVroom also offers some relevant news, tips, and product reviews.

Inside Mac Games

www.insidemacgames.com

So you've installed a Mac mini in your car to keep the kids happy on long trips. Movies can keep them happy for a while — until you run out of movies. Games, on the other hand, can keep them occupied until you've parked the car and unloaded the trunk. (Okay, I know that you really want games for yourself, to play on your Mac mini–based home entertainment center. Don't worry, I won't tell.)

Inside Mac Games is the best Mac gaming site that I know of, mostly for the wide variety of its content. You find oodles of game reviews with screen shots, and of game-control hardware such as joysticks and gaming pads. The game reviews have a Buy Now button that you can click to place an order. You can keep current with news reports of upgrades and new releases. You can talk to other gamers in the chat area and in the discussion forum, where you can find troubleshooting information.

The next time someone tells you that there aren't any games for Mac, send them to Inside Mac Games.

Radio Shack

www.radioshack.com

Radio Shack isn't much of a Mac mini Web site. All right, it has nothing to do with Macs. But it does have a lot (if not all) of the tools and materials that you need to do the mods and hacks that I describe in this book. The site is comprehensive, with a large number of items. When your Mac mini gets old and the internal battery dies, you can buy a replacement here. If you don't have a Radio Shack retail store or another electronics or hardware store near you, the Radio Shack Web site is the next best thing.

Tom's Hardware Guide

www.tomshardware.com

One way to shop for the best price on Mac mini parts and peripherals is to check multiple Web sites and then compare the prices that you find. This involves a lot of Web surfing and copying different prices. Sometimes different Web sites use different terminology for the same parts, which means that you have to figure out whether two or more terms refer to the same piece of hardware. But, if you have a lot of time on your hands and love Web searching, go ahead and use this method.

A much better way to comparison-shop for hardware is to go to one Web site that gives you the prices from multiple Web vendors all at once. You can then pick the cheapest one, check the shipping cost, and place your order. Several sites do this across the Web. One of the easiest to use is Tom's Hardware Guide — where you can find hard drives and DVD burners, both internal and external, as well as printers, scanners, and other computer hardware.

Finding the best price for a piece of hardware at Tom's is basically a three-step process:

1. **At the home page, type a search phrase that describes what you're looking for.**

   For instance, if you're looking to replace the Mac mini's internal hard drive, type **2.5" hard drive** in the search field. You see a list of models of differing capacities from different manufacturers.

2. **Click the Compare Prices button to look at prices for a particular model, say, the Hitachi Travelstar 100GB hard drive.**

   A table opens that lists two dozen Web vendors, along with their prices.

3. **Click a link in the table, and it takes you right to the Web page for that item at the vendor's site.**

You can also use Tom's Hardware Guide to search for RAM, but it's tougher to figure out which type of RAM to search for to use in the Mac mini. A better way to comparison-shop for RAM is to visit RamSeeker (www.ramseeker.com). Here, you simply select your Mac model (the mini) to bring up a table and compare prices.

Chapter 22

Ten Other Uses for the Mac mini

*T*he compact, complete, and inexpensive Mac mini invites new uses. They couldn't all fit in this book, but some are at least worth mentioning. You won't find some of the more expensive ideas here, such as tiling your kitchen floor with Mac minis or building a mini supercomputer array. The ideas presented in this chapter are doable, as well as cool and zany, with a few practical ones thrown in for good measure.

Safe Surfing Box for Window Users

For many Windows users, the Internet is not the carefree experience we Mac users enjoy. Windows users are constantly beset by various evil or annoying forms of software and must constantly be on guard, lest one of them get in and literally take over their PCs. Some software can even spy on you, reporting to spammer HQ what you've been doing, and can even record what you type.

Mac users don't worry about most of this. Apple gets some credit for this for coming up with an operating system that has good built-in security. But the Mac is by no means hack-proof. It's just much less of a target than a Windows PC. The creators of *malware,* as it's collectively called, focus on the Windows operating system because there are several hundred million Windows users and only several tens of millions of Mac users. Programmers on the dark side want to put their efforts where they can do the most harm.

So how does this help your friend who won't (or can't) switch to a Mac? Tactfully suggest that your friend consider the mini as an Internet surfing accessory for the PC setup. Your friend already owns the needed displays, keyboards, and mice. A PC owner is unlikely to buy this book, of course, so you might loan him your copy. (Or hey, it makes a great gift. . . .)

The idea is this: Keep on using the PC for whatever it is the PC does, and use the mini for Web surfing and e-mail, but use the same keyboard, monitor, and mouse for both. Connect both machines to the keyboard, monitor, and mouse using a USB KVM switch, a gadget that lets you run two computers from the same keyboard, mouse, and display. Your Windows-using friend can read about KVM switches in Chapter 2. Chapter 2 also describes how you can use a PC keyboard with a Mac. The PC needs to have a USB port, but for people with really old PCs, a dual PS2-to-USB adapter costs $15. Files for e-mail attachments can easily be moved between the two machines via an Ethernet cable.

The mini has built-in DVI output and comes with a free VGA adapter. It works fine with most USB keyboards and mice. Even the bottom-of-the-line mini is plenty fast for most uses, and it's Internet-capable right out of the box. If your friend's house is set up for wireless networking, getting an AirPort WiFi card with the mini can provide a lot of flexibility.

And the Mac mini is small. It's a bit bigger than a stand-alone CD burner, at 2 inches high. It weighs less than 3 pounds, offers less clutter, puts out less noise, and has less to break. The shipping container is smaller than many cereal cartons. You can take it home in a grocery bag with room to spare. You don't need to ask for help carrying it up or down the stairs. Unplug the keyboard, mouse, and display from your PC tower and plug them into the KVM switch; then connect the switch to the PC and the mini. In five minutes tops — *boing,* you're in business!

Is it worth $499 to a Windows user to have the mini as a safe Internet surfing appliance? You wouldn't ask this question if your PC had slowed to a crawl due to 68 malware programs sucking the sap out of the processor, and as a result, you had to spend big bucks to send your PC to a computer doctor to remove the bad stuff.

No, you wouldn't ask that if this happened to you. But it didn't happen to you because you're using a Mac mini to access the Internet, and you've never had a computer virus.

Electronic Scoreboard

A mini connected to a large-screen display or projection TV (at least indoors) can serve as a scoreboard for schools, as well as for Little League teams and other teams who play in locations without one. Most such systems have a VGA port, which the Mac mini can connect to using the VGA adapter that comes with it.

You can use presentation software, such as Apple's Keynote and Microsoft's PowerPoint, to display the score and play special effects. If you have a digital camcorder handy, you can show instant replays on the big screen.

Computer on a Rope

One big advantage of the Mac mini is its small footprint. It takes up very little space on your desk or electronics shelf. But maybe you have so little working room that any space is precious. Well then, try hanging your Mac mini from the ceiling. With WiFi for your network connection, Bluetooth keyboard, and mouse, the only wires you need to run to your mini are the power cable from the AC adapter and the display cable. If you are up for modding the mini's enclosure, you can attach a (short) eyebolt to one side of the mini.

Alternately, you can fabricate a harness that goes around the mini using nylon webbing. You can even do the same for the display, using two ropes to keep it steady, suspending both over your kitchen island (see Chapter 11). A pulley arrangement can raise or lower the units, or you can tie an adjustable knot like a Boy Scout taut-line hitch.

To ensure that the mini hangs straight, find its center of gravity by balancing it on a pencil before attaching a permanent hook. Also, be sure that the line in the ceiling is anchored to a stud or rafter, not just plaster (unless you use a Molly bolt, of course).

And unlike that spider plant or fern you've been meaning to rid of, you never have to water a mini-on-a-rope.

Boat or Small-Plane Mac

The same reasons a mini is great for car installation make it a fine addition to boats and small planes as well. GPS navigation and charting software is available. Much of what is covered about installations in Part V applies to boats and planes as well. The electrical systems in boats and planes are trickier than those in cars. In a boat, a professional installation is a good idea. In a plane, you need a licensed airframe mechanic to make electrical and mechanical modifications.

Most aircraft electrical systems are 24-volt DC. Some have AC voltage available, but it's usually 400 hertz. DC-to-DC converters that can work in this situation are available, although not cheaply. Skip the optional WiFi and Bluetooth. You don't want them to interfere with the aircraft's radio and navigational instruments.

Boats have their own issues, too, which mainly have to do with water. Computers don't like water, especially salt water. You can keep the mini in a watertight locker with power routed to it. The mini's small size is an advantage here. A waterproof keyboard is a sensible idea. Chapter 11 describes these devices.

Of course, any moving vehicle is a candidate for a mini: trucks, farm tractors, and parade floats. A motorcycle mini would be awesome.

Mobile Podcast Studio

A journalistic revolution is in progress right now. People no longer get all their news from the teams of paid reporters and editors at newspapers, television, and radio. Blogging, podcasting, and open-licensed Internet news sites, such as wikinews.org, are challenging traditional media. If you want to try your hand at samizdat publishing, turn your car, van, or minivan into your Mac mini–based mobile studio for blogging, podcasting, or online video production. (See Part V for information and ideas about installing a mini in a car.)

The mini-mobile can take you to where the action is. If a car is parked away from road noise, its interior can be a better recording studio than a home office or den. A car has lots of sound-deadening material and no right-angle corners to echo the sound. Feed your field-recorded audio and video into the mini and edit it with Apple tools such as iMovie and Final Cut. High-quality USB audio mixers are available for about $300. You can even improvise a musical soundtrack with Apple's GarageBand or a MIDI keyboard.

When your news program is finished, upload it to your blog or Web site via a cell-phone modem or a WiFi hot spot in a Starbucks parking lot. Enable your Web site to podcast it, and iPod users everywhere can listen to your take on things as they ride the subway.

Pro Recording Studio

You may have heard that you can plug a guitar into the Mac mini and use GarageBand to create your own songs. You can go much further with some additional software, peripherals, a big FireWire hard drive, and maxed-out RAM. The Mac mini could be the center — the *portable* center — of a studio where you create, record, mix, and produce music.

Add a USB-to-MIDI interface to connect to electronic keyboards (the kind with black and white keys), synthesizers, and analog instruments such as guitars and mics. MIDI gives you editable digital music, where you can adjust individual notes, tempos, rhythm, and other musical parameters. Add an analog-to-digital converter for analog instruments, such as guitars and mics (if the MIDI interface doesn't already have one built-in). Then, add an audio mixer to blend microphone and audio-signal instruments in, and amplifiers and speakers out.

Graduate from GarageBand to Apple's Logic Pro MIDI sequencer/multitrack audio editor/effects processor. Logic Pro is to GarageBand what Final Cut Pro is to iMovie.

Electronic Sculpture

The Mac mini's packaging is a work of art in itself. It's even more so if you follow the lead of some of the chapters in this book and paint it, cover it in red leather, or glue plastic army men to the top of it.

Build the mini into an organic piece of artwork that includes video displays or computer-controlled mechanisms. Computers that control kinetic or video art shouldn't be hidden in a closet or built into a pedestal. They should be *on* the pedestal, and the mini is the right machine for the job.

Digital Picture Frame

In Harry Potter's world, pictures of wizards and witches in picture frames don't just stand there — they move around, smiling and waving at you. You can do Harry one better by having your picture frame magically change the picture to display all your loved ones, your favorite scenes, or the works of great masters. Use the Mac mini to drive a digital picture frame.

If you have the mini in your living room connected to a flat-panel TV mounted to a wall, give it something to do when you're not watching it. Or, mount a flat-panel monitor on the wall. You can even mount the monitor inside a picture frame for a more authentic look.

The killer app here is the Mac OS X screen saver, with its Ken Burns effect slideshow. Load iPhoto with photos of the kids and your best nature photography, and get it going like this:

1. **Select Desktop and Screen Saver from System Preferences.**
2. **Click the Screen Saver tab.**
3. **Select your family iPhoto album from the list on the left.**
4. **Click the Options button, and make sure that every check box but Keep Slides Centered is selected.**

   If the panning and zooming make you dizzy, deselect the Zoom Back and Forth check box and select the Keep Slides Centered check box.

After you do this, screen saver puts on a heart-stopping display of the photos, full-screen. Also, set the Energy Saver in System Preferences to wait a longer time before going to sleep.

TIP

You don't have to limit what your picture frame displays. Unlike Harry Potter, you have the entire Web at your disposal. Envision software from Open Door Networks (www.opendoor.com) goes to the Web and displays a slideshow of images — and only images — from a Web site of your choice, again in full-screen. If Hubble Space Telescope images nebulae and galaxies are your thing, choose NASA. If you want great works of art on your wall, you can have them. You can customize Envision to present what you want. And unlike the Mac OS X screen saver, Envision lets you set the time that an image remains displayed.

For extra credit, you might write a script using OS X Tiger's Automator feature to check your .Mac account for new photos and download them to the mini. That way, when you take new photos of the kids, they appear on your mini within hours.

Not bad for muggles.

Treffpunkt

Many airports and train stations in Europe follow the intelligent practice of putting up a sign in some central hall designating that spot as a "meeting point" (*treffpunkt* in German). There is even an international symbol for meeting points. If someone is supposed to meet you at the airport and you forgot to mention where, the meeting point is the place to go.

The one problem with this great idea is that it doesn't work too well for large multiterminal airports in major cities. Unless you know what terminal the person is arriving at, a single meeting point doesn't work. The obvious fix is to create kiosks at the meeting point in each terminal with a Mac mini and an Apple iSight camera, videoconferencing to all the other meeting points in the airport. Then if you wind up at the wrong *treffpunkt*, you can see your family waiting for you on the mini's screen.

Such a system should be cheap to build. With a secured WiFi connection to the airport's network (more airports already have WiFi hot spots), there would be no expensive cabling to run. For cities with more than one major airport, you could connect all the meeting points, enabling visitors and hosts to connect, even if they went to the wrong airport.

Bar Punkt

In 2005, the mayor of San Francisco proclaimed that the government would implement free WiFi service throughout the city. Not everyone was happy with this idea. This was a time of budget deficits, when bus service had been reduced and funding for the elderly slashed, and the lack of funds to fix the city's fire hydrants was front-page news.

Most unhappy, however, were the numerous coffeehouses that provided WiFi service to draw in customers.

You can help here — at least, with the coffeehouse problem. Take the virtual meeting point idea (described in the preceding section) into the cafés, as well as into bars and nightclubs. Patrons would call up the video-enabled virtual meeting points in nearby or far-away watering holes to hang with the hipsters there. The mini could be set up and rented out for "five-minute virtual dating," for example. Thus, the coffeehouses would make up for their loss, and San Francisco could maintain its density of 11 cafés per voting precinct. If we could only find a way for the mini to fix the fire hydrants. . . .

Appendix

Keeping the Mac mini Running Smoothly

In This Appendix

▶ Troubleshooting preferences file problems

▶ Repairing permissions for a more stable Mac mini

▶ Detecting and fixing hard drive problems

▶ Fixing hardware problems

*I*n a perfect world, a computer would work all the time without needing your help. In our world, however, we need to tune up and fix our cars, service our appliances, and yes, maintain and fix our Mac minis. Your Mac mini is probably working right now, but that won't continue indefinitely.

Not only that, but if you've done some of the projects in this book, you've had your Mac mini in pieces all over your desk. This in itself isn't a bad thing, but it does expose the hard drive to electromagnetic charges that it might not see when left undisturbed deep inside the Mac mini. (If you have leftover pieces after you've put it back together, that usually *is* a bad thing.) You may also have been hacking the operating system and installing some unusual software that may not play nicely with the versions of software that are already installed in your Mac. Heck, even a new version of Mac OS X direct from Apple can wreak havoc on older installed software.

This appendix takes you through the problems and snags you're likely to run into. I take you through troubleshooting to find the source of a problem, and then through the repair procedures. A large chunk of this appendix is devoted to the hard drive, which is the source of some of the most serious problems. There are also tips for regular maintenance that can prevent some of these headaches.

Troubleshooting Problems

The process of looking for a problem entails applying a potential fix and determining whether the fix works. If the fix doesn't work, you haven't found the problem, and you need to move on to the next possible fix.

The best troubleshooting strategy is to first try fixes that are the easiest and that present the least risk to your data. This is roughly the order in which you might try them:

1. Repair permissions with Disk Utility.

2. Remove preferences files.

3. Repair the drive with Disk Utility.

4. Reformat the hard drive, and reinstall Mac OS X and your settings, software, and documents.

Always start trying to fix a problem by repairing permissions. I begin the next section with removing preferences files, however, because repairing permissions and the drive both involve using the same tool. Also, removing preferences isn't always necessary. Reformatting the drive is always a last-resort measure.

These procedures all deal with software problems. You also may encounter some hardware problems, which I discuss at the end of this appendix.

Troubleshooting Prefs and Other System Files: Fixing Spinning Beach Balls and Other Maladies

In small doses, the spinning beach ball is a minor annoyance. Your cursor turns into this animated icon, a kind of busy signal to let you know that your software will be with you shortly. When the beach ball starts preventing you from doing anything with your application, it becomes the Spinning Beach Ball of Death. You know you're in trouble when you open the Force Quit dialog (by pressing ⌘+Option+Esc), and it tells you that your application is not responding, as shown in Figure A-1. The only recourse at this point is to force-quit the application.

Figure A-1:
A perpetually spinning beach ball shows up as a nonresponding application in the Force Quit dialog.

This happens to everyone from time to time, but a frequently-appearing Spinning Beach Ball of Death is a sign of a problem. That problem could be a corrupt preferences file. Deleting the corrupted preferences file often fixes this and other problems.

Preferences files are small files written in the XML language. They store information about changes you've made to the application, including the type of toolbars and palettes that are displayed, the last files you opened, and even where your windows are located on-screen. These files also hold settings that you've made to the application, and sometimes can hold the registration code for the application.

When preference files become corrupt, you can experience annoying problems such as chronic Beach Ball of Deathism, applications that frequently quit without warning, and applications that have trouble launching.

Identifying and locating preferences files

You can identify some preferences files by their filenames. The filenames often begin with `com.` and end in `.plist`. They usually contain the name of the application and the manufacturer. For instance:

```
com.microsoft.Entourage.plist

com.apple.mail.plist

com.adobe.Photoshop.plist
```

Not all applications use this naming scheme, however, so looking for a preference file may not be this simple.

Most preference files reside in the Library folder of your home folder. The first place to look is in the `~/Library/Preferences` folder.

In a path name, the squiggle before a slash indicates the home folder. Figure A-2 shows this Preferences folder. Most applications store their preferences here.

Figure A-2: The Preferences folder in the home folder.

You can find more preferences files in the Library file at the root level of your hard drive. Look in the `/Library/Preferences` folder.

Preferences files can also be located in one or more folders within the Preferences folders.

Troubleshooting problem preferences files

If you have a misbehaving application, removing a corrupt preferences file may fix the problem.

Removing a preferences file from the folder that it normally resides in causes the application to create a new preferences file the next time you launch it. With the new preferences file created, the application reverts to the default settings. If the removed preferences file was corrupt, the application should run trouble-free with the new one.

To find a defective preferences file for a single application, follow these steps:

1. **Quit all open applications.**

2. **Locate one or more suspect preferences files using the guidelines in the previous section.**

   Look in the Library folder in your home folder first.

3. **Remove the preferences file from the Preferences folder and drag it to the Desktop.**

   An application can have more than one preferences file. There may be more than one preferences file associated with an application.

   Don't trash these preferences files just yet. You'll want to put them back if they aren't causing problems.

4. **Launch the offending application and check for the problem.**

5. **If you removed more than one preference file and the problem has been fixed, quit the application, put one of the removed prefs files back where it was, and relaunch the application.**

   Keep repeating Step 5 to see whether you can isolate one of the files as being the defective file.

If you're having general system problems, such as spinning beach balls everywhere you turn, isolating a single preference file takes more work. In this case, try removing all the com.apple preferences from the `~/Library/Preferences` folder. You should restart the Mac mini after doing this. If the problem goes away, you could try putting some of the prefs files back, a few at a time, in the attempt to retain as many of your settings as possible.

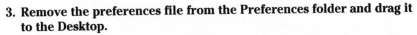

A tool is available that can make preference troubleshooting *much* easier. Preferential Treatment is a free AppleScript that can identify corrupt preference files for you, as shown in Figure A-3. After quitting all your applications, you can then remove the listed file or files. If removing the files fixes your problem, go ahead and delete them. If removing the file doesn't fix the problem, Preferential Treatment might have found a preference file that is just a bit, um, different, but still functional. This is rare.

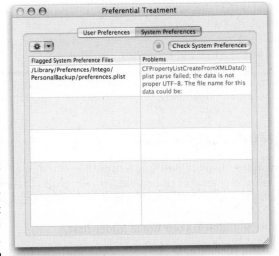

Figure A-3: Preferential Treatment can help identify corrupt preference files.

You can download Preferential Treatment from this Web site:

```
http://homepage.mac.com/jonn8/as/html/pt.html
```

Preferential Treatment is not guaranteed to find every bad preferences file, and you may still have to use the manual method that I describe earlier to locate the bad file. But Preferential Treatment can go a long way to troubleshoot preferences files, and the price is right.

For those who think that graphical interfaces are for wussies, you can also check for corrupt preference files in Terminal. This line of code checks the home Library folder:

```
sudo plutil -s ~/Library/Preferences/*.plist
```

Then, to check the other Library folder, leave out the ~ character, as follows:

```
sudo plutil -s /Library/Preferences/*.plist
```

You get no benefit from using Terminal rather than Preferential Treatment other than the feeling of hacker-worthiness. Preferential Treatment is easier to use (with one click instead of two lines of code to type) and presents the results in a simple format that is easier to read.

Whether you are using Preferential Treatment or not, after you identify and verify that a preference file is corrupt, you can move it to the Trash.

Troubleshooting flaky fonts

If your fonts aren't working properly, you may have one or more corrupt font caches. These are also kept in the Library folders.

A $10 shareware utility, Font Finagler, can detect and delete corrupted font caches. You can get Font Finagler at the following URL:

```
http://homepage.mac.com/mdouma46/fontfinagler/
```

A printer problem-solver

One thing that Macs have always done way-better than Windows PCs is print. Your Mac mini can print any kind of document, usually with good results. Occasionally, however, a Mac can experience printing weirdness, particularly if you're using a lot of different printers. You might be having a tough time adding a printer, or maybe you can't seem to open Printer Setup.

Maintenance utilities

A little preventative maintenance can go a long way in Mac OS X. In fact, the system has Unix routines designed to clean up various system files. However, these routines are set to run after midnight, probably when your Mac is turned off. And if you happen to be working on your Mac at that time, the maintenance tasks wouldn't run.

A number of utilities let you run these maintenance routines whenever you want, and without having to open Terminal. These utilities can also do other things, such as repair permissions without having to open Disk Utility and delete old cache files. One of the best is Cocktail ($15, www.macosxcocktail.com), which has a clean user interface and very thorough coverage of the Unix cleaning functions. Macaroni

(www.atomicbird.com) is a $9 utility that can run the Unix cleaning routines automatically. Other choices include the $8 version of TinkerTool (www.bresink.de/osx/TinkerTool.html), which also does some of the Finder modifications that I describe in Chapter 18. Control Freak (http://home.comcast.net/~jeff.ulicny/software/) is another maintenance utility that offers some ability to tweak. It's free, although the developer asks for a donation.

Because these are shareware or freeware utilities, you have no guarantee that the developers will release timely updates for new updates of Mac OS X. If one is acting weird, try another. You can try most of them for free.

Printer Setup Repair ($25, www.fixamac.net) looks in a whole bunch of different places and cleans up, deletes, or fixes files related to printing all around the system.

Repairing Permissions

Repairing permissions is the first step of hard drive maintenance. It's a procedure that is quick and easy to do, is risk free, and can prevent and fix hard drive problems.

Permissions are settings that are associated with each of the thousands of visible and invisible files, folders, and applications on your hard drive. Permissions identify which users or operating system entities are allowed to read or make changes to a file or folder.

You can see the operating system entities that exist in the Info window of any file by clicking the Ownership & Permissions section, then clicking Details, and finally clicking the Owner pop-up menu. (You may have to click the Lock icon to unlock the Owner pop-up menu.) You may see your username listed, as well as entity names such as system, appowner, and deamon. These are software processes that interact with some of the files. If one of these processes can't access a file that it needs to, or makes a change to a file it's not supposed to, you can have problems.

Damaged permissions can cause slow performance, problems opening files and folders, and other types of weird behavior.

When to repair permissions

On the following occasions, you should repair your drive's permissions, both to fix problems and to prevent them:

- ✔ **General weirdness or slower performance than usual.** Repairing permissions is the first step in trying to fix just about any problem you're having. This includes files or applications that won't open and preference settings that refuse to change after you set them.
- ✔ **After a hard restart (pressing the power button without shutting down) or a system crash.**
- ✔ **After you install new software or software updates.**
- ✔ **As a part of routine monthly maintenance.**

Even if everything seems hunky-dory, if you don't repair permissions, you can cause hidden problems to fester and grow.

How to repair permissions

Unlike repairing the disk (described in the next section), you can repair permissions right from the hard disk that's used to boot the Mac mini. You don't need to repair permissions of CDs and DVDs. (Disk Utility also doesn't let you.)

To repair permissions, follow these steps:

1. **Open the Disk Utility in the Utilities folder.**

   In the Finder, you can select Go⇨Utilities.

2. **Make sure that the First Aid tab is selected.**

3. **If you have more than one hard drive with Mac OS X installed connected to the Mac mini, select the drive that you want to work on in the left column.**

   The buttons that start the process are grayed out if the disk you select is not a startup disk, or if it is a CD or DVD.

4. **Click the Repair Disk Permissions button.**

Bunches of messages scroll by, telling you which permissions were repaired. Disk Utility tells you when it has finished. The whole process should take just a few minutes, and you don't need to restart that Mac mini.

Repairing the Hard Disk with Disk Utility

The act of "repairing a disk" with Disk Utility isn't actually repairing the physical hard drive. It means that Disk Utility fixes the information on the drive that enables the hard drive to locate files and function properly.

Repairing a disk with Disk Utility fixes more serious problems than does repairing permissions. It's also more difficult because you need to start the Mac mini from a CD or DVD (or another hard drive) that contains Mac OS X.

When to repair the hard disk

You should repair the hard disk on these occasions:

- **When the mini doesn't boot.** If you get a blinking question mark when you try to start the Mac mini, it means that the Mac can't find a startup drive, probably because of a hard disk problem.

- **At any sign of hard disk problems.** This includes weird behavior, such as files that won't open properly, applications that don't act properly, or software that continually tells you to install an update that you've already installed.

- **When the Mac mini seems to be running slower than it used to.**

- **During quarterly maintenance.** Repair your hard disk regularly to prevent problems or to prevent little, unseen problems from growing into big, annoying problems. Nip 'em in the bug.

Repairing a hard drive is a bit more trouble than repairing permissions because restrictions exist on what you can repair. Specifically, you can't test or repair these kinds of drives or discs:

- **The disk which the Mac mini is currently booted.** This means that you need to restart the Mac mini with something other than the hard drive you want to fix.

- **Write-protected discs, including nonrecordable CDs and DVDs.**

- **Hard drives with open files.**

You *can* repair hard drives that don't have Mac OS X installed on them, such as an external FireWire drive that you might be using to store video. It's a good idea to run Repair Disk on these types of drives every few months.

For a disk that meets the above criteria for repairing, use the Disk Utility application; it's located in the `/Applications/Utilities` folder.

Running the Repair Disk function

To repair your hard drive, you need to restart the Mac mini from another hard drive or optical disc that has Mac OS X and Disk Utility installed on it. This is known as a *bootable disk*. To start up with a bootable disk, hold down Option while starting up. In a few minutes, you'll see icons for drives or discs that have Mac OS X installed. Select one and click the right arrow, and the Mac mini will start up using the drive or disc you selected. You can also restart while holding the C key to boot from a DVD or CD.

If you haven't created a bootable disk, you can use the system DVD (called Mac OS X Install Disc 1) that came with your Mac mini to boot and run Disk Utility. Follow these steps to do so:

1. **Back up your hard drive or important files before repairing the drive.**

   Chapter 7 describes what to back up; see the "Saving your software and settings" section.

2. **Insert the Mac OS X Install Disc 1.**

3. **Restart the Mac mini while holding down the C key to start up from the DVD.**

   The Installer program appears when the Mac mini has rebooted.

4. **Choose Installer⇨Open Disk Utility.**

   Disk Utility opens.

5. **Make sure that the First Aid tab is selected.**

6. **Select the drive that you want to fix in the left column.**

7. **Click the Repair Disk button.**

   Disk Utility checks and, if necessary, repairs the selected drive. It displays its progress in the lower-right quarter of the dialog, as shown in Figure A-4.

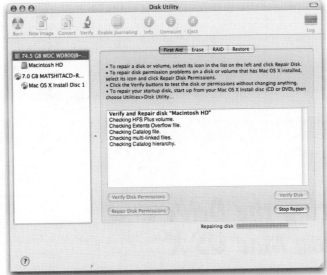

Figure A-4:
Disk Utility
displays its
progress
and tells you
whether it
fixed the
problem
when it's
done.

8. **If Disk Utility finds and repairs a problem, run the repair again.**

9. **Restart the Mac to boot from the hard drive.**

If Disk Utility tells you that it couldn't fix that problem, try running it again. If Disk Utility can't fix the problem, you may need to run a third-party utility such as Disk Warrior from Alsoft (www.alsoft.com). This utility can catch problems that Disk Utility sometimes can't.

A shortcut for repairing the disk

If you don't have a system DVD when you need to repair the disk, you can do without it, if you don't mind typing some commands. You can repair a boot volume by starting up the Mac mini in single-user mode and running a Unix utility. Single-user mode is when the Mac starts up without a graphical user interface — you see a black screen with white command-line text.

To start up in single-user mode, hold down ⌘+S while starting (or restarting) the Mac. When you see the Unix prompt, type this command:

```
fsck -fy
```

This runs `fsck`, a repair disk routine that is similar to the one in Disk Utility.

To restart, type the following command:

```
reboot
```

With both of these commands, make sure to use all lowercase letters.

If every utility that you use tells you that it can't fix a problem, you may need to erase the drive and reinstall all your software and files, as I describe in the following sections.

Reformatting the Drive and Reinstalling Mac OS X

Erasing the drive and reinstalling everything — operating system, applications, settings, iTunes music, data files, and so on — doesn't sound very appealing. It isn't. It should be a last resort, *after* you've tried everything in this appendix previous to this section and your Mac mini still isn't performing correctly. Chapter 7 has information and instructions on backing up and restoring a hard drive. In the following sections, I give you some reminders.

Backing up the hard drive

First, back up your drive. Chapter 7 goes into what items on your hard drive you should back up. If you have SuperDrive, you can back up to a set of DVDs. If you don't have a DVD burner, backing up to a set of CDs is tougher. The easiest backup media to use is an external FireWire hard drive.

I can recommend two backup programs that will make a complete copy of everything on your hard drive so that you can create a bootable drive on another hard drive. This is known as *cloning* the hard drive. Carbon Copy Clone (www.bombich.com) is "donationware," which is free to use, but a small voluntary fee is requested by the developer. SuperDuper ($20, www.shirt-pocket.com) has a variety of backup methods and has a user interface that tells you what each option does.

Erasing your drive

To erase (reformat) the hard drive, you need to start up from a system DVD, such as the one that came with your Mac mini, or one that came with a copy of Mac OS X that you may have bought. After you boot the Mac mini from the DVD, choose Installer⇨Disk Utility.

Select your drive on the left of the screen and click the Erase tab. Choose Mac OS X Extended (Journaling) from the Volume Format pop-up menu. Give the drive a name in the Name field, and then click the Erase button.

Restoring the hard drive

The easiest way to restore the operating system and everything else to the new hard drive is to use a program that you used to back up the Mac mini (such as Carbon Copy Mac or SuperDuper). The software must be able to create a bootable drive. This means that it copies all the invisible files as well as those that are not hidden.

You can also use the Restore function of the system DVD that came with the Mac mini — this also installs the Apple applications such as iTunes and iMovie. Then, if you've backed up everything to an external FireWire hard drive, use the Migration Assistant in the Utilities folder to move your settings and files.

Migration Assistant doesn't move all settings and files, however. You have to re-create settings for Bluetooth, Energy Saver, and printers, for instance.

Hardware Problems

Up to this point in the appendix, everything is related to manipulating bits of data. Unfortunately, with hardware, the only remedy is to pull the bad actor out of the Mac mini and replace it with a new one. This applies to two items, the hard drive and RAM.

When the hard drive fixes don't work

Most hard drives have a long, happy life, but all are mortal. If even erasing and reinstalling software doesn't solve a problem, or if you can't get Disk Utility to erase the hard drive, the drive may be physically dead. In that case, it's time to replace the drive.

If your hard drive is dead and your Mac mini is still under warranty, get Apple to replace the drive. Apple's tech support will want to know that you've tried everything in this chapter in an attempt to fix the drive. If Apple agrees to replace the drive, an Apple technician will ask you to send that Mac mini back. Certain Mac models have had a run of bad drives that need to be replaced while still new. The Mac mini hasn't been one of those models, fortunately.

If your Mac mini is no longer under warranty, buy a new 2.5-inch hard drive (hopefully one that's faster and bigger than the original) and install it yourself. Chapter 7 shows you how.

RAM problems

You find two kinds of RAM problems: those that don't let the Mac mini start up and those that do.

RAM that doesn't let the Mac mini start up

If you try to start up the Mac mini and get a nasty buzz instead of the happy startup chime, this is a sign that there is a real hardware problem.

If you see a black screen at start up, you've probably just installed or replaced RAM. That's because RAM modules rarely "go bad." Unlike hard drives, RAM modules can live forever. RAM contains no moving parts, after all. The problem could be that the new RAM you bought is defective. The fix is to send it back to the manufacturer.

It could also mean that the RAM module is loose; you didn't press down hard enough when you installed it. In the Mac mini, the two clips should pop up to the notches in the sides of the RAM module. (Chapter 7 has more details about installing RAM.) If this is the cause, reseating the RAM module will fix the problem.

RAM that lets the Mac mini start up, but crashes it

Not all bad RAM prevents your mini from starting up, however. Sometimes a particular RAM module is more sensitive to heat than is usual. Signs of this include frequent kernel panics. This is when the screen freezes and is covered with white-on-black text. This could occur with certain applications running, or it could occur randomly.

Fortunately, the Mac mini doesn't run particularly hot, the way PowerBooks do. But the mini will run warmer if you've overclocked it, as I describe in Chapter 20.

To fix RAM that is causing kernel panics, replace it with another module. If it's still under warranty, send it back to the manufacturer to get a new module.

Before you do, however, make sure that you aren't inadvertently restrictin0g airflow into the Mac mini. The air vents around the bottom of the mini should be open, and the mini should be sitting on a solid surface, not on a soft surface such as a towel or your lap.

Another way to detect bad RAM or other bad hardware is to run Apple Hardware Test, described next.

Running Apple Hardware Test

The Mac OS X Install Disc 1 DVD contains a utility called Apple Hardware Test that can check for bad RAM. It's a good utility to run when you're experiencing frequent kernel panics. Apple Hardware Test displays an error code when it detects a hardware problem. RAM is usually the cause of an error code, though another hardware problem could be responsible.

To run Apple Hardware test, do the following:

1. **Unplug USB and FireWire peripherals from the Mac mini, except for the keyboard and mouse. Also unplug an Ethernet cable if you're using one.**

2. **Insert Mac OS X Install Disc 1.**

3. **Restart the Mac mini while pressing Option.**

   The bootable disks appear on-screen.

4. **Click the Apple Hardware Test icon and click the right arrow.**

   The Mac mini will start up using a special Apple Hardware Test partition on the DVD. The Apple Hardware Test dialog will appear.

5. **Follow the on-screen instructions to run the test.**

If the mini passes the test, then your problem is probably a software problem. If it fails, it will present an error code. This could point to a RAM problem. If your Mac mini is still under warranty or you have an AppleCare support contract, write down the error code and report it to Apple when you report your problem.

Index